The Wanderer a...

Born in Glasgow and raised on the west coast of Scotland, Kenneth White studied French, German and philosophy at the Universities of Glasgow, Munich and Paris. He was first published in London in the mid-sixties (*The Cold Wind of Dawn, Letters from Gourgounel, The Most Difficult Area* – all at Jonathan Cape), but broke with the British scene in 1967, settling in the Pyrenees, where he lived in concentrated silence for a while before beginning to publish again, this time in Paris. A whole series of books – narrative, poetry, essays – won not only wide-spread recognition in France, but also some of its most prestigious literary prizes: the Prix Médicis Etranger for his book *La Route bleue*, the Prix Alfred de Vigny for his poetry, the French Academy's Grand Prix du Rayonnement Français and the Prix Roger Caillois for his work as a whole. These books have been translated into several languages. Since his return, via Scotland, to the English-language context in 1989, White's work has been published by Mainstream (Edinburgh): *The Bird Path, Handbook for the Diamond Country, Travels in the Drifting Dawn, The Blue Road, Pilgrim of the Void*, and by Polygon (Edinburgh): *On Scottish Ground, House of Tides*. When Birlinn Ltd (also of Edinburgh) took over Polygon, its first act was to publish White's collected poems, *Open World*, as a gateway to White's complete work. From 1983 to 1996, Kenneth White held the Chair of XXth Century Poetics at Paris-Sorbonne. In 1989, he founded the International Institute of Geopoetics, which now has centres in various countries, including Scotland, and he directs its transdisciplinary review, *Cahiers de Géopoétique*. Kenneth White lives at present with his wife Marie-Claude, translator and photographer, on the north coast of Brittany.

Other books by Kenneth White

The Cold Wind of Dawn, poems, London, Jonathan Cape, 1966.

Letters from Gourgounel, narrative, London, Jonathan Cape, 1966.

The Most Difficult Area, poems, London, Jonathan Cape, 1968.

The Bird Path, collected longer poems, Edinburgh and London, Mainstream Publishing, 1989; also in Penguin paperback edition.

Travels in the Drifting Dawn, narrative, Edinburgh and London, Mainstream Publishing, 1989; also in Penguin paperback edition.

Handbook for the Diamond Country, collected shorter poems, Edinburgh and London, Mainstream Publishing, 1990.

The Blue Road, narrative, Edinburgh and London, Mainstream Publishing, 1990.

Pilgrim of the Void, narrative, Edinburgh and London, Mainstream Publishing, 1992.

Van Gogh and Kenneth White, an encounter, Paris, Flohic Éditions, 1994

Coast to Coast, interviews, Glasgow, Open World Editions and Mythic Horse Press, 1996.

On Scottish Ground, essays, Edinburgh, Polygon Press, 1998.

House of Tides, narrative, Edinburgh, Polygon Press, 2000.

Open World, Collected Poems 1960-2000, Edinburgh, Birlinn-Polygon, 2003.

Across the Territories, narrative, Edinburgh, Birlinn-Polygon, 2004.

KENNETH WHITE

The Wanderer
and his Charts

Exploring the Fields of Vagrant
Thought and Vagabond Beauty

First published in Great Britain in 2004 by Polygon Books

Polygon an imprint of Birlinn Ltd
West Newington House
10 Newington Road
Edinburgh EH9 1QS

British Library Cataloguing in Publication Data

A catalogue record is available on request from the British Library

ISBN 1 904598 15 3

Typeset in Scotch Roman by Koinonia, Manchester
Printed in Great Britain by Creative Print and Design, Ebbw Vale,
Wales

Contents

Preface   vi

Part I Portrait of the Intellectual Nomad
The Nomadic Intellect   3
Rimbaud, Glasgow and Ways West   17
On a Ridge between Two Seas   23
The Ruins and Lights of Ezra Pound   30

Part II Place and Space
Letter from the Pyrenees   41
Aquitanian Affinities   47
Meditation in Winter   59
Reflections on a Logbook   66
The High Line   74
Writing the Road   94
Along the Atlantic Coast   111
A Wave and Wind Philosophy   129
The Complex Field   139
Elements of a New Cartography   149

Part III A Cultural Project
The White Bag of Books   169
The New Europe   182
The Re-mapping of Scotland   197
Aesthetic Considerations on the Calton Hill   208
The Music of the Landscape   223
An Outline of Geopoetics   229

Preface

For an overall sense of the context in which I work, it is useful to go back to Toynbee's *Study of History*, where, in the section 'The Prospects of the Western Civilization' he alludes to wanderers in the Western wilderness and to Western navigators steering a course through difficult straits, trying to make their way into open waters, an open world.

In more abstract terms, Toynbee wonders if it may be possible to open up a 'post-modern' space (the word, later so much abused, originates in these pages), beyond the slump into which civilization has fallen, beyond all the *ad hoc* socio-political remedies, and beyond all the material piled and piling up in the name of 'creativity' and 'culture', most of which is no more than a mirroring of the rundown situation.

Toynbee himself winds up, religiously, with a franciscan brand of spirituality. I was not attracted to any such harbour.

I kept outside, with the calling of the navigator–wanderer, the terrain of the difficult territory, and a sense of ongoing itinerary. The intellectual nomad (the term used, in passing, by Spengler in his *Decline of the West*, and whose scope I was to develop), is engaged, outside the glitzy or glaury compound of late modernity, in an area of complex co-ordinates. He is trying to move out of pathological psycho-history, along uncoded paths, into fresh existential, intellectual, poetic space.

The initial part of this book lays out the theory of intellectual nomadism, as I began to conceive it in Glasgow, engrossed there in multiple investigations of the latter stages of Western metaphysics and the farther reaches of poetics with, as examples alongside me, the itineraries of Nietzsche, Rimbaud and Ezra Pound.

Thereafter, the book moves over to the Continent, into an experience of place represented (always in conjunction with my original territory, Scotland) in the first instance by the mountain area of the Pyrenees and, later, the sea coast of Brittany. The readings and the soundings (via cartography, meteorology, biology and other such methodologies) of these places, open out on to a space which it is difficult to define, but the approach to which I came to call geopoetics.

Finally, in the third part of the book, after a summing up of the whole itinerary, geopoetics is presented and proposed, from various angles, as a viable cultural project.

The texts, written at various times whenever I felt the need to get my bearings, are essays, that is, as I see the form, attempts at fast, clear, cogent thinking. Live thought is erratic and erotic in its nature, full of tentative exploration and existential energy, and the essay-form proceeds by a series of intellectual sensations and logical leaps. Poetic thought is more dynamic than philosophy. I have worn my pants out on the benches of philosophy in Scotland, Germany and France, but the first philosopher who meant anything to me, Friedrich Nietzsche, announced a new type of philosopher, the artist–philosopher (the poet–thinker, thinker–poet) trying to evolve in a space that had largely been *left out* when official philosophy began.

What this book presents are fields of vagrant thought with maybe, here and there, something of what Kant calls 'vagabond beauty'. This thought is always connected to sensed space, a lived existence, and tries to be in constant association with poetic force.

K. W.
2004

We all follow an eccentric trail and there is no other way
possible from childhood to completion.

(Hölderlin, *Hyperion*)

The frontiers of the mind, you'll never find them, though you
travel all the roads, so deep is the *logos*.

(Heraclitus)

And it came to pass that the next day about evening we saw,
within a kenning before us, towards the north, as it were,
thicker clouds, which did put us in some hope of land.

(Bacon, *New Atlantis*)

PART I

Portrait of the Intellectual Nomad

The Nomadic Intellect

The stranger's out on the road and well ahead. He isn't just
wandering about, with nowhere to go. All the time, he's coming
closer to a place he can call his own.

(Martin Heidegger)

1

Imagine a Winter's night, in the year of grace 1535, in Carpentras, south-eastern France. The bishop of Carpentras is in
his library, deep in study, when a knock comes at the door. It's
his chamberlain saying that a young man has just turned up out
of the dark.

'What does he look like?', says the bishop.

'A bit wild and travelworn', says the chamberlain, 'but he's
wearing a scholar's gown.'

'Oh, well, better show him in', says the bishop, keeping his
forefinger crooked in his book so the visitor will understand
he's interrupted something and not hang about too long. When
the wandering scholar has entered the library, the bishop asks
him where he comes from.

'*Scotus sum*', is the reply.

'Ah, so you're from that country away up on the edge of the
world!' exclaims the bishop. 'What brings you here?'

'I have heard of your learning and piety', says the *Scotus
vagans* diplomatically, 'and I've been told you're looking for a
good teacher.'

In no time at all, Florentius Volusensus (alias Florence
Wilson), who was born in Moray, near the town of Elgin, on
the banks of the bonnie River Lossie (*In Moraviae provincia, ad
Losaeum amnem amoenissimum, haud procul ab Elgino oppido*,
as the old Latin text says) and who had studied first at Aberdeen, then at Paris, was appointed professor of eloquence and
rhetoric at Carpentras. In later years, Wilson wrote a book,
first published in Lyons, entitled *De Animi Tranquillitate*. It's
a dialogue, or rather trialogue, among three young men climb-
ing up the heights of Fourvières, above the confluence of the
Saône and the Rhône, the question being how to get out of
anxiety (literally, narrowness of being) and achieve some peace

3

of mind amid the bloody mess of history and the deadly disputes of religion. The mind of man is described therein as moving from one place to another, either furiously irate or enthusiastically exultant, following out uncertain wandering paths so as to find a way of living and a place to stay ('*Nunc huc, nunc illuc, iratus et ejulans, furiosa et incerta erratione se proripit ut inveniat*'). There's the Scot abroad, and intellectual nomadism, *modo scotico*, at the time of the Renaissance.

Wilson was one among many. In Renaissance times, France was hotching with Scots. You couldn't travel twenty miles between Calais and Marseilles without coming across somebody from Glasgow, Edinburgh or Aberdeen. But if France was, as Irving says in his *Lives of the Scottish Poets*, 'the favourite place for wandering Scots', they didn't restrict themselves to there. They were all over Europe, and in lands beyond Europe, and there was a continual stream of them throughout the centuries. Robert Bruce, born at Kinnaird in 1554, educated at St Andrews, then in France and Flanders, attacked the British Crown from his pulpit, for which he was exiled – a century or so later, his descendant, James Bruce, was exploring Abyssinia. Some, mistakenly and sadly, went no farther than London. Thomas Dempster, born 1579 in Banffshire, educated at Aberdeen and Paris and who was to weave his own way through Louvain, Rome, Toulouse, Nîmes, Marseilles, Florence, Bologna, met up with one such, James Halkerstone, soldier, scholar and poet: 'In the year of grace 1615, I saw Halkerstone in London, and called him by his name, wondering at his haggard look and threadbare cloak. Turning to me, he said: "What ill fate brings you to this country which regards not worth or learning – *Fuge crudeles terras, fuge littus avarum* [Flee these miserable lands, flee these miserly shores]."' Which is exactly what Dempster did, finding the time in his wanderings to write a huge ecclesiastical history of Scotland (*Historia Ecclesiastica Gentis Scotorum*), in which he sets out to prove that the Holy Ghost was Scottish and, later, a massive, all-inclusive study of Etruria, *Etruria Regalis*. Even when, in the latter days, these Scots were ostensibly only the servants, the frontline servants, of that Empire on which the sun never set (and on which, as someone roguishly added, the light of reason never rose), there was a deep unrest at work, and a great desire feeling its way out across the territories. Take Mungo Park. For fifteen shillings a day, he treks alone along the banks of the Niger, 'the river that flows to the ends of the world', as a Bambara told him, trying to reach Timbuktu, one of Africa's great culture-centres.

There's an erratic logic in it all, as well as what you might call erotic research work, if you're ready to give the word 'erotic' its full scope – remember that in Greek mythology, *eros* is the son of *penia*, necessity, and of *poros*, the maker of passageways. There's flight in it also, in the sense of fleeing from, but also in the sense of the plenitudinous deployment of energy. The energy-field may go right back to the Eurasian steppes, where Celt rubbed shoulders with Cimmerian and Scyth, sharing the same great, unroaded, uncoded space, and the same perception of fast movement, whether it be of flickering fire, agile flanks or the fluttering of a bird's wings. What these minds were fleeing from, in the first instance, was a mental, social, political complex started up under the name of Britain, which was the insular, largely English form (though English minds here and there would be against it, and some Scots minds would be among its staunchest upholders) of a certain stage in the development of Western civilization. The whole movement is described in the verse of an English poet perfectly at home in that complex, John Cleveland (seventeenth century), who, in 'The Rebel Scot', has this:

> Like Jewes they spread and as Infection flie
> As if the Divell had Ubiquitie [...]
> Thus do they live as rovers and defy
> This or that place, rags of geography.

In the book *On Scottish Ground*, particularly the chapter 'The Scot Abroad', I give many more examples of the 'nomad Scot' than those I've evoked and will evoke in the context of this essay, from the travelling monks of the early Middle Ages up to Robert Louis Stevenson saying in his letters that he would 'always be something of a nomad' and that he loves 'flashing from one end of the world to the other, both in mind and body'. What I want to do in this essay is go into the *nature* of the nomadic intellect, from a Scottish point of view, with Scottish references. Having opened up Scotland, we'll see the nomadic intellect of Scotland joining a whole stream of continental drift and world-change, but without losing any of its local mind or land – on the contrary.

2

If anything has marked the Scottish mind over the past four centuries, it's the Bible, as presented in the 1611 version sponsored by James VI (and I), which was to be the bottom line of the Presbyterian Kirk. It practically killed the old Scottish literature, with only exceptions like Urquhart of Cromarty holding out eccentrically on the Black Isle. The Bible fulfilled several functions. Along with the religion it backboned, it was something to cling to in a period of turmoil and stress. It provided a force of resistance, and it was a basis of theory, even if that theory was always fundamentally theological – even Enlightenment Common Sense thought in Scotland was still rockbottomly theological. Often the theory would be reactionary. For example, when Newton brought out his *Principia*, a Scotsman, Hutchinson, brought out a book, *Moses' Principia*, to prove via the Bible that gravitation was wrong. But not always so.

Take a case in point: John Glas (eighteenth century), originally from Galloway, but who found himself for long years in a little village on the north-east coast with a lot of time, and the Bible, on his hands. He began to read and think. That the Catholic Church was not the original church of the Testament was, to the Protestant (*pro testamento*) Glas, obvious enough. That the Episcopalian Church was not the original church was also evident. But Glas began to wonder if the Church of Scotland itself corresponded at all to the original church. He began to write pamphlets that were carried round the country by the chapmen. The General Assembly got wise to him and, instead of giving him the apostolic 'kiss of peace' that Glas wanted to see in the streets, sent him packing in 1729 for 'speculative tendencies'. He left for Dundee, and while his teaching went across the Atlantic, where it helped on the American revolution, he died away, day by miserable day, latterly in Perth. During this time, his son, George Glas (it's a phenomenon frequent enough; we've already seen it with the Bruces: speculation followed by travelling), trained as a surgeon, voyaged to the West Indies and later explored the coast of

Africa between Cape Bojador and Cape Blanco.

Other speculations concerned the status of the natural world. For some, if in the beginning 'it was good', after the Fall it was evil, God himself having said 'cursed be the ground'. These people saw mountains and all desert places, not only as uncultivatable and useless, but as downright damned. Others again, however (Calvin himself, for example, but not many Calvinists), would say that the Fall concerned only man, and that the outside world was still God's creation, still good.

I was very speculative myself at one time about the Bible. And I'd say that, if it doesn't drive you completely round the bend, it can be a good introduction to nomadism.

At least in its Old Testament, by far the best documented and the most substantial (it's the one in which the Scottish mind was always the most interested), the Bible is a book of beginnings, based largely on a dialectic of nomadism and sedentarization. The question is for a bunch of Aramaic tribe-folk to get out of built-up, enslaving precincts such as Babylonia and Egypt and make their way to Canaan, open country, the promised land. At least to start with, the word God pronounces the most is 'go'. Genesis 11 is all about 'getting out', 'going away', 'passing through'. 'Leave your country, your homeland, your father's house', says Jahweh to Abraham in Genesis 12, and Moses in Exodus gets the same message, along with a chart (charter) written on rock. It all concentrates then in the story of Cain and Abel, where the dialectic I evoked is most acute, and where the internal trouble starts. 'Let us give ourselves a name, lest we be scattered over the face of the earth', we read in Genesis 11. There's the beginning of identity ideology, proprietorial genealogy, and so on. Cain has a name: 'smith'. Abel has practically no name: the word used to designate him means something like 'the useless wind'. Abel is the nomad, moving in the wilderness from well to well. The nomad territory is a network of wells – the well-being of the pastoral nomad depends, literally, on wells. Cain builds the first town, giving it the name of his son, Tubal-Cain, 'the father of all who work bronze and iron' (Genesis 4). With Cain, man becomes a townsman, a citizen, a maker of history, a constructor of enclosed culture. Jahweh prefers Abel to Cain, because nomadism opens humanity out on to something non-human (what that is exactly, beyond the folk-story and the folk-religion, will be the big theme of theology and philosophy). In the Bible, wayfaring is seen as more radical than rootedness.

Going now a step farther, I'd say that biblically nourished Protestantism, which often leads to existential incarceration, with the mind staring dementedly through the bars, can also, more openly read, be a good starting base for *intellectual* nomadism. In the early days, being in a risky position, the Protestant would tend to live in frontier towns or sea-towns – ready to make a quick getaway. Then, since landed property was easily occupied and confiscated, he would tend to go in for business with easily movable cash. My mind goes from that image to the image of an intellectual on the borders, a writer at the limits, moving fast over the territories, working at something outside the properties and the proprieties and that has no 'rooted' name.

3

Whatever the long-term antecedents may have been, intellectual nomadism began for me in a precise kind of way when, around the age of thirteen, I was reading the essays of Emerson that, by some chance or other (I think my father had picked them up from a second-hand bookbarrow in Glasgow), formed part of the family library. In a short paragraph, which he doesn't develop, Emerson describes intellectual nomadism as the faculty of seeing far in all directions, going on to say that the house of the intellectual nomad is a chariot in which, like a Kalmuk, he will traverse all latitudes, never forgetting his own 'inner law'. The image stuck in my mind, which is perhaps why texts from Mongolia and adjacent territories were later to constitute a significant section of my own pretty extensive library, including that marvellous album of documents printed by Roland Bonaparte in Paris in 1895 (I picked it up at Guenther's in the rue Vavin): images of gateways and roads, and patched manuscripts in six languages (Sanskrit, Prakrit, Chinese, Tibetan, Mongol and Uigour).

As a student in Glasgow, I had digs in Scotstoun, just above Dumbarton Road. I knew my Glasgow because, when I wasn't reading books, I was hoofing through its streets, but I also knew I was just next door to an even older place, Alclyd, 'the rock on the Clyde', which the Gaels of the north had called

Dumbarton, 'the fortress of the Brythons' and which Macpherson's *Ossian*, read in Fairlie (my little Ayrshire village), called 'the halls of Balclutha'. That was the time for me, while going farther into French, German and Latin, with a little Spanish, Italian and Gaelic on the side, to start learning Old Welsh: '*Yscinvaen beirt bit butic clydur*' ('The poet of the limits finds no solid banks'), as it is written in *The Book of Carmarthen*.

It must have been about the Winter of 1955 that, there in Glasgow, I came across Spengler's *Decline of the West*. These were the days before Glasgow was 'miles better', and the city on the Clyde seemed a very appropriate place to read that book. In the section 'Cities and Peoples' of his sketch of a 'morphology of universal history', after evoking the figure of man in anthropological, ethological terms as 'a wandering animal', then tracing a historical development through agriculture, sedentarization and civilization, Spengler suggests that we are now living in the end times of civilization and that the human being is returning to the condition of nomadism – but with less space and energy at his disposal: he prowls around in the restricted precincts of the city, deprived of any real contact with nature at large, his mind playing about or fantasizing in a vacuum. It is, for example, at its best, James Joyce's Stephen Daedalus flanked by Mr Bloom. I enjoyed Joyce's remake of *The Odyssey* in Dublin, but more and more the work turned into a linguistic rigmarole with only the faint cry of a gull at the end of *Finnegans Wake* ('A gull. Gulls. Far calls. Coming, far!') to suggest the possibility of something else: something with more space, more energy, more amplitude.

It was that *something* else I was after. Something that would be less like endless bouts of logorrhoea and more like a logbook. Which is why I turned away from Spengler, and from Joyce, to Rimbaud and Nietzsche.

During my student years in Glasgow, I read mainly Arthur Rimbaud and Friedrich Nietzsche. I read a lot of other stuff, but only in the bygoing, to pass the exams – Rimbaud and Nietzsche I read for ecstasy and intellectual evolution. Over those years, in Glasgow, later in Munich, then in Paris, I saw Rimbaud and Nietzsche as being the first, the one departing from the literary precinct, the other from the philosophical, to leave what I tended to think of more and more as the Motor-

way of Western Civilization, laid down and directed by Platonic
idealism, Aristotelian classification, Christianity, Renaissance
humanism, Cartesianism and Hegelian historicism, to mention
only a few major stages in its progression. They left the motorway, set out on roads that were no more than tracks, and on
tracks that were no more than a series of traces, trying to open
up another space. Both ended in disaster. But this kind of
endeavour, even culminating in disaster, was infinitely more
interesting to me than the literature of the motorway, which
consists most of the time only in offspins and subproducts of
the above-mentioned stages.

I myself was writing at that time in what you might call
flamboyant Gothic. I had a whole host of characters: Mungo
Reilly, the arch-Glaswegian, and his sidekick, Archie Pelago,
an Italo-Scottish seaman. Another was called Aristotle Mac-
kenzie, an uncommonsensical Scottish Enlightenment philosopher. Yet another was Anacharsis McCracken, republican
anarchist. His pedigree went like this. First of all, there was an
activist in the French Revolution called Jean Baptiste de
Clootz who, after reading a book by Abbé Barthélémy called
Voyage du jeune Anacharsis ('The Travels of Young Anacharsis'), relating the journey of a young Scythian through the
Greek republics in the fourth century BC, changed his name to
Anacharsis Clootz. Carlyle in one of his essays says that he
'dropped baptisms and feudalisms and wandered over the
terraqueous planet seeking, one may say, the paradise we lost
long ago'. I liked the sound of that, and got hold of Clootz's
book, *Base constitutionnelle de la république du genre humain.*
It was then I invented Anacharsis McCracken and brought
him into my Sauchiehall Street saga. At that time, I was going
about Glasgow dressed in a black anorak I'd bought in Munich.
The word 'anacharsis' had in it for me that 'anorak', along with
'anarchism' and 'catharsis'. I think the last chapter of my sprawl-
ing manuscript was entitled in fact: 'Catharsis in Cathcart'.

I had a great black-and-red, cathartic time in Glasgow.

But it was going to take me years more, and much more
moving about, before I would get into the mental sphere and
the kind of writing I really wanted.

That has meant a certain type of poetry (poetry that 'gets
through to the white' and flows in open space), a certain type of

narrative writing (the waybook, that goes beyond both novel and travel-writing), and the practice of the essay (often devoted to figures that the culture-process has neglected, doesn't know how to use).

4

One of these neglected figures is Duns Scot, whom I have mentioned here and there, but of whom I have never spoken in detail. This is the appropriate moment to do so.

In Cologne, Germany, there is a tombstone on which can be read an inscription in Latin, beginning *Scotia me genuit* ('Scotland is where I was born') which, Englished, might go something like this:

> *Scotland saw my birth*
> *England made me a Franciscan*
> *France perfected my education*
> *Germany will see my death*

This stone marks the resting-place of John Duns Scot. Born in the village of Duns, to the south-east of Edinburgh, in 1266, John the Scot probably did his early studies at Dumfries and in the Scottish *studium* at Northampton, before going to Oxford, at that time an interesting enough Franciscan study-centre, where he completed his bachelor's degree. From Oxford, he went to Paris, where he spent four studious years (1293–1297), before coming back to Britain, living and working at Cambridge, then at Oxford. By 1302 he was on the move again – back to Paris, studying this time mainly under Gonzales of Spain. From there he returned to Oxford, then went back to Paris where he took his Doctor's degree. It was in 1307 that he left for Cologne, where he died in 1308.

While these movements are impressive and significant, they are not enough in themselves to turn Scot into an intellectual nomad of the first order. For that, we have to look at his works. Of the *Opera Omnia* (published in Paris between 1891 and 1895, then, at Rome, from 1950 on), written all in Latin, but an idiosyncratic Latin, with neologisms being created all along the way, I'll mention here only the *Opus Oxoniense*, the Oxford Opus, which contains John Scot's commentaries on the *Sentences* of Peter the Lombard (a standard text-book of the period), the

Tractatus de Primo Principio ('Treatise on the Primal Principle'), the *Questiones Quodlibeticae* ('The Quodlibetical Questions'), and the *Reportata Parisiensia* ('The Paris Reports'), which consist mainly in notes taken by others on John's Paris lectures. I stop bibliographical detail there, in order to insist rather on the position of Scot's work within the intellectual context of the time, and on the singular nature of that work.

The scattered archipelago of Scot's work not only stands out from the massive mediocrity of his contemporary situation (in this case, scholastic), which is the mark of all primal work, it stands opposite, indeed in opposition to, a work which was not at all mediocre, which amounted in fact to a conceptual cathedral, with a massive Aristotelian basis and elevated, Christianly divine towers: the *Summa Theologica* of Thomas Aquinas. Scot is the anti-Aquinas (in the same way as Schopenhauer was to be the anti-Hegel), and it is there that he appears as an intellectual nomad.

In the face of Aquinas' institutionalist massiveness, Scot is a wanderer in the desert, concerned with following tracks and pathways rather than with building edifices. For Aquinas, the city and the family go without saying, they are foundations (he has with him not only the *ecclesia*, but the philosophy of Aristotle, for whom man is essentially a political animal). For Duns Scot, the city is a late institution and, like the family, it is not principial, it is merely contractual. He's out for something more fundamental than the foundations of Aquinas' theology and Aristotle's metaphysics, and politics in the city-state or municipal sense (what he wants is something that could inform and inspire a *new* politics). In the place of philosophical (institutional) theology, he practises revelatory (investigative) theology. And the accent is on practice – *praxis*.

Scot has beliefs, and professes those beliefs, but it's obvious from an attentive reading of his texts (in one of them he speaks of 'theological persuasion, going from one believed thing to another') that for him there is a life outside belief and a thought outside theology – which is why his active thought has validity and value outside any strictly theological context. With regard to philosophy, he can 'do it' (he also studied thoroughly Plato and Aristotle), but he has no confidence in those whom he calls the *philosophantes*. And it's not only a question of lack of confidence, or a feeling that strictly philosophical discourse can go on *ad infinitum*, it is, more radically still, the fact that philosophy does not satisfy his intellect. That doesn't make him a total lughead or a logical positivist. It makes him something like a mathematician such as Cantor, who gets out of the infinite series of finite numbers and penetrates into the region of what he calls transfinite numbers. Neither finite, nor infinite, *transfinite*. We're concerned with a new category. Scot isn't content simply to make a point, or to develop a demonstration concerning the existence of universals, or the infallibility of the Pope, or the divine right of kings (though he could do a very nice job with the Immaculate Conception if put to it), he has a *praxis* leading to delight and delectation (*fruitio*, he says). His intelligence is extremely active, sensitive and intellectual at one and the same time. He works, not with beliefs, or with axioms, or with psychosocial realities, but with perceptions and insights, in a highly operative field. He has a fast and flickering way of thought. Ernest Renan, no fool, and a man with his own merits, but closer to Aquinas than to Scot, diagnoses in Duns a 'violent temperament' and an 'uncultured genius'. There is no violence, but there is an energy, a quickness, a dynamics. As to 'uncultured', no – not in any active sense of the word 'culture'. Scot is 'uncultured' in the sense that, as an active (non-denatured) intellect, as a free spirit, he stands outside the communal glue-job commonly called 'culture', but he is very much concerned with culture, in the sense of *growth* – and sudden growth, enlightened growth. Scot's thinking takes place outside the *ens commune* (established mental structures – 'common sense'), it is occupied not with *ens* (being, identity) or with *quidditas* (definition, taxonomy), but with what he calls *haecceitas*, thisness. Thisness can appear in anything, in next to nothing, in a stone, for example (stoniness may in fact be a good first locus: Scot refers to it in the *Opus Oxoniense* and in his Paris lectures) – it will be no less thisness for that, just as (as Scot says elsewhere), the whiteness of a moment is just as great as the whiteness of a year, or, for that matter, of eternity.

Situated at the limit of Aquinian theology and Aristotelian metaphysics, Scot is a wanderer at the limits who opens up an unedited space of thought (at the beginning of his *Primal Principle*, he evokes Moses' search for a 'promised land' – a metaphor later used also by Husserl for his investigations in phenomenology). This was felt in the Middle Ages, when he was known as *Doctor Subtilis*, 'the doctor of subtlety'. That, in later times, Britishers should have used his name to designate stupidity ('dunce') is no reflection on his thought but every reflection on the opaque dullness of certain civilizations.

One of the first Britishers to get into the Scotic thing in English was Gerald Manley Hopkins. Hopkins can at times be over-febrile but, given the scope of his investigations and the intellectual excitement they involved, given also the constraints he imposed on himself out of religious conviction and discipline, this is understandable enough. In August 1872, still flush from his first reading of Duns Scot, he was on holiday on the Isle of Man. In his note-book, for 10 August, we have this:

> I was looking at high waves. The breakers always are parallel to the coast and shape themselves to it except where the curve is sharp however the wind blows. [...] About all the turns of the scaping from the break and flooding of the wave to its run out again I have not yet satisfied myself. The shores are swimming and the eyes have before them a region of milky surf but it is hard for them to unpack the huddling and gnarls of the water and law out the shapes and the sequence of the running.

There you have Hopkins' sensation of the world, and it can lead to science on the one hand ('lawing out') and poetry on the other ('turns of the scaping'), both connected in a semantics that can bring together ecstasy and exactitude in quick, dynamic movement.

In later times, Duns Scot was really to come again into his own. Since the end of the nineteenth century, philosophy in Europe has been going through a radical crisis, with questions being raised as to its limits and perspectives. Among the foremost in this discussion and investigation was Martin Heidegger, trying to find ways into 'regions philosophy has never heard of', and Heidegger's doctoral thesis was based, precisely, on Duns Scot. In the cognate country of poetics, if we remember Ezra Pound's declaration at the entry to the unmarked field he felt opening before him at the beginning of the twentieth century that there was 'no Aquinas map', we can see the relevance of Duns Scot to this whole new area, which could lead maybe to a new era.

Having indicated a few focal points of energy, a few modes of questioning and a few lines of movement, it's that whole area I'll now enter into.

5

Even from its beginning, civilization was never, except by some, who saw in it a means of financial profit and political power, considered as an unmixed blessing. Hence Golden Age myths on the one hand, and Utopia visions on the other. But by the eighteenth century, criticism was not only coming faster, it was becoming more incisive. I'm thinking there of Rousseau. In the nineteenth century, Melville's Ishmael (the nomad) thinks to flee civilization by embarking on the *Pequod* for the Pacific, while Mark Twain's Huckleberry Finn 'lights out for the territory'. In Europe, Charles Fourier says that, if civilization took over from barbarity, it's time now to go from civilization to what he calls harmony. In the twentieth century, there's Freud's *Civilization and its Discontents* and Valéry's admonition, in his *Crisis of the Mind*, that our civilization is mortal – maybe, shall we add, mortiferous.

Along with this critique of civilization has gone a radical re-reading of history, seen no longer simply in terms of event and story, with more or less causal explanation and teleological perspective, but as a mathematical formula containing, above the line, politics, economics and technology, and, below the line, a psyche either flaccid and wobbly, or stunted and contorted.

That criticism is necessary in this context is something I go with. But criticist discourse tends to become a process in itself, integrated into the system. The result is a vast accumulation of studies and statistics that give the impression of being valid and up-to-date, but get nobody anywhere and tend to simply clutter up the space of manoeuvring.

A quicker procedure is required.

Now it's at the crises of civilization that the voice of the nomad is once more heard in the land. The figure I call the intellectual nomad has not only gone critically through all this context, he is the bearer of at least the beginnings of new language and new space. He has broken his way out of the labyrinth and moves in what may at first seem a void, but which is perhaps the high-energy field in which could emerge a (new) world.

The intellectual nomad will tend to find more confirmation for his activity and thought in science than in most of what is taken to be 'culture' (literature and art). That is normal, since most contemporary culture, when it is not simply a re-shuffling of the old habitual cards, is the expression of the diminished context that is in question, or tries to satisfy its lack in simplistic ways, whereas science advances with less encumbrance and, at least in its outer reaches, opens on to the space-field, the proto-world in which the intellectual nomad lives, moves and has his becoming.

The idealistic structures have collapsed and crumbled – leaving in their wake, most of the time, only confusion, fantasy, horror or irony. But work has gone on, in a reality sensed and known as complex, moving, subtle. To take only some Scottish examples, Maxwell's thermodynamics and Robert Brown's 'brownian movement' are relevant here. We're at the frontiers of a closed system, at the limits of the validity of classical description. To get into the total energy of the universe, seen as an open thermodynamic system highly heterogeneous and unstable, demands more than classical and local description. Diffusive movements, unforeseen trajectories, wave functions lead into new complex fields. Interest concentrates on erratic behaviour: fluctuations, bifurcations, dissipative structures. It's when it moves out of stability that matter gains new properties. We hear of randomness, chaos-maps, matrices of density. We hear too of new forms of coherence: auto-organization, auto-poetics. We come to what Thoreau, the intellectual nomad of Walden, calls 'a larger sense than common sense permits'. We're in a new epistemological landscape. It's like a complex, moving seascape, with a headland of conceptual possibility, and poetry in the air like the wings of an albatross.

This is the real field. And the question is how to integrate it into existence and culture.

It will take a combination of resistance, research and regrounding; it will take a lot of mobile, tactical, strategic thinking; it will take long-term policy in place of shifty, superficial, myopic politics; it will take a really grounded, openly moving poetics. A tall order. But it can, perhaps, be done.

What is certain is that trying to map it out is the greatest intellectual pleasure around.

Rimbaud, Glasgow and Ways West

Me, I walk the roads, that's all.
                              (Arthur Rimbaud)

1

In his determination to become a *voyant* (a man of vision) or, to
use the old Vedic language in which such a project was formu-
lated for the first time, a *rishi*, Rimbaud threw himself body
and soul into his method. Wanting to find the 'real meaning' of
the self, which meant regaining the 'primitive state of a son of
the sun', he set out on what the Veda calls the Northern Route:
'As for the sun-world, it is to be arrived at on the High North
Road, by means of research on the self.'

For such an enterprise, nobody was better qualified than
Arthur Rimbaud. He had the necessary physical robustness:
'For eight days I had worn out my shoes on the stones of the
road.' He had intellectual energy and clarity: 'Where thinking's
concerned, I fear no one.' And he had a certain moral hardness: 'heartless Rimbaud' he called himself.

And yet, what a welter of tears and sobbing. For, however
excellent his personal qualities, Rimbaud is the product of a
culture: that of a certain narrow-minded, bourgeois, stifling civilization. Despite his efforts to become a 'barbarian', this culture
(based on Christianity, with a whole superstructure of moral
values), never lets him alone: 'I'm damned by the rainbow.' It's
this culture which casts the colours of hell over his enterprise,
and it's the 'realism' of the mentality it engenders which finally
gets the better of his revolt: 'I'm here, I'm still here.'

The end of the nineteenth century in Europe saw three
radical attempts (beside which most art pales) to get out of the
dull and constrictive state-of-things, three focal points of
incandescent energy: Rimbaud, Van Gogh, Nietzsche. Rimbaud,
the comet; Van Gogh, the crazy sun; Nietzsche, the aurora borealis. They all die young. They all live in solitude, and two of them
go mad. After his 'Faustian' attempt, all Rimbaud feels, deep
down, is an overwhelming boredom, while opting, on the surface,
for the realist solution that Goethe found for his Faust by
turning him into an engineer. Between the 'millions of golden

17

birds' of Rimbaud's primal vision and the 'eight kilos of gold' of the final period, the gold that was going to enable him to settle down with a little peace in the world, you have the whole history of European revolt. A tragic story, not without melodrama.

Where are we, a hundred years or so after Rimbaud?

We? Since I know no one better than myself, as Thoreau says in the first chapter of *Walden*, I'll formulate that question differently: where am I? Talking about oneself isn't always such a hateful enterprise, so long as you go about it radically enough. It's the only way to get anywhere beyond flat sociology.

2

At one time, Arthur Rimbaud represented for me the *nec plus ultra* of poetry and life, and I read his work in Glasgow with enthusiasm, but not without lucidity. Phrases of his such as *l'aube exaltée ainsi qu'un peuple de colombes*, 'the dawn exalted like a people of doves', *oiseaux clabaudeurs aux yeux blonds*, 'clamouring birds with blond eyes', 'blew my mind', as we used to say. I was living in Glasgow, at that time one of Europe's hell-holes, where I wandered about obsessively by day and by night, but now and then I'd leave the city on foot to walk the thirty or so miles down to the coast.

'Ever since it became nominally christianized', writes Rémy de Gourmont, 'Europe has only survived thanks to a few drops of pagan elixir saved from the jealousy of its converters.' It was that elixir Rimbaud was out to recover. That's what he thirsts for, all his life a 'comedy of thirst', as he says, stemming from a refusal to drink the 'civilized concoctions' he was offered. He often conceives of that elixir as a dew, and his poems are full of images of dawn and morning freshness, with a nostalgia for the streams of the Ardennes. In June 1872, he writes from Paris to his friend Ernest Delahaye:

> Strange, the life we lead in this cosmorama. The provinces, where they feed on meal and mud, and guzzle down bad wine and country beer, I'm not homesick for that. [...] But this place: all distillation, synthetic living, narrowness. And the damned summer weather: it's not just that the heat never lets up, it's to see that everyone loves the 'fine weather', and since everyone is a pig, I loathe the summer, it kills me whenever it makes its appearance. I've got a thirst on me as if I was dying of gangrene. The Belgian and Ardennes rivers, the caves, that's what I feel the loss of.

18

Rimbaud, 'the man of our lands as he was before the Greco-Roman yoke clamped down', says André Breton somewhere. At least potentially, and as project. Rimbaud is both potency and project. But the yoke was there. And the yoke won.

In a very real sense, Rimbaud isn't 'French'. He's too abrupt and rough to be French. He comes from farther back. He tended to see himself as a Gaul, and that's maybe so. What's sure is that it's hard to fit him into the categories of classical French literature. In fact, when set up against a figure like Rimbaud, the very notion of French literature pales into insignificance. When he mentions Rimbaud, a very French mind like Mallarmé adopts an attitude of ironical distance. Gide feels uneasy in the presence of Rimbaud, suspecting that, in comparison, all his living and thinking is artificial. Rimbaud can't be gauged in purely literary terms. His energies go way out beyond that circumscribed sphere. And we should be able to speak of it without dragging in all kinds of religious, metaphysical, occultist paraphernalia as has so often been done.

3

But let's come back to Glasgow, and to my 'Rimbaud period' in that city with its bituminous deserts and its sinister fog.

I'd often go up to the Necropolis, the graveyard hill that looks out over the old quarters of the town: grey-black stone, rows of yellow chimneys, steeples groping hysterically for the heavens, a desperate sun, scattered flights of starlings. As for the gravestones themselves, they were mostly made of a soft grey stone so worn by age and weather that the features of the angels sculpted on them had become sharp, vicious, devilish.

On the south side of the river, in the Gorbals, which had been Jewish before they became Pakistani, there was a whole Orient: women in multi-coloured saris trailing about the wet, dirty streets; and in the local library there were books in Hebrew that made me think of the centres of Hassidism. At the corner of any street, I might have met, in the guise of some old Glaswegian in a murky gaberdine, the rabbi Elimelekh or the Baal-Shem himself.

I was right in the middle of a transcendental trip.

I read like a demon all the most extravagant literature I could get my hands on: theological, mystical, philosophical – not because I was looking for truth, but because they gave me matter that I could burn. It was less a question of information and culture than of *combustion*. Those readings and those walkings helped me to *take off*.

'Where is the way?', asks Faust, and Mephisto replies: 'There is no way, you are doomed to wander throughout endless solitudes...'

And then, suddenly, all that theopathic atmosphere broke up, and in its place there was an emptiness:

> *Then came the emptiness*
> *watching the red sun*
> *in the winter sky*
> *and the bare branches*
> *('What do you see on the tree, ô Arjuna?')*

It was the second stage beginning – at least that's how with hindsight I see it now. I had a big room with whitewashed walls, but not much light got through:

> *All along the winter*
> *in that dark room*
>
> yatra na anyat prashyati
> na anyat shrinoti
> na anyat vijanati

Yes, it was emptiness ('Where you hear nothing, see nothing, know nothing'), but without the plenitude the Sanskrit text speaks of. When I looked at the wall, it wasn't my 'original face', as the Zen texts speak of, that I saw. It was just blankness.

What had happened? I don't think you can interpret such breaks simply in terms of biological growth – the end of adolescence, for instance. That's the paternalist interpretation. Biology certainly has something to do with it: the amount of vital energy spent in such transcendental errancies is enormous and can't be continued indefinitely. The fast transitions between exaltation and depression are also exhausting. But there was also an intellectual realization: the becoming aware of the fact that the 'search for the self' can in reality lead nowhere. There was and is no self. So, nothing at all? Just the performance of duties, or a game to be played? End in any case of the transcendental landscape, the metaphysical mindscape.

4

That, I think, is what happened to Rimbaud. That's where the second stage of his life and of his peregrinations begins. From now on, he's no longer in search of 'the place and the formula', he's hounded by more immediate necessities. Psychologically, he's a vagabond of vacuity.

'M. Arthur Rimbaud, Hôtel de l'Univers, Aden'. That's his address. And the phrases that turn up again and again in his letters are of the type: 'My life's a nightmare', 'Well, let's just hope for the best.'

If only, one finds oneself wishing, he'd been able to continue his radical explorations, but with other means, over there on the 'incandescent shores' of the Red Sea. The Arab countries might have provided him with elements for a new formulation of his quest. But he seems to have left all of his early movement behind him. All he's concerned with now is business, desperate commercial transactions. All that remains of the first movement is the energy, now expended on body-racking desert trails. But there are also the geographical reports. And that 'curious album' he sometimes refers to. Would it just have been full of 'curiosities' more or less exotic, or...

I felt I had to start again. From the ground up. I had my 'companions' behind me: Rimbaud, Van Gogh, Nietzsche, with Whitman and Thoreau before them. It's good to have companions, to believe in the possibility of a community. But at bottom you're all alone, and there comes a time when you know it.

It was the winter of the mind. A cold wind was blowing from the cosmos. Nietzsche had talked about the death of God ('Isn't it getting colder all around? Isn't it getting darker?') Less mythologically, less religiously put, what was going on was the last throes of transcendental transcendentalism, the last throes of a metaphysically based culture. I'd become 'absolutely modern', as Rimbaud said. With my feet on the ground and my brain bare. Evolving in an emptiness:

> *In this world*
> *always harder and more acrid*
> *more and more white*
>
> *you ask me for news?*
>
> *the ice breaks in blue characters*
> *who can read them?*
>
> *I talk grotesquely to myself*
> *and the silence answers*

I still tried to say, in as bare a way as possible, where I felt I was maybe going. Or at least where I was at. Apart from these odd scrapings of my own pen, the poems that spoke to me most were haiku:

> *The sea's so cold*
> *even the gull*
> *can't get to sleep*

> *A snowy morning*
> *and here I sit*
> *chewing dried salmon*

And then, very gradually, things seemed to get in movement again, in a different way:

> *If the great frost*
> *has not bitten the branches*
> *how can plum blossom*
> *be fragrant?*

Without in any way denying my earlier 'companions', I'd found new ones: Dogen, Hakuin, Basho, Sesshu – all those who walk on the 'path of emptiness' (*sunyavada*).

5

Let's come back for a moment to Rimbaud. If, re-reading his writings today, I often find them too 'poetic', the man remains for me more than a poet, he is one of the ontological heroes of modern culture.

Hart Crane, moving desperately between Brooklyn and Key West, said that Rimbaud was the last great poet our civilization would know. Even if that were true (and I don't think it is), it would not matter. The real question, of which 'our' civilization has hardly an inkling, is elsewhere. To be recognized as a 'great poet' by this civilization, according to its rundown categories, is neither here nor there (cf. Nietzsche: 'Do what goes beyond praise and even all understanding'). The real work consists in changing the categories, grounding a new anthropology, moving towards a new experience of the earth and of life. *The Book of Chao* puts it this way: 'Rising above symbols and entering the naked region.'

One single beam of white light annihilates the culture-comedy.

On a Ridge between Two Seas

Like one suddenly raised to the heights and given wings.
(Friedrich Nietzsche)

1

There's a passage in the fragments Nietzsche wrote for a projected *Birth of Philosophy*, a passage in which he evokes the earliest of the early Greek philosophers: Thales, Anaximander, Parmenides, Empedocles, Heraclitus... In those times, he says, such minds were recognized, acknowledged and listened to. Whereas, at other times, 'the philosopher is a solitary traveller, placed by chance in a hostile environment, wandering about from place to place [...] he is like a comet, an astonishing phenomenon, but not allowed to shine like a star in the solar system of a complete culture.'

Nietzsche in this text is obviously enough describing his own situation, his own existential and intellectual activity, and our times.

2

If we speak in terms of philosophical or cultural anthropology, the type of the artist–philosopher, or philosopher–artist, to which Nietzsche feels he belongs, which he manifestly represents, sometimes to the point of rhetorical grandiloquence, but most often with incisive irony, an aphoristic–anarchistic intellectual energy, and a poetic conceptualization, will in the first instance be expatriate, fatherlandless. How, he asks, can 'a son of the future' feel 'at home' anywhere today? No ideal whatsoever can make him believe in the possibility of a homely settlement, whether it be an ideal of the past (conservative) or an ideal of the future (progressive), whether it be an ideal of general world-wide humanitarianism, or an ideal of specific nationalist identity; the result, given the ground, will only, and inevitably, be mediocrity of one type or another. The artist–philosopher is too well-informed and too far-travelled to be, in this context, a partisan and spokesman of one or the other

23

camp. So he will prefer to live 'on mountains' and 'in the margin'. Far, however, from satisfying himself with any kind of easy scepticism, or being an eternal no-sayer, he will, within his distance and his silence, undertake a certain type of work: a work that will involve both wide-ranging investigation and poetic creation.

Not only would this work not easily fit into the categories of the time, but, if it were listened to at all, it would, in varying degrees, be misunderstood. Its relevance would be seen only when the age of nihilism (which, from the late nineteenth century on, would last about two hundred years) had been thoroughly worked out, and when the culture would see the need for new paths, new maps. Nietzsche said he himself would begin to be understood by about 1901 – maybe there he was being over-optimistic: the worst misinterpretation of his work would come in the twenties and thirties.

3

I first came across the work of Nietzsche in Glasgow during my second year at university (but outside the university curriculum). 'Do you wish, brother, to seek the way to yourself? Then linger a while and listen to me', he says in *Thus Spake Zarathustra*. I lingered a while. In fact, during those years, I read everything he wrote, or at least everything published in what were then called the Complete Works.

I saw Nietzsche, radical poet–philosopher, stressing, for a fundamental start, physiological and elementary factors such as the food you eat, the air you breathe, the physical space in which you live and move. He considered, for example, that a German diet of boiled meat, vegetables cooked in fat, pastries and alcohol, would make a brute even of a potential genius. As to a British diet, somewhat similar, it would 'give the intelligence heavy feet', making it inclined to lounge in cerebral indolence and viscerally reject anything at all resembling intellectual adventure. The same goes for air (atmospheric and cultural) – usually thick, heavy and noisome: 'German intellect is my bad air, I breathe with difficulty in this foul psychological atmosphere'. 'The book of mountain air' is how, on the contrary, he describes *Thus Spake Zarathustra*. With regard to place, in search of a climate propitious to vitality and intellect, he pointed to Provence, Jerusalem, Athens – regions of sunlight and clarity (some of those he evokes are no longer so). He himself lived his most creative period in the mountains of northern Italy and Switzerland: 'I have a predilection for those places where in all directions one can drink from swift-running streams.' It was there – around Genoa, the Ligurian coast and farther up in Sils-Maria, that he wrote those extraordinary books that are *Dawn, Thus Spake Zarathustra, Untimely Considerations, The Twilight of the Idols, Ecce Homo.*

For Nietzsche, something had gone drastically wrong with European culture. The nineteenth century was a mess, and, unless something was done fast, the twentieth would be worse. So he undertakes an analysis of the whole of Western civilization. Things began to get out of kilter when the original Greek *phusis* was lost, leaving the mind high and dry. That's where Socrates starts up: rationalist dialectics. But if Nietzsche is anti-Socrates (ratiocination) and anti-Plato (idealization), he is much more anti-Christian. For him, the introduction of Christianity was the beginning of a very long and dreary end: 'Two thousand years of hostility to nature and the violation of humanity'. For Nietzsche as psychologist, any belief in God stems ultimately from a weariness of life, a weariness (alternating with salvation-army type joy) that 'wants to get to the ultimate in one leap, in one fatal leap', whereas the only way to get to the ultimate (if it is useful even to entertain the notion) is by a long existential–intellectual path. But it is not mainly the theology of Christianity, its ultimate answer, that Nietzsche attacks, it is its everyday morality, a morality propagated by 'that perfidious order of goblins': priests, pastors, ministers, evangelists and general do-gooders. With Christianity, everything is banalized and reduced to the lowest common denominator. With Nietzsche and his Zarathustra, on the contrary, morality has to yield before the need to augment one's own life. Life-values come before the moral law, always upheld most vociferously and narrowly by those who have a grudge against life, or who merely use it to camouflage sordid interests. Christianity would last a long time, but in its wake, contemporaneous with its survival here and there, sometimes in forms not overtly using its name, would come its legacy, a numb and mindless nihilism. 'The destruction of the moral interpretation of the world, which has no longer any sanction, results in nihilism', writes Nietzsche in *The Antechrist*. Once the pillar to which humanity had clung for two millennia had collapsed (and it had begun to fall with the investigations of Copernicus), men would be helpless and bewildered, stumbling around (the short-sighted leading the blind) in an undefined X. One could foresee philosophies of the absurd, religions getting into all sorts of contortions in order to survive, political follow-ups to religious millenniarism, all kinds of paroxystic outbursts from mind-starved multitudes, and a culture Nietzsche describes as a disgusting stew in which float bits of this and bits of that the very dogs wouldn't look at. A hundred years after he wrote this, one can hardly say his predictions were false: they have been verified practically all along the line. But unlike, say, Spengler, Nietzsche is neither resigned nor reductive. There is, with him, a possibility not only of resistance, but of clearance.

The propagators of new space would in the first place be 'Hyperboreans', living in distance, but in that distance working at a potential general space. Having educated and cultivated themselves, education and culture being for Nietzsche 'the means to promote inside and outside of ourselves the development of the philosopher and the artist, and thus to work at the perfection of nature' (another lapidary phrase puts it this way: 'We want to be the poets of our life!'), they would be able to come forward as educators of a society.

Where could this essential, educative–cultural work be done? Not only did the educational system Nietzsche knew not encourage this work (see his essay: 'On the future of our educational institutions'), it was based more and more on principles of comfortable mediocrity, with quantity and extension its main criteria. Nietzsche himself worked for ten years within the context of a philological seminar at the university of Basle, till illness released him from it. After that, he was on his own, and blessed his illness for the liberation, for if he had stayed in that context, he might never have developed, might have remained definitely under-developed, like, he says, Kant: 'A university scholar can never become a philosopher, for even Kant could not do it, and remained to the end, in spite of his innate genius, in a quasi cocoon stage.' Nietzsche then was out on his own, accompanied only by his shadow, and by ghost-figures such as Zarathustra, Ariane and the Overman. But the idea of new institutions never left him. As late as the *Ecce Homo*, that thunder-and-lightning little autobiography, he was writing: 'One day institutions will be needed in which men will live and teach as I understand living and teaching.' In Basle, he imagined a group meeting in some 'owl's cave' on the outskirts of the city. Later, he projected a 'new Greek academy', a 'council' in the Grisons, an Institute (*Anstalt*) of culture. Throughout his wanderings and writings, he comes back to the idea again and again: 'I know that in the not too distant future, many Germans will feel as I do the desire to live for one's education free from politics, nationality and newspapers... There must yet be circles such as the monastic orders were, only with broader contents.'

'Germans... in the not too distant future'. There again was the expression of one of Nietzsche's more optimistic moments (it is hard to do without at least some *occasional* optimism...). If the need Nietzsche evoked was to be felt 'in the future', it would be in no national context. The work of the radical precursor he was would be appreciated publicly in Denmark before it was noticed at all in Germany. Which did not prevent Nietzsche from pursuing it 'far from the market place and fame', 'six thousand feet above men and time', struggling at one and the same time against the modern will to nonentity, its aversion to original thought, and his own 'black floods'. That work consists, materially, in a series of books that are so many poetic–philosophical essays (trials, attempts), written in a sharp and saltatory style, aimed in the first instance at clearing away all hindrances, encumbrances and entanglements, and thereafter at revealing a new–old ground of existence, an auroral space–time, which is the place of that 'humanly super-human well-being and goodwill' Nietzsche exemplified in Zarathustra: an area of physical, ethical and intellectual radiance.

That, roughly summarized, is what I got from Nietzsche when I first read him, in entirety, years ago, and it is what I still retain, for it remains, to a large extent, 'inactually actual'. Nietzsche is one of the indispensable companions for anyone who, intellectually and artistically, is out to do more than function automatically within a debased system or contribute to the entertainment industry.

4

Looking at him now from afar, I see Nietzsche as walking a high ridge between two seas. The 'high ridge' is the one he evoked in *The Birth of Philosophy*, that 'ridge line' that must be maintained if culture is not to subside into total confusion and platitude, if fertile and brilliant contact is to be kept up between the past and the future. As to the two seas, they can be interpreted differently according to various points along the path.

At one point, we can see them as the sea of art on the one hand, the sea of knowledge on the other. Nietzsche was all for knowledge: the human sciences and the natural sciences. They had been necessary to transcend the belief and faith of the Middle Ages, and they were still useful aids against all kinds of recurrent mumbo jumbo. But knowledge was not sufficient in itself – it can become heavy and cumbersome (think of Zarathustra's camel), so, against knowledge, Nietzsche stresses the necessity of art and an aesthetic sense of life. On that ridge of his, you have something going on that is beyond art and knowledge, without being anything like a (Hegelian) synthesis.

The two seas, at another point along the path, can be seen as poetry and philosophy. Nietzsche is hard on poetry, and rightly so, if poetry is to get rid of its habits and facilities. He loathes lyrical sentiment, declares that poets lie too much and that, to write good prose, you have to be a poet who knows how to fight against poetry – and at the same time he calls himself 'a poet, to the limit of the word'. As to philosophy, whose birth he salutes, and of which he wishes a re-birth, hardly any philosopher finds favour in his eyes except Heraclitus – all the rest are talking sophisticatedly out of a blockage or a sickness. More abstractly, he will say that the task of the philosopher, as he envisages it, is to 'have resound within himself the universal symphony, and project it outside himself in the form of concepts'. But elsewhere he will say that there is, at times, an 'immediate evidence' that is difficult to get at by means of concepts and reason. Again, on the ridge, something is going on that is beyond both poetry and philosophy as commonly understood.

It is possible also, at another point, to see the two seas as East and West. We know that Nietzsche was attracted to what he could find of Eastern thought. He speaks of 'the heights of the Hindu atmosphere', and as epigraph to *Morgenröthe* ('Dawns'), quotes the *Rig-Veda*: 'There are so many dawns that have not yet shed their light.' Eastern references abound in his work. At the same time, he was critical of Buddhism as being too negative: concerned only with the cessation of suffering, not with the dance of existence, the poetics of life. The fact is, Buddhism came to him via the Schopenhauerian version – he knew nothing of the higher reaches of the Mahayana. But had he done so, I think he would have been delighted. So that in his walk along that high ridge, I see him meeting now and then Dogen, or Hakuin, or the Taoist Chuang-Tzu.

Farther along again, we can see the two seas as homeless-ness on the one hand (uncertain wandering), and on the other, a new situation, a new grounding and founding.

And finally, the two seas are those of serenity and madness.

5

I've spoken of something 'going on' along that high ridge, something that doesn't fit easily into the categories, something that goes on above all the quarrelsome dialectics, the localist squabblings, and the fantasias of less developed minds. This 'going on' is not simply a series of works, the marks of a career. It is a life-path, a wayfaring, and it comprises projections and conceptions as well as artefacts. Philosophically, it is something that does not merely pose problems (academic philosophery) or ask questions (socratic philosophism), it goes through *askesis*, psychodrama and existential exposure. Poetically, it evolves from an act of writing that, with its energy, agility and acumen, leaves most literature standing and looking rather foolish. 'Let every body become a dancer, and every mind a bird!', Nietzsche cries. Let's say that Nietzschean writing is a faster and faster wing-beat across wider and wider spaces.

One last remark. No one, I think, will fully understand Nietzsche who cannot see why, one day in the streets of Turin, he flung his arms round the neck of a poor old tired cab-horse.

The Ruins and Lights of Ezra Pound

> Only in the high air and the great clarity can there be a just estimation of values.
>
> (Ezra Pound)

1

Like his hero, Odysseus the wanderer ('the live man among duds' – *Polite Essays*), Pound carries with him more 'flames and voices' than most writers. He is animated by that energy which makes a man want to go outside the existing categories, create, or at least transmit his apprehension of, something that goes beyond himself and may transfigure the all-too-human context, enliven dead time.

What Pound, with his 'flames and voices' is concerned with is no less than a civilization, a world: 'Quite simply, I want a new civilization' (*The Exile*, no. 3, 1928). This obviously implies other men, hence attempts at communication. No communication, no world. If we can say that the poet, as pure artist, is content to sing the 'flames and voices', leaving it more or less to chance whether other men listen in and comprehend or not, a man may go out actively to communicate the energy and the message of these 'flames and voices'. At that moment, he becomes a teacher.

To become a teacher in *this* sense requires confidence *vis-à-vis* the world, perhaps even a certain amount of presumption. Pound is not lacking in either. And it is no accident that he should take as his models the Confucianists, those most presumptuous of teachers, those most instilled with a belief in the value of education and in their educative capacities.

Such a teacher, who is presenting more than a fragment of utilitarian knowledge, rather a totally new apprehension, is bound to come up against difficulties. His presumptive assertion, while some will kindle to it, and attempt to live by it, will be irritating to those more restricted in their outlook (those who proceed by a steady tick-tock, as Nietzsche puts it). His conception, unverifiable by the constituted logic (though Pound takes pains to prove that he has mucked about in history,

30

adducing historical evidence and citing moments of earlier culture to show that his notion is grounded), will be looked at askance by dealers in more positivistic discourse. The cultural bureaucracies, as well as the media of mediocracy, will try to keep him in cold storage – until such time as he can be safely brought back in, as a culture-corpse. Then too, as Pound says, any glimpse into what he calls the Paradiso, which changes radically a man's whole outlook, is enough to deprive him of worldly consideration, because he will be too far out for normal apprehension. That is all in the order of things.

Yet it is from teachers such as these that the vivification of human life, human society comes, if it comes at all. Without periodical 'revivifications', implying the instilling of new conceptions, the creation of new values, a new 'active image' (Hegel), civilization would lapse into one vast mechanical platitude, with recurrent outbreaks of agitated commotion or mindless violence as sole human manifestation.

2

At a time when Europe (and not only Europe) seemed to be definitively losing its energies and settling into monstrous platitude, Nietzsche gave what still remains the most radical diagnosis of its state. Without going into all the aspects of this diagnosis, it is useful, in the present context, to remember that, in the universities, he sees an absurd and sterile accumulation of dead knowledge (cf. Santayana, *Interpretations of Poetry and Religion*: 'the most minute and comprehensive studies do not teach us what the spirit of man should have learned by its long living'), while in society at large what passes for culture is a vague stew (going one better, Pound speaks of 'stale sewage'). The fundamental dearth in the culture-area will never be seen by the 'cultivated people' (sometimes called 'the elite'). Satisfied with what Nietzsche calls a culture-skin (*Bildungshaut*), they are part of the rot, their culture being at the level of cosmetics, not cosmos. It is certain too that a merely sociological point of view will never get us very far. From a flatly sociological standpoint, there is always 'a culture' As Borges says of the Yahoos, through the voice of Brodie (in *Brodie's Report*): 'They have institutions, a king, they use a language founded on generic concepts, they believe, like the Hebrews and the Greeks, in the divine origin of poetry and have an intuition that the soul survives the death of the body. They also believe in punishments and rewards. In short, they also represent culture.' The list of characteristics could be changed, the point remains. In the face of the lack of a living culture – a lack felt neither by the savants, nor the consumers of mass-culture, nor the cultivated, nor the culture-sociologists – Nietzsche's answer is education, education towards culture defined socially as 'a unity of style in all the life-manifestations of a people' (*Untimely Considerations*) or, more personally, as high individuation.

For the education he envisaged, Nietzsche saw the necessity of new institutions, beyond the dictates of the state. With the idea of a new 'Greek academy' in mind, he made an attempt to found at Nice an institute that would gather together the first 'good Europeans', free spirits beyond the nationalist nexus. Similarly, Pound aimed at various times to found an Arts College in London, with the same intellectual impetus as the Renaissance academies; a Paideuma Institute in the States; and a centre of advanced studies (the 'Ezuversity', as he jokingly refers to it) at Rapallo.

The *Guide to Kulchur* can be seen as one of the textbooks of Pound's never founded super-college (others would be H*ow to Read, Make it New*, and his Confucian translations). Presented jocularly in a letter (February 1937) as 'all wot Ez knows, for seven and saxpence', it is dedicated to those 'struggling in the desert' (that 'desert of our exhausted culture' – Nietzsche, *Birth of Tragedy*) and it is meant to provide the basis of a living culture, i.e. 'the gristly roots of ideas that are in action'.

3

A word first as to the method. This pedagogical guide to culture is the work of a poet. We might even speak, no doubt at the risk of scandalizing the 'serious', of *poetic pedagogy*. It is a book written by an active intellect, and if it is recalled that the term for active intellect in Aristotle is *nous poetikos*, this will help perhaps to show up the word 'poetic' in its true light.

As to pedagogy, let's listen to Sir Philip Sidney (sixteenth century):

For suppose it be granted (that which I suppose with great reason may be denied), that the Philosopher in respect of his methodical proceeding, doth teach more perfectly than the Poet: yet do I thinke, that no man is so much *Philophilosophos,* as to compare the Philosopher in moving, with the Poet. And that moving is of a higher degree than teaching, it may by this appeare: that it is well nigh the cause and the effect of teaching. For who will be taught, if hee bee not moved with desire to be taught? And what so much good doth that teaching bring forth... as that it moveth one to doe that which it doth teach? For as Aristotle sayth, it is not Gnosis, but Praxis must be the fruit. And howe Praxis cannot be, without being moved to practise, it is no hard matter to consider.

The way Pound goes about getting the mind of the student in movement is analogous to Nietzsche's method in philosophy: proceeding by aphorism, and quick but illuminating jumps in and out of sundry matters in various fields ('Does any really good mind ever get a kick out of studying stuff that has been put into watertight compartments and hermetically sealed?'). Pound himself calls this method the Ideogramic Method (elsewhere: The Method of Luminous Detail), defined so: 'The ideogramic method consists of presenting one facet and then another until at some point one gets off the dead and desensitized surface of the reader's mind, on to a part that will register.'

Before going further into Pound's practice, let's look, for a recommendation of the aphoristic method, to someone considerably less volatile than Pound: Francis Bacon. In *The Advancement of Learning* (Pound had this in mind, as well as the Confucian *Ta Hio,* The Great Learning, when he wrote his *Guide,* the original title of which was *The New Learning*), Bacon states that 'the writing in aphorisms hath many excellent virtues, whereto the writing in method doth not approach.' 'Made out of the pith and heart of sciences' (Pound himself, quoting a Chinese student's definition of poetry, speaks of 'piths and gists'), and going outside 'discourse of connexion and order', the aphoristic presentation of knowledge takes the student into an area where he must act himself – it 'points to action'. 'Representing a knowledge broken' it 'invites men to enquire further', whereas 'methods carrying the show of a total, do secure men as if they were at farthest'.

Pound's method is out for a vision of ensemble, but he makes no claim to a total discourse, to exhaustivity. As he takes pains to point out, his book is a guide *to* culture, not *through* culture, and all he is providing are a few axes of reference, lighting up a field which cannot be laid out objectively, and merely learned, but demands the student's informed, and wide-awake activity. The book might in fact best be seen as a kind of gymnastic preparation for the leap into poetry.

Which brings us back to that much-vexed word, and to the content of Pound's teaching.

4

Pound sees the poet working 'at the very crux of a clarified conception' (essay in *The New Age*, 1912), moving in and through sense impressions towards a concept and from it back to sense impressions. Reading what he writes in the *Guide* about Sigismundo Malatesta's Tempio, one of his cultural 'highs': 'If the Tempio is a jumble and junk shop, it nevertheless registers a concept, there is no other single man's effort equally registered', we inevitably think of the *Guide to Kulchur* itself, and of Pound's effort in general. What we are presented with in the culture-book (not to speak here of the *Cantos*), is an apparently heterogeneous miscellany of impressions and disorganized references, with no genetic connection, a rag-bag of random comments. The word 'guide' would seem to be a misnomer, maybe a joke. And yet, knowing as we do that Pound as poet, in all his work, is moving, struggling to move, towards a 'clarified conception', and that the way to it for him is not logical and linear, but through a welter, we can at least give him the benefit of the doubt, and ask ourselves whether this conception cannot in fact be in-gathered from the disorganized mass. Whether the *Guide* itself succeeds or not in the move towards clarification is debatable (at the very least, it awakens desire), but here we prefer to consider the general theory. For even if Pound himself failed in his practice (and if he did, even as according to his own estimation he did, failures such as this make success *within the system* look ridiculous), other 'horrible workers' (as Rimbaud called them) can carry on where he left off. To the present writer, any work of poetry (to speak only of poetry) situated below the Poundian effort (i.e. refusing it or neglecting it), may well be part of the 'successful' literature of the times, but it is not at the cutting edge of poetic movement, and will not open up that area of energy and light which is lacking both on our cultural map, and in our living.

Implicit in Pound's poetry, as in any poetry worth its salt, there is a philosophy (not, as Pound says, 'merely a philosophism' – *Guide*). This statement, and the use of the word 'philosophy' already requires some qualification. It is not as if the 'philosophy' were a separate body, which the poetry would merely illustrate – a philosophy with its own logic, which poetry would 'translate' into its own terms. Such a separation is itself perhaps the symptom of an unhealthy state of affairs. If Pound refuses the philosophy of Socrates, with its discursive logic, it is because he sees it (letter to Katue Kitasono, 1940) as 'a mere splitting, an impoverishment of understanding' (though it led to the establishment of particular sciences). What he is concerned with is a more sense-bearing philosophy, a philosophy of energy and light rather than logic and formalism (Fenollosa was to use 'logicianised' as a pejorative epithet). As representatives of such a philosophy he sees, within the European sphere, Scot Erigena ('Erigena had a nice mind, full of light and had perceived quite a lot' – letter to George Santayana, 1940), and Richard of St Victor (the Scots theologian who spent most of his life at the abbey of St Victor in Paris) whose definition of contemplation as radiating from a centre, like light from the sun, and reaching out in an infinite number of ways to things related or dependent, was to be central to Pound's poetic practice. A lot of the thinking Pound finds most germane to his concerns went on in fact in the medieval church (though he has no sympathy for 'dead cod about God' – *Guide*). It is against this background that he reads Dante's *Commedia* (and the *Cantos* were meant to do the same work for the modern age) as 'a symbol of mankind's struggle upward out of ignorance into the clear light of philosophy' (*The Spirit of Romance*).

5

But it is in Confucius that he finds the body of thought most congenial to him. What Pound appreciates first and foremost in Confucius (or, rather, the Confucian Classics – in which, by the way, there is more Taoism than Pound realized) is a sense of co-ordination which he finds lacking in the two culture-movements which have largely shaped the mind of Europe: Greek philosophical thought, which Pound criticizes as being utterly irresponsible; and Christianity, which he says was never a balanced system. The final outcome might be described succinctly as dessicated intellectuality, a psychological mess, and a general lack of balance – with nothing (except at rare moments and sporadic attempts by individuals or small groups) like the Great Digest (*Ta Hio*), or The Unwobbling Pivot (*Chung Yung*), to keep things in a coherent equilibrium. If there is this sense of co-ordination in Confucius, it is because there lies at the centre of his thought the idea of one principle, 'the total light-process' (elsewhere translated by Pound as 'the transforming and nurturing processes of Heaven and Earth'). This principle changes its mode of operation according to context – so that, for example, the clear energy of sunlight is the same force as sincerity in man.

It is an awareness of this principle, and its branching out, that make for realness in the individual, and, through the inter-action of individuals, the warp and woof of society, and, beyond society, the very foundation of the world. Cosmos, world, society, individual are gathered together in one vast inter-locked activity, that basic principle (*tao*) working subtly through-out: 'The spirits of the energies and of the rays have their operative virtue.' And it is the business of the Confucian scholar, allied to the poet (it is no mere personal whim or infantile nostalgia that makes Confucius consider poetry as indispensable to education) to 'make the action of heaven and earth shine forth' (Couvreur's translation). And this is how Pound conceives his own work, and any work of art worth the name: 'The work of art is a door or a lift permitting a man to enter, or hoisting him mentally into, a zone of activity, and out of fugg and inertia' (*Guide*).

'Splendour, it all coheres', Pound has Heracles cry in his translation of Sophocles' *Trachiniae*, and, if his own aim (see *Drafts and Fragments of Cantos CX–CXVII*) is 'to make cosmos' (this is one of his final definitions of the poetic enterprise, going beyond his earlier derision of the extollers of 'kawsmos', at a time when he needed to cut his way out of a certain sloppy sub-Whitmanism), he knows that one doesn't 'get through hell in a hurry', hell being the nightmare of history, and a world in which, in Donne's words: ''Tis all in peeces, all coherence gone/ All just supply and all relation.' The *idea* was that, gradually, the chaos of references and impressions, in the poems and in the essays, would draw together, the associations forming a constellation, the whole becoming 'whitegathered' (Pound's word). The way of poetry is from 'realities perceptible to the sense', interacting by a kind of fertile logic, towards a 'radiant world', a 'world of moving energies' (essay on medievalism, in *Make It New*).

If there is Confucianism in this, there is also Platonism (or Neo-Platonism), and Pound is aware of the attraction: 'What we can assert is that Plato periodically caused enthusiasm among his disciples. And the Platonists after him have caused man after man to be suddenly conscious of the reality of the *nous*, of mind, apart from any man's individual mind, of the sea crystalline and enduring, of the bright and as it were molten glass that envelops us, full of light' (*Guide*).

6

This brings us to the question of the Republic, the transference of this paradigm of reality into the social arena. Plato's *Republic* attempts an answer. The Confucianists had theirs. Pound had his, inspired by the former – and it led him to that cage in the prison stockade north of Pisa.

It may be possible to retain the live, total scheme, but with other methods of socio-political realization.

For a chance to realize his Republic, Plato went to the tyrant Dionysius of Syracuse. The Confucianists apparently never got beyond the notion that the only person to set things in motion and keep the movement coherent was an authoritarian ruler. Pound went, with monumental naivety, to Mussolini. But he recognizes himself that the authoritarian method is not the only one: 'A democracy run by clean men, decent men cd. or shd. attain *Kraft durch Freude* quite as well as a dictatorship. Naturally a foetid and sham democracy doesn't. This is due to foetor, not to its -ocracy.'

If Pound, like many another, was attracted to Fascism, it was because he reasoned like Sorel (letter to Croce, 1921): 'At the present moment, the adventures of fascism are the most original social phenomena in Italy, going well beyond the manoeuvring of the politicians.' Everybody nowadays is well aware of the illusions of such thinking. The criticism of Fascism has been pretty thoroughly done, the lessons of history, I trust, retained, and Pound's monumental error could only add, at most, a picturesque and pathetic chapter.

The final question, the *live* question, is whether, in Pound's words, a 'modern Eleusis is possible in the wilds of a man's mind only' (*Guide*), or whether a social realization is feasible. But those who continue to believe in the latter possibility, pursuing the work of education and activism, would do well to bear in mind the wisdom of Confucius, in the *Analects*:

'If my principles prevail in the world, that is good. If they fail, that also is good.'

PART II

Place and Space

Letter from the Pyrenees

When life becomes unlivable, the need will arise for a movement beyond humanity and humanism. This move, which may
make some headway among us, will open up a horizon as yet
hardly conceived of.

(Kostas Axelos)

1

It's a strange life, this life of mine, full of ups and downs, distance and silence, refusing to separate, for the sake of some
facile unity, the near and the far, the sublime and the grotes-
que, the self and the not-self, the human and the non-human.

Here I am at this present moment on a sandy shore of the
Landes, just up from the Basque country, and in a few days'
time I'll be back in my room in Pau, drinking a glass or two of
Laphroaig (a whisky I drink for ethnopsychological reasons
when the moon is full) and conversing familiarly with my
ghosts in Glaswegian. So I go, chaos-cosmically, from a Scotch
novel (say *The Master of Ballantrae* or *The House with the
Green Shutters*) to a Chinese dictionary, from there to a map of
the Transcaspian Railway (do you know the K country, that
goes from Krasnovodsk to Kashgar, passing through Kizyl-
Arvat, Ashkabad and Boukhara, with lateral thrusts to Khiva,
Kerki and Tashkent?), a study of the *Avatamsaka Sutra*, ending
up with the geology of Cape Wrath, which is connected in my
erratic mind for more than just alliterative reasons with Key
West, where Wallace Stevens pondered imaginatively on the
question of order.

This 'so-called self', say the Buddhist monks (I adopt and
adapt their principles without sharing any orthodoxy). In the
mobile geography of identity, we Westerners (writers included)
are content with very little, pitifully little: a little dose of
personality, preferably altruistic, and on that flimsy basis, you
make it, whether the 'it' be social life, business or literature. A
lot of writers, few authors, said the undefinable Rimbaud, lost
between the blue streams of the Ardennes and the fiery desert
of Abyssinia, between the rotten Christian he felt in the marrow

41

of his bones and the potential man of light. Author? Being a man who had not altogether forgotten his Latin, Rimbaud knew that an author is a man who (*augere – auctum*) augments. Who augments what? Let's say: the sensation of life. For that, you need an identity that is much more *extravagant* than the one we normally run our lives on. With such extravagant movement, there's always the risk of madness, of course – unless you find the *poetry* of that movement. When I say 'poetry', I'm thinking of fluxes, of tensions, unknown architectures. Nothing at all to do with those who are content to paraphrase their paralysis.

2

Now I'm back again, this Autumn evening, in my Pyrenean study. Around me, books, many books, and piles of manuscript on the floor, each pile topped by a lump of quartz. A dragon is singing in the silence (it's an old Chinese kind of evening), but I've decided that tonight I'm going to try and answer a question put to me several days ago by a literary journal concerning my relationship to present-day British culture.

My relationship to present-day British culture... It's as if somebody asked Dante (forgive the comparison) to talk about the Sunday Supplement. The Sunday Supplement is, of course, part of 'culture' – like all the rest that's printed and distributed. But who can accept being part of 'culture' in this sense? *Paulo maiora canamus*! – let's sing something a bit larger!

In Britain, at the present moment, culture is represented largely by a crowd of novelists all producing regularly three hundred pages of turgid platitude (with sometimes a little puritan perversity thrown in for spice). Alongside them, a handful of very timid intellectuals, mostly biting their toenails in university staffrooms, and more or less neurasthenic poets who cluster round pale poetry reviews and drink beer in dingy pubs waiting for the day when they'll be a Book Society Choice. It's the depressing tail-end of the tradition.

Fortunately, there's always been a line of outsiders. I'm thinking of Shelley, Oscar Wilde, D. H. Lawrence, James Joyce... The first thing you notice is that they all fled the country at some moment in their lives, and some of them felt less and less the need to define themselves with respect to it. Joyce fulminates against Ireland, the 'old sow devouring her litter', but on his mental map, England simply doesn't exist: it's *beneath* critical attention. For about the last two hundred years, as soon as a British-born writer had any guts and brains, he chose expatriation. If one or two did stay at home, only one course was open to them: alcoholic oblivion (witness Dylan Thomas).

Another thing that has to be said is that America, a land of expatriates, at least at the beginning, before it concocted the most simplistic patriotism conceivable, took over in some sense the great English tradition. I'm thinking of Thoreau, Melville and Whitman. This transfer of energies into a new space brought a second wind to English literature. Which is why it was to Americans I first turned when I really began to get interested in writing. Melville is very much a transatlantic Scot and, with very little exaggeration, one could say that American literature had its main source in the correspondence between Ralph Waldo Emerson and Thomas Carlyle. The tradition of English literature benefited, then, from this American prolongation. But in America, as we know, things go fast, and it looks as if, only two hundred years after its start, that prolongation is running short. Which is why it's necessary now to find another space transcending both frontier and tradition.

But for the moment, let's continue analysing the state-of-affairs in Britain.

Take general ideology to start with. British ideology (which is specifically *English*, other mentalities being reduced to defence and reaction), is still very strong. It's all the stronger for being less apparent. It isn't institutionalized, as is the case in France, for example. It has no Academy, and if there are intellectuals posted pathetically here and there, there is no intelligentsia. British ideology has never been theorized. Not only does it never reach the level of theory (that would mean coming out into the open), it's only with difficulty and at rare moments that it achieves articulation. Mostly it is vehiculed by bulldog grunting, nose-sniffing, the raising of eyebrows and other epidermic manifestations. Hardly articulate, which is to say never open to argument, it is omnipresent and insidious. It's like fog or cotton-wool, you can't attack it, it slowly stifles you.

British civilization? Business, sport and, yes, literature – in that order. There undoubtedly is a *lot* of literature. But great quantities of printed matter do not necessarily make for a culture in the dynamic sense of the word. On the contrary, such proliferation may be a pathological phenomenon. And the massive presence of mediocre literature stifles the few more interesting growths that emerge, despite all, here and there, even in Britain. It is these growths which, given space to develop, might bring about cultural transformation and augment the sensation of life. By the way, much reference is made to 'life' in Britain. The two most widespread criteria of value are 'close to life' and 'popular'. But the 'popular' life in question is that heavy platitude referred to above, a context from which any real popular energy as well as any clarified living is absent. It's life in the suburbs of existence.

The last intellectual brightness to radiate in Britain occurred around 1930, and it was largely due to an erratic American, Ezra Pound. It's interesting to note that, with very few exceptions, the most interesting manifestations are ex-American (Pound, Eliot), or else they emerge, sporadically, from the Celtic margins of the country: Oscar Wilde, George Bernard Shaw, W. B. Yeats, Dylan Thomas, James Joyce. The most scathing and vociferous criticism of the Anglo-British cultural morass of these past few years came from a Scot: Hugh MacDiarmid. For MacDiarmid, British civilization was marked by a congenital frustration. Given that as a basis, its literature could only be flat and superficial: never the leap in the void, never the energy that via many modes and in the midst of contradictions achieves a hitherto unimagined unity. As for Scotland itself, it had been provincialized out of all recognition ('Scotland has nothing clear in its own mind'), but there were in it latent energies and resources. Which is why MacDiarmid set about creating a nationalist movement and inaugurating a cultural Renaissance. MacDiarmid's own work, however unequal (often it looks like a cantilever bridge with most of the bolts missing), is all in all fascinating, from the early lyrics, earthy and eerie, to the later poems, long screeds packed chock full of heterogeneous information, written at lightning speed in a desperate but exhilarating effort to break the sound barriers of thought. But the trouble with a nationalist movement is that, while gathering together a great deal of first-class material from the neglected past, it tends very soon to settle down into too narrow definitions and complacent channels, not to say canals. Instead of taking advantage of the fact that the national reality is in rags (it's when the national culture is broken up that the individual can emerge, relieved of history's heavy weight, and open new space), the attempt is made to re-create an identity and force things into a unity that can only be artificial. And then there's the bandwagon phenomenon. Look what happened to the Irish movement (at the end, Yeats preferred to walk alone and naked) and Scotland, with MacDiarmid rampaging ahead, fell into the same trap – and the same claptrap. In order to convince itself that it exists, a national movement is obliged to push onto the scene writers who are no doubt true sons of the nation and full of the most praiseworthy intentions, but who are too often quite simply and obviously second rate. That was the kind of context Joyce wanted out of. So did I.

3

'My situation is very special and it will be difficult to live it out to the full. I'm free, I'm independent. I belong to no country, no nation, no social group. I love the whole world and at the same time I despise it. Understand me – I despise it in the name of poetry-in-action, for humanity is all too prosaic. A lot of people return the compliment. I just laugh.' Years ago I copied out those lines from Blaise Cendrars on a piece of paper, and that piece of paper has long been stuck on the wall just next to my writing table.

So I jumped the Channel at one point and have been living and working in France. That doesn't mean I've been 'converted' to French culture and am trying to fit myself into another scheme of things. No, what it means in effect is that I'm living out a paradoxical situation, a real little transnational atopia. I'm thinking of what Roger Caillois says in his essay on the theme about dissymmetry: 'In any constituted symmetry, a partial and non-accidental break can occur, which tends to complicate the established balance. Such a break is what I call a dissymmetry. *Its effect is to enrich the structure or the organism in which it arises by endowing them with a new property, making them move up to a superior level of organization.'* (My emphasis.)

Let's get one or two things straight before, temporarily, concluding. If I've apparently turned my back on Britain, it's maybe in order to find it again, at a deeper level and in a wider context. And if present-day British culture seems to me superficial and trivial, I don't forget that it wasn't always so, and maybe it won't always remain so. I even persuade myself at times that I see signs of a change, or at least the desire for a change, a radical change, here and there.

In the meantime, I continue on my own roads, working in a transcultural context, trying to open a larger, and deeper, world.

I'm speaking of roads, and at the beginning of this letter I evoked the Transcaspian Railway. If, after leaving the Transcaspian, you pursue your way across the desert, you arrive at the Tien Shan mountains. And if you push on farther, you come to the Tarim Valley, an important stage on the old Silk Road, where all kinds of culture came together: Hellenic, Iranian, Indian, Chinese... In one of his long info-poems ('In Memoriam James Joyce'), MacDiarmid evokes that valley: 'For unlike you, Joyce, I am more concerned with the East than with the West, and the poetry I seek must be the work of one who has always known that the Tarim Valley is of more importance than Jordan or Rhine in world history.'

It's in a kind of Tarim Valley that I've been working for years.

Aquitanian Affinities

I don't paint being, I paint passages.
(Michel de Montaigne)

1

I'm sitting down to write this essay in my Pyrenean study. At my side are pinned prints and photographs of other work-places dear to my mind: Thoreau's cabin at Walden, the inn frequented by Nietzsche at Sils-Maria in the Engadine, Spinoza's workshop at Rhynnsburg, a Taoist hermitage in the mountains – and Montaigne's library: 'It's on the third floor of a tower, [...] a round room, with just enough flat surface for my table and chair. [...] It is sixteen paces in diameter and has three wide views of the surrounding countryside. [...] That's where I'm at home. That's where my real power lies.'

I first read Montaigne in Glasgow. I read him in an icy little room on the heights of Maryhill, then, later on, in more spacious, almost comfortable digs in Scotstoun. I did those early readings out of duty, because Montaigne was on the French studies curri-culum of Glasgow University. But the more I read, the more duty turned into delight, and this delight became enthusiasm when I realized one day that the author I was reading with fervour at the time, Friedrich Nietzsche, had unlimited admira-tion for Montaigne. In his essay, 'Schopenhauer as Educator', he has this to say: 'The very fact that such a man should have taken his pen to write increases the pleasure of living on this earth.' I continued reading Montaigne in Germany, at Munich, where I had three lodgings in turn: a baroque chamber rented out by a duchess, a wooden hut on the edge of the Englischer Garten, and a cosy middle-class room with an enormous leather arm-chair in a flat on the Prinzregentenstrasse owned by a woman from Switzerland. Later on still, the essays of Montaigne were among the handful of books I thought fit to gather together at Gourgounel, the old farmhouse I had in the Ardèche (it had a little tower something like Montaigne's...), and I'm deep into the *Essays* again here at Pau where, from a studio in the Trespoey district, I have a wide view over the Pyrenees.

I thought I'd begin this essay with the Pic du Midi d'Ossau, seen from the window of my workroom. But it so happened that, the day after I had the idea of it, I'd been wandering about for an hour or so in the sixth quarter of Paris when, in the Rue Saint-André-des-Arts, there in the window of a secondhand bookshop specialising in history, I came across the *History of Scotland* by George Buchanan, translated into English from the original Latin.

For those who may have forgotten the fact, George Buchanan was the Scottish poet and scholar who taught Montaigne Latin at the Collège de Guyenne, in Bordeaux. But that's not his only claim to fame. And since an essay, by definition, has to be diverse and fluctuating, before coming back to Montaigne, it seems appropriate to take a look first at the life and times, the itinerary and works, of this exiled and extravagant Scot.

2

George Buchanan was born at Killearn, in 1506 – that was the year when Luther burnt the papal bull and when Magellan passed through the straits that ever since have borne his name. A brilliant pupil at Glasgow Grammar School (towards the end of his life he was going to donate 'twenty Greek books, annotated by his hand' to the university of that town), he was sent, at the age of fourteen, to study in Paris. Now in Paris at that time, a student could be lodged in several ways: if he was rich, he'd be a *camériste* (with private chambers and a tutor); less rich, he'd be a *pensionnaire* (he'd live in a residence usually run by a professor of repute); if he was a *boursier*, a bursar, he'd live in one of the various colleges; if he was downright poor, he'd be a *martinet* (a house-martin), he'd live alone in some attic and make the best of things. I like to think of Buchanan as a house-martin, flitting about the quays of the Seine, wandering round the Place Maubert or strolling up the rue d'Écosse...

The Faculty of Arts in Paris was divided into four nations: the French nation (including in fact all of southern Europe), the Norman nation, the Picard nation and the German nation. As a Scotsman, from the north of Europe, it was to this last nation that Buchanan naturally belonged. Classes were held in dingy, dirty little rooms, with straw and reeds strewn on the floor.

But the New Knowledge, that of the Renaissance, was in the air. The idea was to free minds of the heavy load of medieval theology (Melanchton and Erasmus make fun of it, Erasmus proposing as a good theme for theological debate: 'Is the idea that God is a pumpkin as probable as the idea that God is a man?'), and get out of the literary bog (the expression is Buchanan's) of Miracles and Moralities. After his first stay in Paris, Buchanan went back up to Scotland, and enrolled as a student at St Andrews. But, after Paris, the existential and intellectual environment of St Andrews seemed dull indeed. The local light was a man called John Mair. Rabelais had already made him a laughing stock by including among the books Pantagruel found in the St Victor library in Paris an imaginary one: *Majoris, De modo faciendi puddinos* ('Mair, or How to make Puddings'). In the same vein, Buchanan threw out at Mair one of those epigrams for which he was to become famous, saying that he was major in name only and that there wasn't one vigorous page in all those he had written. To say the least, Buchanan did not ingratiate himself in the eyes of the local intelligenzia, and, well aware that he really had nothing to do with them, he decided to leave again for the Continent so as to rejoin the band of the New Knowledge men.

A bursar at the Scots' College, he received the degree of Magister Artium in 1528, and in 1529 was elected regent of the famous college of Sainte-Barbe. In one of his poems: '*Quam misera sit conditio docentium litteras humaniores Lutetiae*' ('on the sad condition of those who teach humanistic literature in Paris'), he describes his daily round and grind. Up at 4 a.m., with classes starting at 5. All the students are not as enthusiastic as himself about the New Learning – some pretty obviously couldn't care less: one yawns prodigiously, another is engaged in solemn contemplation of a hole in his sock. At midday, a meal, followed by classes again till supper-time. Buchanan then retires to his room, and studies till midnight. If you add to the severity of this programme the fact that Buchanan's diet was in all likelihood vastly inferior to anything his dear Virgil or Horace had known, it comes as no surprise to see him, after three years of it all, accepting a post as tutor in the household of the Duc de Cassilis, who was about to leave on a diplomatic mission to Scotland.

So Buchanan found himself back in his home country. But he still didn't fit in easily, and he did nothing by way of appeasement. On the contrary. Hardly had he set foot on Scottish soil, when he composed a ferocious satire against the Franciscans, whom most folk up there at the time admired no end. The result was that Buchanan was firmly invited to go back where he came from, which now meant Paris. Buchanan left without tears. But the new Scottish ambassador in Paris was Cardinal Beaton, and Beaton not only couldn't thole Buchanan, he was out for his blood. Which is one of the reasons why Buchanan left Paris for Bordeaux.

At Bordeaux, Andreas de Gouvea had set up a school of the New Knowledge, the Collège de Guyenne. Buchanan was to occupy the chair of Latin. He already had a reputation both as scholar and as poet – Scaliger, Henri Estienne and other great humanists held him to be the best Latinist poet of his time; Milton later admired him a great deal; and his portrait hung on the walls of Tycho Brahe's observatory. Buchanan was to enjoy his life in Bordeaux, and we'll come back to it.

But he hadn't been there long when the King of Portugal invited Gouvea to introduce the New Knowledge into his own home country. Buchanan was one of those Gouvea invited to go with him to Coimbra. All went well till the Scotsman, as we might have expected, began to attract the attention of the Inquisition. So much so that he was locked up in a monastery at Lisbon, to think things over, a quiet period he used to get on with his literary work. Finally managing to get out of the clutches of the Inquisition, he left Portugal in 1552. Over the next nine years, he was moving between England, France and Italy, working all the time at a long cosmological poem, *De Sphaera*.

In 1562, he was back up in Scotland, closely involved in politics and history, since he was tutor, first to Mary Stuart herself, then to her son, James VI. He also set about reforming the teaching at the university of St Andrews before having a try at reforming the State itself, with an incendiary text, *De Jure Regni apud Scotos*. And it was at this time too that he undertook a new reading of Scottish history, *Rerum Scoticarum Historia*, which, to say the least, didn't suit everybody's taste. If Mary herself soon became convinced that Buchanan was a

'downright atheist', the Scottish Parliament condemned him as
a 'very pernicious author'. When he died in Scotland in 1582,
he was practically a pauper – it was the city of Edinburgh that
saw to his funeral.

But to come back to Bordeaux. I think those Bordeaux years
were the happiest in Buchanan's life. For one thing, he'd be
drinking better wine than the vinegary stuff of the Scots
College in Paris. As to the Leonora of his erotic poems, she
was maybe all imagination, but who knows: some lively little
Basque from the Bidassoa? Then, he was teaching the way he
wanted to teach, and in good conditions. For the benefit of his
pupils, among them Michel de Montaigne, who enjoyed acting
in them, and retained respect and admiration for the 'great
Scottish poet', he staged the plays he wrote. And he could
pursue in peace, with no Inquisition breathing down his neck,
his Greek and Latin studies: he read Plato, Plutarch's *Moralia*,
Eustathius' commentary on Homer, Proclus' commentary on
the *Timaeus*, the *Argonautica* of Apollonios of Rhodes,
Aristophanes, Basilius Baesariensis, Euclid and Strabo. And he
was composing his own poems, including that one I mentioned
earlier, and which attracts me more than the others: the
cosmographic poem, *De Sphaera*. Let me say in passing that
cosmography (*cosmographia, id est scientia de sphaera mundi*)
was part of the ordinary curriculum of the old Scottish
universities. To top it all there was a circle of intellectual
friends, among them Élie Vinet, who had translated the
Sphaera of Proclus, edited Sacrobosco's *Sphaera* (Paris, 1566)
and was himself the author of *De Logistica* (Bordeaux, 1573).
We'll come up against other Élies later, quite numerous in
Aquitania, as well as the cosmographical question.

But maybe, after this excursion into the life-work of
Buchanan, I can come back to Montaigne, the mountains and
myself.

3

When, in the Autumn of 1967, I arrived in Pau to take up a post
at the university, I wasn't aware yet of all the 'Aquitanian
affinities' that are the subject of this essay. I knew that
Buchanan had lived, written and taught some time in Bordeaux,

likewise Hölderlin. But it was only later I learned of the presence in Pau of Saint-John Perse, and really began to see all the latencies revealing themselves, the whole network coming together.

In the course of the year 1967–68, I was absorbed mostly by the politico-cultural movement of May. It was only in 1969 that I began to pay more and deeper attention to the actual place, which meant first and foremost the Pyrenees.

In a series of poems, *Pyrenean Meditations*, I've gone into my own mountain excursions, both physical and mental. Here I want to speak of other figures I met with on the way, in the course of my explorations.

Among them was George Russell, an Irishman who'd travelled round the world before setting himself up a hermitage in a cave on the Vignemale where he drank champagne in the company of the local bears. Then there was Élie de Beaumont, with his *Lessons in Practical Geology*. And old Ramond, born in Strasburg, but a Pyrenean by adoption, the author, among other books, of *Observations made in the Pyrenees* (1789) and *Journey to Mont Perdu* (1801). What I liked about Ramond was his determination to get away from all the well-known sites ('vulgarly famous', he says), and make rather for the 'secret paths' of the shepherd, the hunter, the smuggler. One has to agree with Sainte-Beuve in his *Monday Conversations* when he says: 'Many a scientist has considered the Pyrenees from some specialist standpoint; none with that mixture of feeling for nature and extensive, diverse knowledge that characterizes Ramond.' I was interested too in Ramond's vocabulary. Speaking of high glaciers, he calls them *serneilhes de glace*, and in place of avalanche, he says *lavange*. That was the kind of thing that got into my Pyrenean notebooks.

And it's this aspect that brings us back to Montaigne. For if I was interested in Montaigne's autobiographical experiment ('I've taken myself for theme and argument – what a wild and monstrous undertaking!'), and I'll come back to it, I was also interested in his language, in the general way he got things down, and across.

In the seventeenth essay of his *Second Book*, Montaigne has this to say: 'Above our heads, up there in the mountains, they talk a Gascon language that is much to my liking: it's brief, uncloying, full of meaning [...]. It's as full of nerve, force and pertinence as the French language is full of grace, subtlety and amplitude.' Now, as luck (objective chance?) had it, way back in 1957, in Munich, at the university, I had attended the linguistic classes of Gerhard Rohlfs, a specialist in Gascon, author of *Studies in Pyrenean Philology*, and in my notebooks I still had lists of words:

asca, an avalanche due to wind
crum, thick cloud
galafre, precipice
eslanbrec, lightning...

Montaigne's allusion, and those notes of my own, made me want to learn more. Which I did by assiduously frequenting the market place of Pau and the valleys of Ossau and Aspe: '*Fier? Je peux te dire qu'il était fier, hils de puta – com un can quan porta tripa* (Proud, I can tell you he was proud, the son of a bitch – like a dog with black pudding in its mouth!)' Then there was a little café, on the Place de la Reine Marguerite, where I could listen in to conversations with my head buried in a book (Montaigne's essays, for example).

There was the vocabulary. But for expression to be really cogent, many other elements are needed, such as rhythm of phrase.

Montaigne 'gasconizes' spontaneously, intuitively. As a fervent Latinist (Buchanan had a role to play in this), he learned a lot concerning 'cuts and cadences' from Caesar, Sallustus, Seneca and Plutarch. So the Latins marked his style, but now he writes in French. What French? A French which, he says, has been 'altered' (denatured) by his 'innate barbarity' – the statement sounds apologetic, but in fact the modesty is purely rhetorical: Montaigne rather likes his 'barbarity'. What does he mean by the term exactly? It doesn't mean a defence of dialect. He's surrounded by the patois of Poitou, the Saintonge, the Limousin and Auvergne, but he finds them all 'flabby, sluggish and floozy'. The only local language he takes to, through his ears and his mind, is Gascon, mountain Gascon. It's as though Montaigne were looking for a language consubstantial to himself: mountain-talk. And it's a kind of home-made 'mountain-talk' he writes, more and more naturally. And this is maybe the moment to say that, of all the phrases and passages I copied out from Montaigne's essays, the one I love most, for its perfect simplicity allied to the height of its tone, is this one: 'When the vineyards frost over in my village...' No sophisticated 'style' can surpass that kind of expression.

4

Let's come now to other affinities.

I hadn't been living long in Pau when I realized that the Reclus family had lived close by, in Orthez. Élisée Reclus was known to me as a geographer (an anarchist–geographer, an anarcho-geographer, like Kropotkin) who had been one of those wide-ranging unclassifiable intellectuals whom Patrick Geddes (himself biologist, sociologist, educator) had invited to the transdisciplinary seminars he ran in Edinburgh at the end of the nineteenth century. I now learned that Élisée had been far from being an only son: he had nine sisters and four brothers. Two of these brothers were particularly close to him: Élie, who became a professor of anthropology at Brussels, author of *The Primitives, Studies in Comparative Ethnology* (on the Eastern and Western Hyperboreans, the Apaches, the Naïr, the Khouds...); and Onésime, a geographer like Élisée himself, and who often worked with him. I began to gather together as many of Élisée Reclus' books as I could get my hands on. Here's the beginning of Chapter 2 of Volume II of his *New Universal Geography*, where he's talking about the Pyrenees:

> Whether we take geology, or the history of its populations, the Pyrenean region presents the most distinct entity within France, the most independent group of provinces. The origins of most of its inhabitants made it already a world apart in ancient Gaul. And nowadays the Catalans of the Roussillon, the Basques of the Saison, the Bidouze and the Nive contrast singularly with their French neighbours, at the same time as, in language and in customs, they resemble the inhabitants of the Iberian peninsula just across the border. But it's mainly because of its highly specific morphology that the Pyrenean zone is a distinct region, requiring special treatment.

To which we should add this, in order to have the whole land and sea context:

Beyond the Gulf of Gascony, the Atlantic is deserted. That's
why the valley of the Garonne has played a less conspicuous
place in history than the valley of the Rhone.

In the writing of Reclus there's an amplitude, an inspired
tone close to Michelet's in history, but with a great deal more
geo-graphical precision. I was particularly attracted to that
'highly specific morphology'. I spent years following out the
morphology lines of that Pyrenees–Atlantic region, moving
along its crests and beaches, exploring it geologically, intellectually, poetically: cosmo-graphically.

But let's continue filling out the affinities map.

5

From the Reclus I went to Élie Faure, who was their nephew.
Here's what Élie Faure, one of the great neglected minds of
France (too vast, too diverse for the little fashion-mongers),
has to say about this affiliation in his book *An Autodidact's
Confession*:

> I was brought up to revere the Reclus brothers by my mother,
> who was their sister. My own forename comes from the elder
> brother, whom she felt closest to, and in whose care she often
> left me when I was young. To say that Élie Reclus is the man
> I've loved most isn't enough. I literally worshipped him. It was
> Élie Reclus that had the most decisive influence on my
> development [...]. It was thanks to him I came to love Élisée
> too, and I think I understood him.

Among the voluminous works of Élie Faure (I'm thinking of
the monumental *History of Art, The Spirit of Form, The
Constructors, The Tree of Eden, The Discovery of the Archipelago, Other Lands in Sight...*), there's a book on Montaigne:
Montaigne and his Three Firstborn Descendants (those three
being Shakespeare, Cervantes and Pascal). In the present
context, it's on this book I'd like to concentrate a little.

It's a well enough known fact that Aquitania was an
astoundingly fertile meeting place for Afro-Mediterranian
civilizations of the south (Cro-magnon man, Ligurians, Iberians,
Saracens...) and civilizations from the north (Celts, Franks,
Visigoths...). And it's Faure's hypothesis that the genius of

Montaigne is at least partly the result of such mingling: an idiosyncratic emergence from the 'floating world' of Aquitania. Analyzing the complex foreground to the formation of a mind such as Montaigne's, Faure does not neglect other factors: physical environment, historical situations, education, social forms, but in his essay 'Three Drops of Blood', he attempts a kind of ethical and intellectual genealogy based on what he calls 'the ethnic anarchy' of Aquitania.

We enter with him then into 'an unknown country', on the edge of the ocean. It's a land of rain, knowing nothing of the burning droughts that characterize the region that stretches down the Rhone towards the Latin Sea. But the Latin is attracted to it, he moves in its direction along the gully of the Garonne, he comes in with his produce, his ideas, his customs, meeting there the pale-faced men from the mists of the fjords. Moors and dunes separate this territory from the Basque country and the lands of Navarre, but it's open to the rude and poverty-stricken hordes of Iberia coming along the mountain gorges, fighting and trading. The hills of the Double cut it off from the tongue of the north, the *langue d'oïl*, but its waters carry oak, poplar, elm and ash, those north country trees, down to the vast sandy estuary that recalls the pampas of America. The reindeer hunter out from the caves of Périgord following the Dordogne corridor finds himself caught up in the swirling ethnic flood brought in along the roads of Spain and the Languedoc. If to this basic sketch, you add the presence of the Iberian Celt, and a semitic type stemming either from the remnants of Arab armies after Poitiers or from Jews fleeing from the Spanish Inquisition, and an Anglo-Norman type after the marriage of Alienor of Aquitania, you arrive at the idea that Montaigne, son of an Anglo-Gascon who was himself the son of a Bordeaux fish-merchant, and whose mother, Antoinette Lopez, was of Portuguese Jewish origin, born then of a triple Celtiberian, Anglo-Norman and Jewish alliance, was the mixed breed *par excellence* of the Entre-deux-Mers, the complex product of a complex region, 'that province of the Western limits that the Romans, with perfect justification, called Celtiberia'.

From this ethnic basis, Faure then moves on to a psychological and intellectual portrait.

What, according to Faure, characterizes first and foremost the 'type' of which Montaigne is an eminent specimen, is an adamant sense of independence, a determined individualism. It was this which made the Bordeaux region one of the hotbeds of Protestantism, and it was this which made it resist the centralizing, Jacobine tendency of the '89 Revolution. And it was this that made of Montaigne 'the first free man to appear in Western Europe, the first autonomous individual'. With the individualism goes a certain pride. If, in more superficial minds, this pride can take the form of bragging and swaggery, in minds like those of Montaigne, it takes rather the form of a quiet, unshakable confidence. Which is to say that with it goes a certain modesty – not a social modesty in the face of other human beings, but a kind of cosmic modesty, concerning the ground of the universe. 'I can't explain the depths of my being', says Fénelon (who has the same origins as Montaigne). And the tendency will be to let the depths alone, leave them undisturbed, since they are too complex for meddling. The thing will be to let life go along, evolve out of these depths, not worrying at or about them, maintaining a contented, indeed joyous frame of mind. I love the way Élie Faure describes Montaigne 'bowel-racked on his saddle, but still eyes open to the space around him and breathing in the dawn'. On the intellectual level, what we see is critical acumen, a power of analysis. This type of mind shatters systems, destroys illusions, not out of any nihilistic rage, but via the natural play of intelligence, and out of a need for lucidity. Having cleaned the decks, as it were, it then undertakes universal investigations – it's Montaigne going to Rouen to talk with an Amerindian chief. We're in the presence of a mind that abandons all the little absolutes, all local culture-contexts, and moves with delight into a great space of relativity, with no partisan bias whatever. Given humanity's propensity for illusions, beliefs, partisanship, intellectual systems, sentimental habits, such a mind will know a certain kind of intellectual solitude. But there are solar solitudes. And it's with such a solitude that this mind will work out its world – sometimes floating, sometimes radiant, always expressive, because it is imbued with a sense of rhythm, word and image. It finally arrives at a poetic conception of the universe, understanding 'poetic' in a wider and wider sense, on a higher and higher plane.

To come back now to 'myself', it's especially on this latter plane I try to work. Involved in a practice, a *praxis*, a poetic *praxis*.

6

Everybody knows that Montaigne wrote *Essays*, but it's often forgotten that it was he who actually invented the word, in order to designate a new type of literature, outside the established ruts, and full of 'strangeness'. In what does this 'strangeness' consist? It means in the first place leaving the harbour of fixed identity in order to plunge into the floating life, following the transformations of the self and the meanderings of thought. It implies also abandoning established genres. The essayist is out on his own, working in the open. Knowing very well that the last word will never be pronounced, maintaining a distance both from dogmatic totality and the detailed report, he makes attempts, *essays*, he tries out ways, he takes soundings. And then, there's a poetics of the essay. It's a form that needs ingenious articulation, co-ordination: no heavy cause and effect sequences, and yet no scrambled mess either. Very few minds have practised it with the freedom, the fire and the acuteness of Montaigne. The form was in vogue with the English writers for a time, but even the best of them (Lamb, Hazlitt, Stevenson), rarely go beyond charming chit-chat and impressionistic rambling. Close to Montaigne, when I started looking into the form myself, I could see only Emerson and Nietzsche, the one flowing peacefully on, like the River Concord under an Indian Summer sun, the other as sharp-angled and discontinuous as mountain rapids.

And here I am now, in my Pyrenean study this April morning, after many an essay, essaying once again. Trying to keep to the high line (the cuts and cadences of the range out there). Trying to open more dimensions than the socio-cultural context usually admits.

In the constant company of the Vignemale, the Maladetta, and the Pic du Midi d'Ossau.

Meditation in Winter

Whatever world that is, it lies far ahead. But its outline, its adumbration, is clear in the landscape.

(Barry Lopez)

1

'Now suddenly there was nothing but a world of cloud, and we were there alone in the middle of a great white plain with snowy hills and mountains staring at us; and it was very still; but there were whispers.' That's the *wichasa wakon* ('holy man') of a Sioux tribe telling of his great vision, his great Winter vision. For the Amerindian, far from being a period of the year smitten by absence and negativity, Winter is 'the season of secrets'. The empty silence of a snowy landscape is an invitation to concentration and meditation, offers the possibility of an expansion of the mind.

It's this concentration and this expansion that modern man lacks most of all. Hustled hither and thither between bureaucracies and circuses, between boredom and distraction, unable to get his bearings in a civilization which, having no deep culture, tries to camouflage its fundamental lack by making a lot of noise and flashing a lot of images, the citizen ends up avoiding any still, open moment when he might, conceivably, contemplate his 'original face', as Zen Buddhism calls it, and, more or less satisfied, but knowing little real joyance, lives on complacently in a well-filled mediocrity.

But there's art. And it's in art, when it's founded and grounded, that is, when it isn't just another aspect of the circus, that we recover, fugitively perhaps (it all depends on the degree of concentration involved and on how consequential we are), that silent part of ourselves that lifts us from the society of noise and lets us participate in the universe.

2

This evening, I propose we take a dream trip and move up into the House of Great Cold, surrounded by winds, where the moon repairs to in Winter. In the House of Great Cold there are trees, and in those trees nest birds. With a little luck you may be able to weave yourself a coat out of their dropped feathers, so as to fly high and far and long. As for the trees, you have to learn to read them, for every tree is a text, just as every profound text is a tree of life. Up there, it's good to meditate on colour, the colours of the five directions: blue (north), red (south), white (east), black (west) and yellow (centre). You can also try to absorb breaths and lights. And who knows, for it doesn't happen to everyone, especially the first time round, you may even meet the mysterious, the highly mysterious Daughter of the Sun and the Moon.

All that, of course, is a bit Chinese. In fact, it's a very specific Taoist meditation called 'the ecstatic excursion'.

Closer to our own context, and in more abstract terms, Mircea Eliade speaks of 'creative imagination', and Henry Corbin of 'active imagination', which has a 'psycho-cosmic function'.

Dream, vision, imagination. We're not talking about psychological delirium or mere fantasia (the ravings of the starved mind in its cell), but of something which is a vital necessity. In *Thalassa*, Ferenczi speaks of the biogenetic frustration of modern man. It would be relevant and cogent to speak also of his psycho-cosmic frustration. Psychic illness is rife, and it's shut up in psychologism. Whereas what's fundamentally required maybe is just a little 'ecstatic excursion' from time to time.

3

Henry Thoreau spent his time walking round Walden pond, near the town of Concord, in New England, at a time when the 'circus' was beginning to spread. Withdrawn from human affairs, he called himself, ironically, 'inspector of snowstorms'. He inspected, he observed, he piled up detail after detail, but any man of science might have done the same, and we'd only have another scientific document to file away. But if Thoreau's deep activity could take in science, it didn't stop there. The question he'd put to himself early on was: how to get the most life? He didn't want just to write up a report, he wanted to get into what Whitman, using a French word as he often did, called *rapport*, relationship. Thoreau wanted to get into the 'great relationship', and he spoke in terms of mythology. Does that mean that he was out to resuscitate the gods, or see fairies in the bushes? No, with Thoreau, we have to think of a non-figurative (and non-picturesque) mythology, maybe we could say a white mythology: a way of perception and a way of thought, a way of being outside oneself and deep in a sensation of the world. Such a sensation could not be expressed in the terms of a scientific report, it could only be expressed poeti-cally, by means of a poetry, an earthworld-poetry that could 'make the rocks talk'. All of Thoreau's work, all of his 'mythological' walks moved towards that kind of poetry: 'On the first day of April, it rained, and the ice melted. Early in the morning, in a thick fog, I heard a lost goose flying over the pond and honking, like the very spirit of the fog.'

4

After Asia and America, let's come back to Europe. Having discarded certain habits, we may be able to look at it with a fresh eye, *rediscover* it.

'Now at last we're outside the gates of the town', says a character in Tieck's *Franz Sternbald*, that most romantic of books – romantic in the strong and original sense of the word, referring to that movement which, with all its faults, was one of the most far-reaching and one of the most beautiful attempts Europe has known to renew its vision of itself and rediscover the world in all its dimensions.

'Men walk on strange and various roads', says Novalis. 'If you follow them and compare them, you'll see other figures coming to life. Figures that seem to belong to that great ciphered writing one can see everywhere: on wings, in clouds, in crystals.'

One of the strangest figures of Romanticism was the poet Lenz. Forty years after he dropped dead in a Moscow street, Büchner devoted a very beautiful text to his memory, a text that tells of Lenz's journey into the Alsace mountains in 1778: 'On the 20th day of January, Lenz started out across the moun-tains. High peaks and plateaus under snow...'

At the beginning of his mountain journey, Lenz is scared of

the silence. His mind feels exposed to a 'desolate chaos' and a 'terrible emptiness'. But, however bare, the mountain landscape ends up by having a beneficial influence: 'If I couldn't go up into the mountains now and then, and see the landscape, I'd go mad.'

One day a certain Kaufmann comes to pay Lenz a visit and the two men enter into a discussion about art. When Lenz praises the most ordinary, the most 'insignificant' reality (which is to say, on a final analysis, the one most free of human projections), Kaufmann objects that in such a context could never be found a model for the Belvedere Apollo or a madonna of Raphaël. 'No indeed', cries Lenz, 'and what does it matter? Works such as these I care little for. I prefer by far the poet, the artist who can render nature in the realest way, so that I feel *something beyond the image he creates*.' (My emphasis.)

5

'Religious man', says Eliade in his essay *The Sacred and the Profane*, 'deeply desires to be, to participate in reality, to saturate himself with power.' There is the real 'will to power' of the artist – nothing to do with any kind of domination. Every authentic artist, every authentic poet is 'religious' in this sense. What may seem, from an exclusively social point of view, egotistic monomania, or narcissistic obsession, is in fact a superpersonal desire to take life to its maximal power. Religions project this power in the form of gods and establish specific places for the worship of these gods. Whereas the artist lives alone in the world, and for him any place can be a place of revelation. Of course there are artists who 'believe' and who are affiliated to specific religions. But to an artist who paints, however divinely, divinities or angels or madonnas, I'll always prefer, like Lenz, the man who paints, without divinity, a landscape that gives me an augmented sense of reality. 'There's the real religion!', cried Van Gogh when he saw for the first time certain Japanese landscape paintings.

To avoid misunderstanding, perhaps I should use a vocabulary similar to that of certain medieval scholastics (all they had was words, so their wordship was sharp), and speak of a religion without religion. It would be the purest religion, the most powerful, but also the most fragile, because it would be the least anthropomorphic, the least built-up. It was Nietzsche who said that it would be only after the death of religion, in the heavy established sense of the word, that there could be any real innovation in the domain of the sacred.

Walking in the landscape, far from the noise of religion, and from the art-circus. Only the cry of a bird, or whisperings.

6

Trying to think beyond religion, beyond metaphysics, beyond science.

I think, therefore I am, said the divine child of the modern intelligence.

I am, completely, therefore I think differently, says the poet–thinker of the 'new landscape'.

How to inaugurate and develop a thinking-in-the-territory (implicated in it, not imposed upon it)? Maybe thought can be like a landscape – with fields and running waters (fluid concepts). A landscape–mindscape. That's maybe what we could map our way towards.

In the course of history, we've gone from religion to science, and we've witnessed their quarrels. But these two disciplines, however inimical they may have been at times, nevertheless have something fundamentally in common: they're both concerned with an explanation of the world. But what if there were another way of approaching, entering into and thinking the world? A kind of thinking that would have no need for explanation. We spend our lives explaining this and explaining that, including ourselves. In other words, we're forever set on changing the landscape into a system of signs. What a circus, what a cinema, what a concert! We try to create the world in our own image, and then we wonder how it comes to bore us so much, so that we have to change toys all the time. But what if we left the world a bit more alone? What if we tried to enter it subtly, getting rid of ourselves (our heavy selves) as we gradually move across and into the territory?

Poetic meditations.

Cosmo-poetic meditations. The primordial dream, which has nothing to do with the dramas of the person. And a cosmic consciousness, where there is no separation between the self and the world, but an experience of continuity.

7

We may have the impression of *coming back home*, after centuries of alienation. We recover lost dimensions. And an expansive thinking, far from all reductionism.

In François Dagognet's 'neo-graphical' study *Une épistémologie de l'espace concret* ('an epistemology of concrete space'), I find this:

> Let's never try to go beyond phenomena! On their surface-skin we can read dramas, discover scars, traces and vestiges that we can prospect, gather and explain. The simple morphology of a mountain-peak, or of an excavation, or of an earth-slide, sometimes a mere lay-out of lines and points, constitute a cosmic writing that can inform us beyond all our hopes and expectations.

Certainly, even in this *neo*-geographical text, one can detect the influence of our limited sense of world and the remains of a reductive epistemology. No doubt to obtain a maximum of knowledge and awareness (enformation and transformation as well as information), one must go still farther out.

But let's retain that notion of *cosmic writing*, already sensed by Novalis.

Painting, like poetry, is cosmic writing. And any reading of poetry, any contemplation of painting that doesn't envisage that dimension is beside the point.

8

I'm thinking now of Wittgenstein: 'My impression is that if all possible scientific questions received an answer, we wouldn't even have begun to touch on the problem of life. Of course, at that moment, there would be no question. And that would be the solution to the problem.'

Professor of philosophy though he was, holding a chair at Cambridge, Wittgenstein often felt the need to interrupt his teaching in order to go away and live for a while in a hut in Norway, or on the Irish coast.

With the world, there, in front of him.

A field, a few trees.

A single tree.

The play of waves.

'The mystery is not the *how*, it's the very fact that it is there.'

Wittgenstein left behind a *Logico-philosophical Discussion* and some *Investigations*. Philosophy continues to be made in his name. But at the end of his life, in 1951, he was already elsewhere.

It's that 'elsewhere' that interests me.

Reflections on a Logbook

It is difficult to read the archives of the earth.
(*Journal* of the navigator Lapérouse, 1787)

1

One of the Pacific's island arcs runs from Halmaheira, south of the Philippines, up to the Kamchatka, via the Pescadores, Taiwan, Okinawa, the Ryukyu and Hokkaido. Volcanic, these islands are part of what has been called the Pacific Ocean's ancient 'fire belt'.

This was more or less the line Lapérouse followed when he left Manila in April 1787, making for the coast of Tartary and the obscure regions of the north-west Pacific. It was an important stage in his expedition (an expedition I'm reading as *mind-journey*), not only because of the cartographic confusion that prevailed in this part of the world, but because it was the only region that had 'escaped the tireless energy of Captain Cook'. Lapérouse was keen not only to make a map, but to make his mark.

So, up by Formosa, as it was called at that time, went the voyage, then past the tip of Korea, into the Sea of Japan: 'We come at last into the Sea of Japan and sail along the coast of China.' The going wasn't easy, the coasts being constantly wrapped in fog, making map-making impossible, with the occasional storm (what the *Journal* calls a 'crisis of nature') worrying Lapérouse as a promise of more to come – he had a lot of work to do, and he didn't have that much time: 'It was important for us to be out of the Japan Seas before the month of June, a time of tempests and typhoons that make that area the most dangerous in the world.'

He continues sailing northward through the fogs ('fogs as thick and long-lasting as anything to be found on the coast of Labrador', he says), waiting for a light-up, and sometimes getting it: 'It's only in misty regions such as these, but then only rarely, that one can see horizons of such a great extent, as though with those moments of extreme clarity nature wished to compensate for the almost everlasting obscurity which prevails in these parts.'

While measuring latitude and longitude as well as he can, taking soundings, he sees 'five groups of rocks with a great quantity of birds flying about them', then a Japanese junk with twenty of a crew all dressed in blue and 'a little white flag with words written on it vertically'.

He would have liked to spend a lot more time hugging the coast of Japan, but time is pressing and he has a wider 'field of discovery' waiting for him.

At 44 degrees latitude, he comes to what the geographers had called the 'Straits of Tessoy'. But Lapérouse finds that the geography is all to hell:

> Those geographers who on the basis of the reports made by Father des Anges and a handful of Japanese maps had traced the outline of the straits and determined the limits of Yezo and the Company Land, had so disfigured the geography of this part of Asia that it was absolutely necessary to put an end to so much useless discussion with a few unquestionable facts.

Landing on the coast, Lapérouse and his men see deer and bears feeding quietly on the shore, and find little baskets made of birch bark ('exactly like those of the Indians of Canada') and snow-shoes. No one to talk to and get information from, so Lapérouse calls the place Bears' Bay, and moves on. At other places, they fish, either in the sea or in rivers, finding it so easy that the fish, in abundance ('cod, gurnard, trout, salmon, herring, plaice') have 'only to hop from the water into our pots'. Birds, they find, are rarer in these parts, but they do get glimpses of 'crows, doves, partridges, wagtails, swallows, fly-catchers, albatrosses, gulls, puffins, bitterns and duck', Lapérouse noting that birds you usually see in bands 'under happier skies', live here alone, on the pinnacles of lonely rocks.

When they do come to meet people, those of the Amur River country or Ainu of Sakhaline and Yezo, they ask them to make maps (is Yezo an island or a peninsula?), and they draw up lists of words: *tebaira* (the wind), *oroa* (the cold), *hourarahaûne* (clouds), *mâchi* (gull), *toukochiche* (salmon). Lapérouse observes that, when drawing, the islanders have no sense of a change of direction and lay out their coast in one continuous line. He takes a liking to the Ainu, even though they know how to drive a hard bargain, saying that they're polite, gentle and intelligent, maybe more intelligent than any nation in Europe – which is a high compliment coming from Lapérouse, who was far from sharing the ideology of the Noble Savage. He appreciates their knowledge of plants, notes signs of some kind of bear ceremony ('a circle of 15 or 20 posts each one surmounted by the skull of a bear'), admires dresses made of salmon-skin every bit as fine as silk, and gets the impression that they live an anarchistic life (which, 'given their gentle manners and their respect for age, is no inconvenience').

'It is very difficult', notes Lapérouse in his *Journal* (entry of August 1787) 'to learn how to investigate and read the archives of the world.' With that phrase, he was summing up not only his researches in the north Pacific, but his whole expedition, and the search for knowledge in general. As is well enough known, Lapérouse's expedition ended in total disaster at Vanikoro. But the *Journal* – because Lapérouse (running the risk that lesser minds would exploit it for their own little purposes) sent it back to Paris bit by bit – survives. And it is a monument. Or better than that: the map of a mind in movement.

2

It was the eighteenth century that saw the first European expeditions round the world, those of Cook, that of Lapérouse – great supra-political circumnavigations, with geographers, ethnologists, natural historians, philosophers and writers following in their wake. The eighteenth century: an age of clear-cut argument, before the nineteenth century's thunder and lightning clouds, and the twentieth's informational confusion (veiling all too often utter deadness of soul and barrenness of mind).

It's an age in which fullness of matter combines with lines of intelligence to create live thought, expressed principally in the form of essays, from Hume's *Essay on Human Understanding* to Fabre's *Essai sur la théorie des torrents*. How much more exciting and stimulating than the novels of Tom, Dick and Harry (and Jane, and Evelyne, and Susan) that were to encumber Europe in the two centuries following!

The main question in the air was the question of order.

On the one hand, there were the partisans of perfect order

and design, represented, say, by Burnet's *Sacred Theory of the Earth*, Süssmilch's *Die Göttliche Ordnung*, De Pluche's *Spectacle de la nature*, Nieuwentijdt's *The Religious Philosopher* or Leibniz throughout his multiple and fascinating works. On the other hand, not Voltaire, whose criticism of Leibniz is no more than journalistic jibing, but, say, d'Holbach, who says that it's in his imagination that man finds the model of order, and, even more radically perhaps, who asks: 'What peculiar privilege has this little agitation of the brain which we call *thought*, that we must thus make it the model of the universe?' Hume is wary of any would-be complete cosmogonies, loathes all talk of 'perfect worlds' (in the art of 'world-making' he sees rather a process, always continuing, of trial and error) and bides by the notion that nature contains 'an infinite number of springs and principles'.

For anyone trying to live a full and living life, with as few preconceptions as possible, and at the same time no facile resignation, no merely flippant scepticism, the 'true logic', as Leibniz calls it, probably implies the sense of a moving mind-world, with a sensation of more or less distant harmony and wholeness, but also a readiness to accept breaks, interruptions, fractures. And the last word of wisdom concerning man's relation to the universe probably comes from Herder, in his *Anthropogeographie*: 'The whole living creation is closely inter-related, and one should act prudently in altering this inter-dependence.'

Lapérouse's *Journal* is part integral of this type of literature, and he was very much concerned with its fate.

First of all, he was fully aware of its value as a contribution to geography. He had determined points that would clear up a lot of confusion and uncertainty, making it impossible for 'cabinet geographers' to fantasize and draw up facile systems. Lapérouse, like Cook, who had also been keen to get 'out there', had a loathing for those system-makers who sit at home and fit reality into their concepts: 'As a traveller, I bring back facts, I lay out differences.' He even goes so far as to say that work such as his, fundamental field-work, will put an end to geography as a science and as a subject of debate, leaving room for something else:

It seems safe to announce that the moment has come when all the obscurities that have attached themselves to particular voyages will be removed. The art of navigation has made enough progress these last few years as not to be stopped by this or that obstacle. Very soon, geography will no longer be a science, because the spirit of dispute and criticism will have become obsolete once all the main points have been given exact latitudes and longitudes, and when all the peoples of the earth know the precise extent of the lands they inhabit and the seas that surround them.

So much for science, and the possibility of another approach to space.

But there's also a literary question.

3

In the edition (1797) of Lapérouse's *Journal* revised by Milet-Mureau, concerning a stream of Sakhaline, we read that it was 'replete with salmon'. If, however, we refer to Lapérouse's original text as published in 1885 at the Imprimerie Nationale (editors John Dunmore and Maurice de Brossard), we see that, in the navigator's mind, the stream in question was '*paved* with salmon', a much bolder expression. It's only one example among many. I'm interested here in the spontaneous writing of a curious, live and exploring mind, outside any canons of taste, outside any literary orthodoxy.

'I could have entrusted the composition of my journal to some man of letters', says Lapérouse in his Preface:

In this way, it would have been written in a purer style, and it would have been spattered with reflections I'd never have thought of. But that would have meant presenting myself with a mask, and I've preferred natural traits, whatever they may be. Reading the last two *Voyages* of Captain Cook, I've often regretted that for the first he borrowed a stranger's pen. His descriptions of the customs, manners and arts of the various peoples have always seemed to me completely satisfactory, and the accounts of his navigation have always given me the *revealing detail* I was looking for as a guide to my own. This is the kind of thing that an editor won't respect: for the sake of harmony of phrase, he'll sacrifice the very word a mariner wants. Besides, in this kind of reading, one likes to put oneself in the place of the traveller, whereas all we get with every line is an actor playing his part, no doubt with greater elegance and with finer manners, but totally incapable of giving us the real thing. The various chapters are not composed according to *the rhythm of the voyaging*, the sailing plans are presented in a uniform way, whereas when you are engaged in a vast space comprising the two hemispheres they are bound to give rise to a thousand variations. We miss the instability that comes from the slightest change in circumstance. *The man of letters ends up by effacing the traveller completely.* [My emphasis.]

Let's get this quite clear. Lapérouse was by no means against a certain cleaning-up of his manuscript: he complains that in the absence of a secretary he had to depend on a series of more or less competent copyists, hence the sometimes shaky spelling and weird punctuation. And he would have been grateful for someone to remove the occasional clumsiness on his part – he says he has a lot to learn about writing. But what he wants is the real, revealing word, that may sound barbarous to an elegant ear, as well as a certain roughness of phrasing. What he most emphatically *doesn't* want is the reduction of a multiple text full of keenly perceived but not necessarily convergent detail to the neat plot and the ironed-out exposition of an 'interesting novel'. He wants no uniformization of the various *plans*, be they of sailing, thinking or writing.

In short, with Lapérouse's *Journal*, we're confronted with a question of poetics.

Let's go into all this a little farther.

A century after Lapérouse, in 1890, Anton Chekhov, a successful author with several plays and a host of short stories to his credit, left for the island of Sakhaline, just across the Lapérouse Straits. He intended to live for a while on his 'isle bound by salty fog', at the far edge of the Russian Empire, and write a book different from any he'd ever tried his hand at before: a socio-ethno-geo-poetico-meteorological kind of book... To prepare himself for this unusual task, he, the elegant man of letters, had turned himself into 'an erudite monster', piling up all the information he could get his hands on in the bookshops and libraries of Moscow and St Petersburg. Once on the island, with more and more direct information coming at him, he was confronted by problems of form: how to bring together all this heterogeneous material, what kind of shape to give it? And then, in touch with the island's situation, structure and atmosphere, he was aware of changes in his mentality:

> Here we are at the edge of the Pacific ocean [...]. Over there, in the distance, lies the coast of America [...]. To the left, across the fog, one can just make out the headlands of Sakhaline [...]. To the right, a stretch of cliffs[...]. And all around, not a living soul, not a bird, not a fly. On these coasts, one is seized, not by thoughts but by meditations. It's frightening, but at the same time enticing. I'd like to stay here, just watching the monotonous waves and listening to their roaring.

There's the beginning of a 'non-literary' literature. How to designate it? The usual categories – 'travel', 'adventure', 'exoticism' – are not only obviously inadequate, in the most interesting cases, they're pitifully inept. Chekhov's *Island* (I'm only taking it as an example, not as a model) comes across as a mass of oceanic prose in which facts, sensations and documents knock together like flotsam and jetsam. Melville did something of the same with *Moby Dick*. And Joyce, if he had lived, after *Ulysses* and *Finnegans Wake*, would have written an ocean-book, a kind of *maximum opus marinum*.

Just as for the Greeks Okeanos surrounded the earth, this literature – outer rim literature – I am trying to speak about is mentally situated at the extreme edge of our culture and its physical movement consists in an attempt to 'approach' the earth in a new way, get in touch with the universe by means of a multiple and simultaneous attentiveness (faster and finer than mere juxtaposition) whose logic, erotic and erratic, has little to do with the logics practised habitually.

For this outer rim literature, most criticism is inadequate. Few critics, whether they go by taste or by (literary) science, are aware of this area and this movement. Melville in his time said there were only five real critics in America, and several of them were asleep. The situation has hardly improved.

Roland Barthes, in France, had the intuition of this thing. After demonstrating, in the *Zero Degree of Writing*, that our 'good' literature is irremediably classicist, in the *Empire of Signs*, he speaks of a 'dream': to know a foreign (and hence strange) language, and yet not understand it, to learn the systematics of the inconceivable, to undo reality by means of new combinations, new syntaxes, to discover new positions of the subject, to displace one's topology. Some chapter in Sapir or Whorf concerning Chinook, Nootka or Hope, some chapter in Granet concerning Chinese, some remark made by a linguist concerning Japanese can open up integral novelty which some modern texts give a sense of, but no novel. Texts such as these allow us to *see a landscape* which our habitual language (the one we own) could never guess at or discover.

Lapérouse spoke about the end of geography, that is, of a time when cartography would no longer be a problem. He was certainly a bit premature there, for even in the simple scientific sense of geography (measuring and situating) there is no doubt still a great deal to be done.

Then, geography can advance, there can be other geographies.

And there can be what I have begun to think of as geopoetics.

The High Line

The permanent lines and character of the landscape.
(Robert Louis Stevenson)

1

I want to begin this 'high line' study by referring to a walking tour that Robert Louis Stevenson did in January 1876, that is, at the age of 26. This was a trip into Ayrshire. In the first place, I suppose inevitably, it's a Burns pilgrimage, with evocations of Kyle and the Brig o'Doon. But it's more than that. It's a psycho-social portrait of Ayrshire as 'one of the most typical regions of Scotland', evoking in this ethno-cultural context a ploughman in a field by the Shanter River, a shellfish-gatherer, and four carters, 'long and muscled, with lean, intelligent faces', talking metaphysics in a pub. But it's more than that again. It's an abstract landscape in black, grey and white, with the lines of the dune-country along the shore from Turnberry Head to Girvan, and the lines of Arran on the horizon. As he walks that road along the cliffs, Stevenson says he has the impression of *following the shores of creation in the void of space*. There you have one of the most arresting and illuminating phrases Stevenson ever wrote.

What great art is concerned with is achieving something like fullness of being and finding a shape for it, a shape with an edge. That's great art, and no live culture, no expanding existence can do without it. We're liable to lose sight of it not only in the humdrum social context, but also in the proliferation of literature and art-objects that... go the rounds.

It's in this context of 'fullness' and 'shape' that I want to reread Stevenson.

I have a great liking for Robert Louis Stevenson. One of the first books to get me interested in writing was his collection of essays *Men and Books* which, while talking of Scottish culture (Robert Burns, John Knox), also talks quite naturally at the same time of French writers (Victor Hugo, François Villon, Charles d'Orléans), American writers (Walt Whitman, Henry Thoreau), a Japanese cultural activist (Yoshida Torajiro), and an English diarist (Samuel Pepys). I have, I repeat, a great liking for Robert Louis Stevenson, and more than a great liking, a fellow-feeling. But, that said, I don't think Stevenson kept to that high line I've just evoked, and which he was always aware of. I think he set, for various reasons, a lot of his writing at a lower level, and I don't think he ever wrote the book he might have written. I have two authorities for saying this. One of them, if I may be so forthright, is myself, after a complete and thorough reading of his work. The other is Robert Louis Stevenson. In a letter written towards the end of his life, Stevenson says that what society offers the writer is 'a box of tricks', saying: play with these. Too much of Stevenson's writing comes out of that 'box of tricks'.

2

Before going on, let me give an example of a box-of-tricks book: *The Master of Ballantrae.*

The starting point of the novel is the house of Durrisdeer ('the Duries of Durrisdeer and Ballantrae were a strong family in the south-west from the day of David First'), and the time is the '45. As was often the case with such big families in Scotland, one son was sent 'out' with the Rebels, while the other stayed loyal to the government. While Henry stays at home, James goes away with the Jacobites. After Culloden, he leaves for Paris, in the company of one of the Prince's Irishmen, Francis Burke, on a French ship, which first gets caught in a hurricane and then, as if that wasn't enough, is waylaid by a pirate. James Durie overthrows Captain Teach the pirate, and takes over the ship. They drift about for a year or more in the north Atlantic, till they decide to make for one of the 'Southern provinces of America', where they slush about for a while in a swamp, till a West Indiaman from Albany laden with slaves whisks them off to New York. There, James' plan is to join the French up by Lake Champlain, in the company of an Indian trader, Jacob Chew, who knows 'the secret paths of the wilderness'. They follow 'a labyrinth of rivers, lakes and portages' till they get to a place where James buries his pirate treasure. He then returns to France, where he lives on the Scots Fund for Jacobite refugees, wrings extra cash from his brother, gets imprisoned in the Bastille, and turns government spy. He then goes back to Scotland. Dire scenes at Durrisdeer: James seduces Henry's wife, and the two brothers have a duel. Thinking he's killed his dearly hated brother, Henry goes off his head. Meanwhile James, not dead at all, the bugger, leaves on a smuggler's boat for France, from where he goes to India, where he meets up with a fakir, Secundra Dass. He then goes back to Scotland. More dire times at Durrisdeer. Henry and his wife, at the end of their tether, decide to abandon the ancestral house to James, and skedaddle to New York. James follows them, in the company of the family steward, Ephraim Mackellar. On the boat, James tells Mackellar (as if we hadn't had enough already) the story about the adventures of a German baron in Rome. In New York, more family conflict. Then James leaves with a band of bloodthirsty ruffians under Captain Harris, an Indian trader, in search of his treasure. Evil deeds in the wilderness. To save him from certain death at the hands of his murderous companions, Secundra Dass buries James alive: he knows a secret whereby if you swallow your tongue you can survive no bother under the earth. No luck, the trick doesn't work. When Secundra Dass opens the grave, he finds a corpse. When he sees the corpse (he finally decided to follow his brother), Henry drops dead. They're both buried in the wilderness. End, thank God, of story.

I saw this novel presented recently in an account of Scottish literature as Stevenson's greatest feat. Such a statement implies a sadly impoverished representation of R. L. Stevenson, as well as a drastic curtailment of the possibilities of literature, including Scottish literature. What it is, quite definitely, is a box of tricks.

Let's come back to Stevenson's *high line*, and, in the first place, to the elements of literary theory one can cull from his essays and his letters. It should go without saying, but it doesn't, that essays can be more creative of new space and be, poetically, more exciting to the mind, than a great deal of what passes for 'creative' literature, usually confined to a broad reach of social fiction and a margin of personal poetry.

3

With very few exceptions, Stevenson took little interest in the literature that was practised around him: that 'sea of banalities', as he called it in a letter. In an essay, 'The Lantern Bearers', he declares that if he had no perspectives other than the mass of little affairs, the mess of puny hopes and wretched fears most British novelists work with, he'd kill himself on the spot. Elsewhere, he has this: 'We are all for tootling on the sentimental flute in literature, and not a man among us will go to the head of the march to sound the heady drums.' He felt that intellectual audacity was becoming rarer, almost extinct – 'Everybody feels obliged to be as boring and stupid as his neighbour', he wrote in an essay of 1876. He had no more liking for French naturalism than he had for British socio-realism. But at least in France, he considered, you could ask questions about style, form and composition, level of logic and intellectual conception. To do so in the Anglo-British context, where, as he said, literature is produced like plum-pudding, is to be an outcast from society.

Well, it's when you're 'cast out' that you really begin to look for new bearings. Writing then isn't something done on an identity card, it's a cartography. In that outside, there are no models, but there are sources of inspiration.

For Stevenson, one of the first such sources was Laurence Sterne, friend of the philosopher David Hume, author of *The Life and Opinions of Tristram Shandy* and of *A Sentimental Journey through France and Italy*. If, by the way, Sterne's journey is 'sentimental', it's in the sense that word had in the eighteenth century: full of volatile feeling and vagrant thinking. Sterne himself describes it as 'a journey to the heart of Nature', understanding by Nature what he calls elsewhere 'the great sensorium of the earth'. Sterne is out to write in accordance with this great 'sensorium'. He loathes the chill conceptions of disconnected minds that can only engender petty, hollow or sordid ideas. The itinerary he follows is irregular in the extreme, full of theses, hypotheses and parentheses. He gives his humour full play and his mind all the scope it can take. From Sterne, Stevenson learned freedom unbound.

Close to Sterne in Stevenson's mind, less eccentric, at least in appearance, but just as far away from the conventional kitchens of culture, there was Hazlitt. 'We are fine fellows, we contemporary authors', wrote Stevenson, 'we are smart, we are charming – but we can't write like William Hazlitt.' Without going here into all the ins and outs of Hazlitt's mind, all the ups and downs of his career (he's one of the most mobile and moving of British writers), suffice it to say that what Hazlitt advocated in writing was a *familiar style* – that is, one that was neither sophisticated nor vulgar: the most difficult style of all.

Then, over on the other side of the Atlantic, there was Thoreau. If Stevenson finds him at times a bit ponderous and puritan, there is no doubt that the river-traveller of the Merrimack, and the hermit of Walden, was a powerful influence on the meditative, wandering Scot, both as to general conceptions of literature and to ways of writing. It was Thoreau who declared that the literary world reminded him of a chicken-coop, and that most literature lacked *winged thought*. For having insisted so much on Common Sense (Thoreau was thinking of certain Scotch philosophers), the age had blunted the fine edge of all the five primal ones. Genius, said Thoreau, isn't a lamp in a salon, it's lightning flashing in open space. And a good book should be like a wild flower, or a lichen.

I'm aligning these influences (Stevenson himself spoke, generously, in his essays about the writers that had meaning for him), for at least two reasons. First of all, just as any river of importance has affluents, no work of any magnitude exists without influences. Then, to lay out such a network is to get out of the history of literature, that dreary, dead and insignificant discipline, and enter into the geography of the mind. But once all that is said, what ultimately counts is the individual flux and flow, the really epoch-making writer being the one who has gathered in, and composed, the most influences and who has been able to project them, energetically, into the largest, most enlightened space.

Having evoked these initial ideas concerning the state of literature and the potentialities of writing, I'd like now to go into Stevenson's biography, because a fully developed mind begins early. That a continuous line of development from child-hood to completion exists is of course rare. But that the first opening and intuitions exist as early as childhood is a constant fact of the greatest artistic achievements.

4

Most people reading this book will be aware of the general outlines of Stevenson's biography, from his early bourgeois-bohemian days in Edinburgh as Velvet Coat to his marooned life on Samoa as Tusitala. But I'd like to go back into it here, rapidly, in order to bring out what I consider to be certain more salient and significant points.

Robert Louis Stevenson had known a fairly typical Scottish childhood: he'd been told stories with a strong religious content that had struck terror into his soul, and he'd worked out battle strategies with toy soldiers. But still early on, he'd shown signs of other propensities. For example, he invented a country for himself, Encyclopedia, of which he drew up a map. And when an aunt showed him the wing of an albatross, describing the flight of the bird over the Pacific, he became strangely silent and thoughtful, as though he was discovering an unheard of dimension of the world. To complexify, if not to complete, this portrait of the young Stevenson, it has to be noted that, if he was never a coward or a shirker, making it on the contrary a point of honour to try himself out physically, his health was never of the best: as a child, he was always coughing, and pretty soon he was to suffer from severe lung trouble. Psychologically, if he was fascinated by examples of rough, adventurous living, which he would at times attempt to imitate, he was not totally exempt from the hysteria and schizophrenia that marked so deeply the nineteenth century.

As a young man, while remaining proud of his forebears, lighthouse engineers ('Whenever I smell salt water, I know that I am not far from one of the works of my ancestors. The Bell Rock stands monument for my grandfather, the Skerry Vhor for my uncle Alan, and when the lights come out at sun-down along the shores of Scotland, I am proud to think they burn more brightly for the genius of my father'), Stevenson reacted against his family, the whole Scottish socio-cultural environment as he knew it, and the general context of Britain, which he esteemed blinkered and blinded by puritanism, class distinction and prejudice. It was at this time he made a slight, but significant, change in his name: from Robert Lewis Balfour Stevenson, he became Robert Louis Stevenson, this 'Louis' looking just a bit French (Stevenson's great-grandmother on his mother's side was in fact French: Marguerite Lizars). At this early period of revolt, he put himself forward as Louis the libertine, Louis the free-thinker, who had given over the Bible for Spencer's *Theory of Evolution*. At the age of sixteen, he had read Whitman's *Leaves of Grass*, which tumbled the world upside down for him, tearing away all the moral cobwebs he felt he was smothering in. A little later, it was Villon (poet and outlaw) and Baudelaire (aesthete and immoralist). This was the time when, dressed in a flamboyant velvet jacket, he frequented the howffs and darker dens of Old Edinburgh. Nights of drunkenness, on burgundy red as a November sunset, would be followed by very pallid dawns.

As was to be expected, Robert Louis had begun, early on, an apprenticeship in engineering, but it soon became evident that he would not be following in the family footsteps. He spoke of writing. This was accepted, on the condition that he study law – after all, his writings might never be profitable, might never earn him a living. Robert Louis gave in to this injunction, studied law and was received at the bar. He would plead only one small case in all his life. But those law studies weren't valueless for the future writer: they gave him insight into human nature as well as sharpening his skill in argumentation and demonstration. In a similar way, his short apprenticeship in engineering gave him a sense of construction in space, a feeling for force and form.

5

From this early biography, I move now on to the notion of travelling.

As a youngster, Stevenson would accompany his father on professional inspection tours of Scotland's ports and light-houses. He got a good deal of pleasure out of these excursions and he saw great advantages in an itinerant existence: you lived in the open air, always a sure cure against what he felt as the closed-upness of urban life; you hung around harbours, a form of activity guaranteed to excite the mind; you learned what it was to cross rough seas and you set foot on wild and lonely islands. In this way, he'd moved along the isolated regions of the Fife coast, gone out to the Hebrides, and traversed the desolate plain of Caithness. In the course of these early travels, Stevenson was piling up all kinds of information concerning topology, geology, tides. He was also gathering in a hoard of vivid, vivifying impressions.

That was travelling in general, but Stevenson was also, more specifically, a walker.

Leaving the family house in Heriot Row, he could in a couple of hours' walk be right in the heart of the Pentlands. From the top of those hills that lie behind Edinburgh, he could see other heights and peaks: the hills of Peebles and Fife, the Lammermuirs and the Ochils. And he could envisage Edinburgh, not as the centre of a little region, but as a boss on the great shield of the earth. And there weren't only the Pentlands. To the south, he could walk to North Berwick and the Bass Rock with its colony of gannets. And one Winter, as we saw, he had done that wild walk in the west, across Ayrshire, following the coast road that, with snow falling on the promontories and over the black, empty waters of the bays, had taken on cosmic dimensions.

In a series of essays, Stevenson developed a whole theory of walking. It's close in many respects to Hazlitt and Thoreau, other meditative walkers, but it has its own particulars and peculiarities.

According to Stevenson, if you put a rucksack on your back and make off, it's to free yourself from the shackles of the past (mistakes, regrets, obsessions), it's to approach a new being in a new world. You're out to put some distance between society and yourself, between your (habitual) self and your (potential) self. You're moving out of time into space, and space is first and foremost the landscape, which is invigorating and inspiring for taste, sensibility and mind. By degrees also, you learn to *read* the landscape. While anybody can look at a painting and understand it, says Stevenson (he was no doubt being a bit over-optimistic there, but we can take his point), only a few can see, distinctly and intelligently, into the apparently confused mass of Nature. Paradoxically, he says, it's by crossing a landscape quite fast that you can read it best: clarity of vision goes with movement, while prolonged sedentary study can make the sight opaque, and dilute, dissipate, efface the vision. Beyond the physical and aesthetic landscape, there's a mental landscape, in close relationship with the first, in fact the two interpenetrate. In order to get into the landscape–mindscape, it's best to travel alone. Total availability, from second to second, right down to the depths of one's being, is an essential factor in any walking that's going to be an awakening. As to movement, better neither too fast nor too slow. There's no sense in exhausting one's energies, but it's no good either to stop every five minutes. The best is a regular rhythm. Gradually (it's a real *gradus ad Parnassum* we're concerned with), the tonus of the muscles has an effect on the tonus of the mind. One *identifies* with the landscape: the body is integrated into it, the spirit breathes in it, and the mind follows out the lines. It's then, says Stevenson, you finally enter into the 'parish of the infinite'.

6

During all these trips, whether they be on foot, or by coach, train, boat, Stevenson was also thinking about literature (wordscape).

Let's look, for example, at his early trip to Caithness. He already had the beginnings of several novels in his desk at Heriot Row, but, once 'out there', once he's moving on the ground, he comes to the conclusion that reality is a lot more interesting. He's not thinking only of his unexpected meeting with the two little Italian vagabonds from the Apennines ('stranger than fiction'), but of his encounter with the landscape itself. Then there's that passage in the *Inland Journey* (the canoe trip he did along the rivers of Belgium and northern France) where he speaks of a certain 'cerebral hygiene' and of the intellectual 'seventh heaven' which this river movement, this body–mind moving in space, enabled him to attain. Up to that moment, at the inns where he and his companion spent the night, he was in the habit of reading the novels published in instalments in the newspapers. But more and more, he felt he simply could not stand this type of literature:

Sometimes when I found a new paper, I took a particular pleasure in reading a single number of the current novel; but I never could bear more than three instalments; and even the second was a disappointment. As soon as the tale became in any way perspicuous, it lost all merit in my eyes; only a single scene, or, as is the way with these *feuilletons*, half a scene, without antecedent or consequence, like a piece of a dream, had the knack of fixing my interest. The less I saw of the novel, the better I liked it: a pregnant reflection.

Again, there's the lesson he got from the little island of Earraid in the Hebrides, practically virgin territory, outside civilization – 'a place older than man'. It's this 'anterior state', outside both civilization and humanity, that fascinates him. The novelist in him wonders if, by integrating these sensa-tions into a work of fiction, he won't be running the risk of deforming them. The novelist silences his qualms, brushes away his doubts. But the reader may well retain them, thinking that, even if the early impressions are not deformed, they are certainly not developed. And he may think this all the more when, with the former text still in his mind, he comes across the island of Earraid again, in the fourteenth chapter of *The Adventures of David Balfour*. David Balfour knows nothing about the sea, nothing about islands – he finds Earraid empty, lonely, desolate, horrible (the pathos is piled up). To say the least, this novelistic hero gives us no real news of the island, on the contrary, he's an encumbrance, a blot on the landscape. He knows nothing and understands less. We can of course (humanly, humanitarianly) sympathize with his plight, and his very ignorance creates drama. We've got all the elements of a novel, all the features of noveldom – but no more. Stevenson himself had knowledge of islands, and had an infinitely finer intelligence of place, but it's not this knowledge, not this intelligence he puts into the novels. In other words, in the novel, he's beneath himself, he's below his possibilities.

Of course, even in the novels, there are traces of the other Stevenson, the 'high line' Stevenson. Even in the more simplis-tic of them there will be flashes, phantasmagorical flourishes, pungent atmospheres, a sense of open space, gusts of vigour, strange emptinesses, snatches of a distant music, but none of that sustained high flying he himself evokes and of which we know he was capable.

There was in R. L. Stevenson a yearning for something other and greater than just spinning a yarn.

7

It's all this biographical background, all those vagrant cogitations about literature and writing that lead up to Stevenson's first really consequential book, *Travels with a Donkey in the Cévennes*. It was, I submit, all this that was going through his head that summer of 1878, as he sat under the trees, in the valley of the Gazeille, at Le Monastier, in the Haute-Loire. He was finishing his book on Edinburgh, which meant a lot of this past life was going through his mind. And he was thinking about the new book, which was to take place there in the Cévennes. How to work it out, how to present things along the way, how to express the farthest experience possible? What he had in mind was a kinetic method that would be like a kaleidoscopic dance of images (as a young boy, he had spent delightful hours with 'Dr Brewster's patent kaleidoscope'). The text would be composed in an elliptical style that would leap over heavy causation without ever losing a subtle sense of logic – an elliptical style that would never become spasmodical. The writing would have to be as naked and direct as possible, never masking the sensation of the real with a veil of phraseology. Then there was that distant music of the landscape. You had to listen close to hear it but, when you did, you could never forget it. To get into the landscape takes thought, you have to study nature in depth till you get beyond analysis into a kind of synthesis. And to cap it all, you have to be able to say it without literary affectation.

It's no part of my intention simply to paraphrase the *Travels*, with a little critical and appreciative comment here and there. What I want to do, bearing in mind all that's been already gathered, is to make a cartography of the book, in concentric circles, according to the orography of the Massif Central.

8

The first circle is geographical.

Stevenson felt strangely drawn to the granite peaks, the schisty escarpments of the Cévennes. Rough and wild, they stretched away there to the south-east of the great Massif Central, the geological core of France. Here lay the sources of rivers such as the Loire, the Allier, the Tarn, the Gard. Here was a whole labyrinth of hills, a complete system of blue crests. Taken as a whole, the Cévennes country comprises mountains, chalky plateaux and expanses of scrubland. But Stevenson was attracted mainly to its central area, around the Espérou and the Aigoual, the chaotic, tormented region that covers the south-east corner of old Gévaudan: the centre of a centre. He had affinities with this land in more ways than one.

For him, these lands were the Highlands of France. At first, this was perhaps only intuitive and analogous. But the comparison is in fact more founded than that. I don't know if Stevenson knew it (living there myself a century later, I was linguistically at an advantage) – but the *vennes* in Cévennes is the same as the *ben* of the Scottish Highlands, just as the *ard* of the Ardèche is the same as the *ard* of Ardlui and Ardrossan ('the heights'). He may not have had these confirmations, but as he made deeper and deeper acquaintance with the country, the parallels that arose in his mind were more and more frequent: Le Monastier reminded him of another 'provincial capital', Maybole in Ayrshire.

In other words, for Stevenson, the Massif Central in general, the Cévennes in particular, were another Scotland. But one that he could observe and experience at some distance, without the cloying associations and the heavy connotations that would accompany any such enterprise back home. This was a distanciated Scotland. The scene was set for something like an operative auto-analysis, to be followed by an auto-poetics.

9

The second circle is historico-cultural. The Cévennes were the country of the Camisards, those French Protestants who were the equivalent of the Covenanters.

It would be totally wrong to think that, if Stevenson wrote such long pages on the Camisards, it was just to fill out his book, provide it with some time-honoured matter, as in those ordinary travel-books where a chapter of contemporary reportage is regularly followed by a chapter on history, and so on. No, the persecution of the Scottish Protestants lay deep in Stevenson's conscience, and in this journey which is also an oblique autobiography, that matter had to emerge, like lava from a volcano. All of Stevenson's childhood had been steeped in that atmosphere. As a boy he'd wandered about in the Pentlands, hiding himself away in his favourite wild spots – 'like a Cameronian at the time of the Killings'. And the first text he ever published (*The Pentland Rising – a page of history*), printed in Edinburgh, at his father's expense, by Andrew Elliot of Princes Street, in 1866 (Stevenson was then sixteen years old), had the Covenanter question as its theme. In the course of his Cévenol peregrination, Stevenson was re-visiting, mentally, the places and the topics of his childhood and early education. The book is at one and the same time a recapitulation and a testament, a trial and an experiment. While staying light on the surface, the text is actually quite complicated, tectonically enfolded. Stevenson was out to get to the limits of himself, going over again known roads, trying to open new ways.

In his baggage there in the Cévennes, Stevenson had a copy of Peyrat's *Les Pasteurs du désert* ('the pastors of the desert') bought at an antiquarian shop in Paris. Regarding the crest of the Mont Lozère, near Finiels, Peyrat writes: 'From this summit one can see in practically one glance the entire dramatic territory of the insurrection.' It was a point Stevenson had placed with particular intent on his itinerary. From up there he could contemplate the whole 'sacred theatre' (it was the title of another book he'd consulted, in the Advocates' Library in Edinburgh: *Le Théâtre sacré des Cévennes*, by Misson, which dates back to 1707), the whole extent of 'the desert', the wild wilderness. 'It is a harsh and savage country, unique in France', wrote Théodore de Bèze in his history of the Reformation. 'And it has seen more prophets and martyrs than any other part of the land.' Obscure and isolated, with craggy heights, full of canyons, ravines and grottos, it was perfect for those who needed a refuge, for resistance movements, and for all those who, for one reason or another, needed to practise what you might call 'ridge tactics' or 'mountain strategy'.

In Stevenson's mind, the parallels between the Cévennes and Scotland were obvious: a similar physical terrain, similar cultural conflict, and a similar psychological context. But the farther he went into the territory, the further he pursued his investigations, the more he saw also a difference, and a fundamental one. It seemed to him that those Protestants of the 'French Highlands' insisted less than their Scottish counterparts on evil and sin. The soul of Esprit Séguier, says Stevenson, was 'like a garden'. Could the reason be climatological? The fact is that, in the Cévennes, alongside the oak, pine, ash and birch of the rocky heights, you also find olive trees, mulberry-trees and mimosa. In any case, the conclusion one comes to, as we leave this circle, is that Stevenson was working his way out from a theatre, to a garden. Leaving the village of Lestampe to cross the mountain in front, he speaks of 'the garden of the world'.

10

The third circle is 'religious'. I'm using the word in a large sense, because that is how it finally has to be understood, but Stevenson's 'pilgrimage' in the Cévennes also passes through the concept in its most institutional forms.

We find, first of all, a dialectic of Protestantism and Catholicism. It's there already in that earlier travel book, *An Inland Voyage*. Going into the cathedral at Noyon, after admiring its architecture (in which he sees traces of mountain and forest), Stevenson doesn't like what he sees as the poor theatricality of the mass. He finds the *miserere* so morbid, so joyless, that it must have been, he says, 'the composition of an atheist', and is of the opinion that the words pronounced within such buildings have never been worthy of them. On the other hand, the place awakens in him the desire to write sermons for himself ('On a final analysis, every man is his own doctor of divinity'), and he leaves it saying (when he read this, his Presbyterian father must have bordered on apoplexy): 'If ever I join the church of Rome, I shall stipulate to be bishop of Noyon on the Oise.' We find a complement to these remarks in the account he gives of his visit to the church at Creil. Good Protestant (or ex-Protestant) that he is, he makes fun of the votive tablets and waxes indignant at the practices of a certain 'Association of the Living Rosary': this dispensation of indulgences, he says, is like 'doing business with God'. But immediately after this outburst, he wonders if his Protestant education has really made him capable of understanding such acts, such signs, and if there might be, even among all the absurdities, deformations and deformities, 'some higher and more religious spirit than I dream'. We have this same confrontation of Protestantism and Catholicism on Stevenson's arrival in the Cévennes. It's the liberty of language that strikes him. Hearing as he did a *fouchtra* here, a *bougra* there, and *moun diou* everywhere, even from women, Stevenson, still to some extent the discreet Edinburghian, had the impression that the Monasterians communicated exclusively via swear-words and oaths. And the Presbyterian Protestant still latent in him was completely taken aback when those pagan Catholics would interrupt what he considered a string of obscenities in order to say a prayer. In Scotland, there was a place for all manner of things, but you didn't mix them! This mixing, though, showed a vivacity he had to admire.

It was in this open frame of mind, in a spirit of relativism, willing to accept the fact that there might be something interesting, even for a Protestant, in Catholicism, and that there might be something to be learned, if only on the level of analogy, from the monastic life (in his head, he had images of hermits contained in Sadeler's *Solitudo sive Vitae Patrum*, a favourite book of his childhood), but not without qualms (he was setting foot, unarmed, on ground that had been papally mined), that Stevenson approached the monastery of Our-Lady-of-the-Snows, which he calls his 'strange destination'.

At the outset, he was agreeably surprised to find that, in this Cistercian context, there was no sign at all of what annoyed him in Catholicism: childish practices, excessive elaboration, decorative pomp. On the contrary, in the monastery of Our-Lady-of-the-Snows, especially in the little whitewashed chapel, he found an austere simplicity, an 'ineffable perfume', and even a kind of poetry. He felt quite at home, not knowing perhaps if it was Catholicism that was attracting him, or something

beyond both Protestantism and Catholicism. On the human
level, he made the acquaintance there of men from the Drôme,
the Haute-Loire, the Ardèche and Savoie who went about
their daily monacal practice in silence. Only one, an Irishman
by the name of Michael O'Callaghan, who went through bouts
of religious mysticism (embarrassing to the other monks) tried,
jocularly, to convert him: 'Become a Catholic, boy, and come to
heaven with the true believers.' With the monks, everything
would have gone well. But it was different with a country
priest and a retired Army man, who were living there at the
monastery on a short retreat. The talk with them was all contro-
versy and acrimony. In that context, Stevenson's Protestantism
re-asserted itself, and his hatred of all bigotry was roused.

Back in his cell, Stevenson tried to think things over coolly,
weighing the pros and cons. On the Catholic side, if there were
bigots and inquisitors, there were also, he knew, broad-minded
men like the bishop of Oloron in the Pyrenees who, right in the
middle of the Huguenot persecutions, had declared that from
one religion to another the differences were too minimal to
merit massacres. On the Protestant side, if there were some
enlightened minds, there were also professional disputants
ready to go to battle over the sense of some Hebrew word
neither party fully understood. The conclusion he came to was
that it would be best to abandon them all, lock, stock and
barrel.

That's why he left the monastery of Our-Lady-of-the-Snows
singing to himself a music-hall song about 'pretty, skitty gals'
he'd heard in Paris.

His reaction was a bit frivolous, a bit superficial, he was
well aware of that. But he needed a little sign of revolt against
the dusty debating, all the terroristic theology, all the murderous narrowmindedness that religion so often implies.

At Le Monastier, in a cooler mood, Stevenson had written a
letter to his friend Charles Baxter, bringing together religion
and literature. He started off by saying that normally he wasn't
much given to prayer, except in the burlesque mode, but that
lately, not only was he more and more aware of the fact that
some prayers took their place among the finest texts in the
world, he was beginning to wonder if prayer wasn't the highest
form of poetry. He even went so far during the Cévennes trip

as to compose a few prayers for himself, asking, for example, the God who guides men in the rain and sun to be with him on his way. These prayers he consigned to the journal, but he didn't take them over into the definitive text. There were probably several reasons for that: the determination to stay light, at least on the surface; the realization that they really weren't very good; an evolution in his thinking. It's this last element that is the most important. Stevenson's thought was in fact evolving rapidly, via a process involving erosion and expansion. There's a linguistic side to this: a slide and a slant. From *pray* he goes to *praise*. And he begins to think that prayers to God could be replaced, advantageously, by praise of place: paradise on earth.

11

The final circle touches on geopoetics.

In an essay, 'Roads', written in 1873, Stevenson was already talking about meandering paths, connivance with a place and the need to study Nature both methodically and deeply. He signed this text: 'L. S. Stoneven', which is of course in the first instance simply an anagram of his name, but which also has a sense: 'on the level of stone', and marks the desire for a radical departure. At about the same time, in France, Arthur Rimbaud was saying things like this: 'If I have any taste for anything, it's for earth and stones.'

It was this radical desire, buried under masses of club conversation (Stevenson was *also* a Scottish writer on the make, looking for favour in London) and layers of light literature (in the British context, it was not the done thing to sound too serious) that, amid psychic perturbation, emerged again during the Cévennes journey.

'The great affair', wrote Stevenson, on the way from Le Cheylard to Luc, 'is to move: to feel the needs and hitches of life more nearly; to come down off this feather-bed of civilization, and find the globe granite underfoot and strewn with cutting flints.'

For this radical exercise, the severe landscape of the Cévennes was perfect.

But, as we've seen, the hill-roads of the Cévennes also

constituted an intellectual way, comprising history, culture, religion, all of them finally transcended.

In a text of 1887, 'The Lantern Bearers', evoking a childhood memory but going beyond it, Stevenson tells the story of a monk who, as he crosses a forest, hears a bird singing, and stops to listen for a moment. When finally he gets back to his monastery, he realizes he's been away fifty years. In his commentary on this story, Stevenson goes on to say that every existence not entirely devoted to mechanical repetition has two strands: the search for such a bird, and the listening to it.

There are several passages on Stevenson's Cévenol way analogous to the monk's listening to the bird.

One is that moment when, on leaving the Trappist monastery, in a spirit of pagan Protestantism, or purified Paganism, soon to become diluted into some more indefinable essence, Stevenson washes in the waters of the Tarn: 'Here, in a place where many straight and prosperous chestnuts stood together, making an isle upon a swarded terrace, I made my morning toilette in the water of the Tarn. It was marvellously clear, thrillingly cool...'

Then there's the night under the pines.

It's maybe necessary to know the hardness of the rock and the harshness of the sun in the Cévennes to be able fully to appreciate a Cévenol night, with its scent of thyme, the unceasing *cri-cri-cri* of crickets, and its big clear sky full of stars. Stevenson knew such a night, and he spoke of it well:

A faint wind, more like a moving coolness than a stream of air, passed down the glade from time to time; so that even in my great chamber the air was being renewed all night long. I thought with horror of the inn at Chasseradès and the congregated nightcaps; with horror of the nocturnal prowesses of clerks and students, of hot theatres and pass-keys and close rooms. I have not often enjoyed a more serene possession of myself, nor felt more independent of material aids. The outer world, from which we cower into our houses, seemed after all a gentle habitable place; and night after night a man's bed, it seemed, was laid and waiting for him in the fields. I thought I had rediscovered one of those truths which are revealed to savages and hid from political economists...

12

It remains to situate *Travels with a Donkey* in Stevenson's work as a whole, see what place it has in his life-line.

It is a book of transition. Just as the Cévennes constitute a watershed, the Cévennes book is a watershed in the evolution of the wandering Scots writer.

As we've just seen, Stevenson was in the process of entering the great relationship, the open world, what he himself called, in the *Inland Journey* (with reference to 'gymnosophy', the Greek word for the physical and mental integration usually called *yoga*) a 'high cold zone'. On the other side of the watershed, there will be stories, novels, tales of adventures, reportage, travel-writing, documentaries – but very little that could be considered the development of what comes over in the first texts and in the essays, almost nothing with their particular perceptions and perspectives, or their subtlety.

The change in his existence certainly had a lot to do with it. When, soon after the Cévennes trip, Stevenson left for the United States, he was going to be burdened with a family – a wife, and two children – a family that would be augmented later, in the Pacific, when his mother joined the group. So that, even if the circumstances were 'exotic', Stevenson was going to be leading the life not only of a bourgeois, but of a humdrum literary bread-winner. To say that a radical departure was turning into a commercial enterprise would be too much (Stevenson remains Stevenson), but there's something of that in the new context: the pressure not only of making a living, but of supporting a whole household, with easily sellable literature, catering, Stevenson knew it and said it, to under-nourished intelligences and dwarfed psychologies.

Circumstances such as I have described are of course common to many writers, who nonetheless manage to produce 'good literature'. But Stevenson wasn't just another 'good writer'. He had set out to travel the high road. He's in another, more difficult, category. Which is why in his case you have to bring in a lot more than 'literary criticism', according to the normal criteria. You have to talk about life-economy, existential and intellectual method, possible far reaches of the mind. A discourse totally different from the one we hear day in day out.

13

Once, however, Stevenson almost got on to the high road again, once 'something else' almost took place.

It was in the Pacific, that 'no man's land of history', as he called it in a letter to his friend Sydney Colvin.

I see the premonition of it, its prefiguration, in the first pages of *The Ebb Tide*, when a silent boat approaches an island where no human being can be seen, no human sound heard: all that is visible is the figure of a woman, white as snow, indicating something with outstretched arm.

What this figurehead indicates is only the object of an episode in the novel, but I'm interpreting the *something* in a larger sense.

In 1890, in a letter to the French writer Marcel Schwob (it was he who described the literary scene as 'a deluge without a dove'), Stevenson said that he was up to the eyes in work. He had two good-sized *novels* on the stocks and also *a big book* about the South Seas.

The distinction is clearly made between 'novels' and this 'big book'.

The 'big book' belonged to a totally different category and was much more ambitious both in conception and in intent. It would try to penetrate into that 'strange place', the Pacific. It would show humanity at its limits. It would move through time and space. It would consist of one kaleidoscopic scene after the other.

This great project was never realized in its entirety, partly owing to lack of time, partly because no one was interested. There was, Stevenson was told, no place on the market for such an undertaking, what the public wanted was novels, more novels, nothing but novels: boxes of tricks. So, in the place of what would have been an immense oceanic and insular panorama, all we have is the mass of prose that bears the title *The South Seas*: fertile *materia prima*, intelligent documentation and commentary, but with nothing of the upsurge, nothing of the tidal movement, nothing of the polymorphic configuration it might have had.

In conclusion, what Stevenson's life-work leaves me with, after the in-depth, outlook reading I've tried to do, is, between the lines, the ghost of a programme.

Writing the Road

It is long, the road most necessary for our thought.

(Martin Heidegger)

1

Where prose-writing is concerned, the massive reference is still the novel, even more specifically, the naturalistic novel, in other words, psycho-sociology in this or that context, with a little fantasy (the infantile form of imagination) or perversity (the legacy of Puritanism) on the side.

If I waste no time on this kind of literature, I have at one time or another read all the recognized great novels and a good number of the less great. I'm thinking of Melville. But Melville I tend to see now more as one straining towards an epic poem than one settled into straight story-telling or any kind of naturalism–humanism. And Dostoevsky. But his work I see as a marathon psychoanalysis interspersed with those moments of 'white-glowing sensation' that Stefan Zweig points to as the real nodes of significance. Then there's Thomas Hardy with that beautiful title *Jude the Obscure*. But Hardy gave up novel-writing and in his later life concentrated on attempts at poetry. I'm thinking of Henry Miller too, but Miller's 'novels' are ongoing autobiography with an underlying gnostic reference interrupted by outbursts of mystico-lyrical exuberance. And at one point, I think it's in *Nexus*, he cries out that he's fed up writing novels, from now on he wants to write for the wild duck.

In other words, over the past century or so, when live minds, with strong life at their fingertips, were writing so-called novels, they were continually striving at and trying to conceive something *outside* the novel.

Another type of writing, another form of literature.

Jean Toomer's *Cane* is often characterized as a novel. That's what Robert Bone calls it, in *The Negro Novel in America*: '*Cane* is an important American novel.' All prose-writing nowadays gets slumped into that big floppy, floozy category. But when *Cane* came out in 1923, nobody knew where to place it.

94

Not only did it mingle prose and poetry, it juxtaposed immediate realism with highflying mysticism. A lot of minds were confused. But one critic, while admitting his bewilderment, hit the right kind of note: '*Cane* is an interesting, occasionally beautiful and often queer book of exploration into old country and new ways of writing.'

I'm interested in books that are often 'queer' and 'occasionally beautiful', books of mental exploration.

Old country, new ways...

Only a few years ago, William Carlos Williams was saying that 'the most of all writing has not even begun in the province from which alone it can draw sustenance', and that 'it is the jump from prose to the process of the imagination that is the next great leap of the intelligence – from the simulations of present experience to the facts of the imagination.'

I'm not sure that 'imagination' is the key word, though it may be part of the process (imagination is the resource of the mind in confined space), but what is certain is that live writing at the present moment is concerned with process, and that in so doing it necessarily goes beyond the precincts of the novel (including, need it be stressed, the de-emotionalized, de-plotted, de-psychologized 'neo-novel').

Let's try to take a closer look at this process, and at the leaps that intelligence has been taking while 'literature' still plodded along with its infantile respect for plot (already Mark Twain in *Huck Finn* was saying that anyone attempting to find a plot in that book should be shot) and its antiquated notions of more or less pathological 'substance', long ago blasted in physics, but still doing their drab and dreary bit in the world of writing.

2

There was a start in Romanticism.

If the word 'romantic' is used in ordinary discourse today, it refers either to sentimental love-contexts, or to the unworldly, otherworldly attitude of someone like, say, Ludwig II of Bavaria in his Swan Castle. Now if love is undoubtedly a part of Romanticism (one of its aspects, like the exploration of the unconscious, to be developed by its late avatar, Surrealism, and finally systematized by Freud), if the female figure, the female principle, is everywhere present in it, so much so that we might speak of an eroto-cosmology, it cannot be restricted to that aspect. Again, if absolute intellectual-aesthetic 'monasteries' turn up in its literature again and again, from Wackenroder to Hesse, such cloistering by no means covers its whole field of energy. What Romanticism meant was a radical crisis in the Western conception of the world, a criticism of its systems, values and ambitions, an encyclopedic search for knowledge in all directions and the groundwork for a new epistemology, as well as a tremendous outburst of creativity.

A lot of this was expressed in what is often referred to as the 'iniatic novel' (Moritz's *Anton Reiser*, Tieck's *Wanderings of Franz Sternbald* or his *Journey into the Blue*), but which, so as to get rid of the trappings of romance and the solemnity of 'initiation', leaving room for new developments, I prefer to call the 'transcendental travelogue'.

The romantic transcendental travelogue (neither mere travel-writing nor adventure tale) moves through a spiritual topography, towards what Hölderlin calls 'completion' (*Vollendung*) and which is often represented mytho-geographically as 'Eldorado' (I'm thinking of Poe) or 'the Orient' (for example, Nerval: 'Where are you going? – To the Orient!'), or symbolically as, for example, 'the blue flower' in Tieck's *Heinrich von Ofterdingen*. It is a journey from self to Self, from confusion and ignorance to a cosmo-poetic reading of the universe.

But more important perhaps than the destination of these transcendental travelogues is their *method*. The idea is to give a sense all along the way of what is open and flowing and cannot be defined in any cut-and-dried fashion.

Many of these books remained unfinished. No book with anything so facile as a conclusion could correspond to the intention these minds had, the opening world they sensed. All is essay, fragment, approach. The creation images are organic: meteorological (nebulae, stars), or botanical (flying seeds).

Projecting themselves outside the normal frameworks, working at a cross-fertilization of sciences normally divided the one from the other (a biologist, Ignaz Troxler, will speak of 'biosophy'), the Romantics were looking for new means of expression: 'The art of writing books', says Novalis in the *Blütenstaub* ('Pollen' – a selection of his 'fragments' made by

Friedrich Schlegel), 'hasn't been invented yet. But we're coming close to it.'

3

A further stage, nakeder, colder:

Nietzsche had no time for the Romantics, loathing their excessive sentimentality and their frothy enthusiasm (*Schwärmerei*), but, seen from a distance, he is working along the same lines. He has the same impatience with most books (shrouds over dead matter, he calls them), has the same concern with a new type of writing (fragmentary, saltatory), and the same preoccupation with a road, a way outside the normal paths and normal destinations. In *Dawns*, he speaks of 'Men who love the hazards of wandering, while others never leave the beaten tracks', and he comes back on the same theme a few pages later: 'Inventive men live quite differently from busy men. It takes time for their irregular, aimless activity to get underway. They don't just follow the beaten track, they grope their way along new experiences, open up new paths.' The image of path and road is omnipresent in Nietzsche's writing: 'There are a thousand paths that have not yet been followed, a thousand types of health, a thousand lands hidden from life. Neither man nor the earth have been discovered yet. Stay awake and listen, you solitaries. From the future you will hear breezes coming, full of secret wing-beats.'

Borrowing a word from Greek mythology, Nietzsche called this 'irregular' path outside the norms the 'hyperborean path'. He speaks of it at the beginning of the *Antichrist*: 'We are Hyperboreans. We are very well aware in what remoteness we live... Beyond the north and ice and death – *our* life, *our* happiness, we know the way, we have found the way out of whole millennia of labyrinth.'

Nietzsche saw the crisis that was to come in Western culture, a crisis that would give rise to half-solutions making things more confused if not definitely worse, before anything like an exit into new existence was found.

Very little literature would get anywhere near that new existence, because to get at it meant, on the one hand, clear insight into the situation (idealism, the break-up of idealism, and its consequence, nihilism) and an energy-thrust that would go beyond both hard nihilism and soft nihilism into different territory. Which is why Nietzsche spurns literature as normally practised, and the 'literary life', looking for new existence, new expression:

> *This is a book, what are books?*
> *Coffins and winding sheets.*
> *The past is the prey of books:*
> *Here lives an eternal today.*
> *This is my will, my promise*
> *This is a breaking of the bridges*
> *A sea wind, the raising of an anchor.*

He himself rarely experienced that other existence, that other territory, on the life-path that led him out of Basle. He knew it maybe on the shores of Santa Margarita, or up in the Engadine: 'A summer on the heights, with cold springs and happy tranquillity', as he says in the *Zarathustra*. But mostly he was labouring in the labyrinth, between exaltation and depression.

4

In 1791, François René de Chateaubriand left for the 'hyper-borean' regions of North America, with the intention of finding the north-west passage. He let himself be persuaded before very long that he was too unprepared and ill-equipped to undertake the task of discovering the hypothetical passage, but he nevertheless moved in his mind a great deal about America, on 'the roads of the New World' (these roads being, as he said 'more traced out than actually laid down'), and he acquired a good sense of American space.

Right from the beginning, his own attitude (questing energy, desire for information, openness to experience) is contrasted sharply with the classical colonialist figure of the governor of Saint Pierre et Miquelon, representative of so many minds 'dropped' on the new continent and devoid of all interest in it. The governor is bored, Chateaubriand is ebullient. The governor wants to talk about the political revolution, Chateaubriand is more interested in the transcontinental passage. And so on. The young Breton sums it up: 'He was in an outpost in the wilderness, but he knew nothing about the Eskimo and all he got from Canada was partridges for his table.'

While he was in America, Chateaubriand went out of his way to learn as much about Amerindian tribal culture as he could. He also piled up information concerning the geology and the botany of the continent. And he has interesting remarks about United States sociology. He asks himself what a Frenchman from New Orleans, a German from New York and an Englishman from Virginia can have in common, and he answers: nothing. In the United States, there is no sense of *patrie* (motherland), what you have are *des compagnies nomades* (nomadic bands), moving across the continent in all directions, every one following its own road. As to literary space, there is none. There are American writers certainly (he mentions Washington Irving and Fennimore Cooper), but they have to come to Europe for appreciation. There is no intellectual ground in the US, the Americans having invested in 'positive' rather than in 'intellectual' values. There is no classical literature, for there are no models. No romantic literature, for there is no past to delve back into. And there is no primitive literature, because the Americans despise the savages.

We are left with the question, the possibility of a literature, a space-and-road literature, left in the air.

5

Only a half-century or so after Chateaubriand's indictment, an American literature was in existence, and it was very much a space-and-road literature.

'A traveller!', notes Thoreau in his *Journal* (2 July 1851), 'I love his title. A traveller is to be reverenced as such. His profession is the best symbol of our life. Going from – towards – ; it is the history of every one of us. I am interested in those that travel in the night.'

But the man who, in the name of America, took the road as his theme and space as his element was, of course, Walt Whitman. What had come to him via Carlyle, and Emerson, was Romanticism (transcendental idealism) but he translated it into Americanese, and gave it a new lease of life. The result was the 'Open Road':

*From this hour I ordain myself loos'd of limits and imaginary
    lines*

Everybody knows Whitman's full-blown enthusiasm, his breezy
declarations, his breathless lists. If it is easy to make fun of
them, he has given more than one mind the impression of
opening a gate, awakening a sense of world outside all socio-
moral constrictions. Equally perceptible is his 'breaking through
copied forms ' (W.C. Williams' phrase), the oceanic surge of his
line, the inventiveness of his vocabulary and these particularly
felicitous moments of contact with the 'cool-breath'd earth',
when the rant and the brag (so irritating to some, so exhilarating
to others, even if they take it, as it must be taken, with a
humorous grain of salt) gives way to a quieter kind of poetics.

But what tends to go unnoticed in the new noise is the
question that never ceased to nag Whitman, even if he kept it
hidden most of the time behind his grandfatherly beard: what,
exactly and essentially, was he after? Sometimes, he'd give
himself an easy answer, as in the 'Open Road' poem: 'They go!
They go! I know that they go, but I know not where they go –
But I know that they go toward the best, toward something
great' (which couldn't convince anybody), but at other times, as
in 'Facing West from California's Shores', he leaves the
question, putting it very quietly within parentheses:

> *(But where is what I started out for so long ago?*
> *And why is it yet unfound?)*

However much he may have been taken as a trumpet-blowing
spokesman of the US, sometimes complacently playing this
rôle, Whitman himself knew in the innermost of his concentric mind circles that he was only beginning something,
something concerned less with 'these States' than with a state
of being:

> *I myself but write one or two indicative words for the future.*

That was written in 1860.

6

In no. 7 of the Mentor publication *New World Writing*, which
came out in 1955, there was a piece by one who signed himself

Jean-Louis, a young Franco-American writer, of Breton origins, which ended so:

> There is no end to the night. At great roar of Chicago dawn we all staggered out and shuddered in the raggedness. It would start all over tomorrow night. We rushed on to New York. 'There ain't nothing left after that', said Dean. 'Whee!' he said. We seek to find new phrases; we try hard, we writhe and twist and blow; every now and then a clear harmonic cry gives new suggestions of a tune, a thought, that will some day be the only tune and thought in the world and which will raise men's soul to joy. We find it, we lose it, we wrestle for it, we find it again, we laugh, we moan. Go moan for man. It's the pathos of people that gets us down, all the lovers in this dream.

Everyone has recognized Jack Kerouac.

It's the Whitmaniac 'open road' figure one hundred years later: Whitman in the age of anxiety, a Whitman who's read Céline's *Voyage au bout de la nuit*, and Breton's automatic writings, an existentialist–surrealist bebop Whitman. And as with Whitman, there are two 'lines': on one, you have the spokesman of the Beat Generation, on the other a 'strange solitary crazy Catholic mystic' concerned with 'old human feelings older than *Time Magazine*'.

I think it's in the novel *You Can't Go Home Again* that Thomas Wolfe has the phrase: 'I know that we are lost here in America – but I believe we shall be found again.' Kerouac used to sing a lyrical version of this lostness theme, this homelessness, without the hope that comes in the second part of Wolfe's phrase. The little song went like this:

> *Home in Missoula*
> *Home in Truckee*
> *Home in Opelousa*
> *Ain't no home for me*
> *Home in old Medora*
> *Home in Wounded Knee*
> *Home in Ogallala*
> *Home I'll never be*

Underneath Kerouac's surface naivety, there is a pathetic desire and a desperate lucidity.

With this homeless (*heimatlos*) feeling in his soul, and with no hope of ever reaching any special place, more or less reconciled to a repetitious wandering about in *samsara* (to use an Oriental vocabulary he affected), but with the chance of a few ecstatic kicks on the way, Kerouac gets out on the road, that road that leads, in his autobiographical sagas, from Lowell to Hoboken, from there to Cincinnati, Chicago, Denver, San Francisco and anywhere...

On the Road... The Dharma Bums... Desolation Angels...
Movement and solitude:

> I was searching for a peaceful kind of life dedicated to contemplation [...] to see the world from the viewpoint of solitude and to meditate upon the world without being imbroglio'd in its actions. [...] I wanted to be a man of Tao, who watches the clouds and lets history rage beneath. [...] I never dreamed I'd be taken in too by the world's action. [...] The circle closed in on this old independent renegade.

One of the most moving texts Kerouac ever wrote about 'the circle closing in' and the gradual disappearance of the American 'independent renegade' is called 'The vanishing American hobo' (it's the eighth and final section of *Lonesome Traveller*):

> In America there has always been [...] a definite special idea of footwalking freedom going back to the days of Jim Bridger and Johnny Appleseed [...]. The American Hobo is on the way out as long as sheriffs operate with as Louis-Ferdinand Céline said 'One line of crime and nine of boredom', because having nothing to do in the middle of the night with everybody gone to sleep they pick on the first human being they see walking [...]. I myself was a hobo but I had to give it up around 1956 because of increasing television stories about the abominableness of strangers with packs passing through by themselves independently [...]. There's something strange going on, you can't be alone any more in the primitive wilderness ('primitive areas' so-called), there's always a helicopter comes and snoops around, you need camouflage [...]. As far as I'm concerned the only thing to do is sit in a room and get drunk. [...] I have no axe to grind: I'm simply going to another world.

So, end of the Open Road, last exits to Brooklyn?

But it's difficult to give up such a fundamental theme so easily.

Maybe, before we come back to the modern context, in America or elsewhere, we should take a look at the road-theme in some of the traditions. Not for the sake of mere erudition, but for the sake of *renewing resources*.

7

In 1932, a little book appeared in the US entitled *Black Elk – the life story of a holy man of the Ogalala Sioux*. The book went unnoticed, till it finally got through to Carl Jung's group in Zürich, who were fascinated by it. News of their interest got back to the US, where the book came out in paperback in the early 1960s. It was to become a little bible during the sixties and seventies. But, as everybody knows, things go fast in the US. And after a few years' enthusiastic reception, the book has probably sunk again into oblivion, any reference to it being a sign of enormous naivety and ridiculous outmodedness. This will probably be the case for some time – till some other 'human sciences' group in Europe (or maybe, say, in China) redis- covers it, or its like, and puts it back on the general map. In the meantime, it's there for individuals concerned about their own lives and their own heads to consult and to use, maybe taking it as a first step into the whole area of Amerindian culture.

For Black Elk, that culture came to a brutal end in 1890, at Wounded Knee: 'A people's dream died there. It was a beauti- ful dream.' Black Elk had seen the dying, the attempt at renewal through the Ghost Dance movement, and the death. He has no illusions: 'There is no centre any longer, and the sacred tree is dead.' But 'the beauty and the strangeness of the earth' is still there, at least in some places, and who knows, who knows, 'it may be that some little root of the sacred tree still lives'. And if that little root still lives, who knows, who knows, some day people 'may once more go back into the sacred circle and find again the good red road'.

8

But the main influence concerning another space, another road, on the modern Western mind from, say, the late eight- eenth century on, came not from American India, but from Asian India.

For the Schlegels in Romantic Germany, to find a perfect

realization of all that Romanticism meant, you had to go East. The same goes for Nerval and Rimbaud in France. As early as 1792, Sir William Jones' translation of Kalidasa's *Sakuntala* was available in Britain, and H.T. Colebrooke's essays on the 'philosophy and religion of the Hindu' followed shortly after. The American transcendentalists were all steeped in Oriental literature, Henry Thoreau saying that he loved to 'bathe his head' in the *Bhagavat-Gîta*.

'The pilgrimage', writes Ananda Coomaraswamy in *The Pilgrim's Way*, 'is a procedure from potentiality to act, non-being to being, darkness to light... and can be expressed in familiar terms by saying that the traveller is on his way to become a *krtsna-karma-krt* (one who has performed the whole task).' In the *Manual of Buddhism*, Rhys Davids says that to follow the way-through-the-worlds is to move into 'a gradual becoming along a More towards a final Most'. I.B. Horner in an essay on *Wayfaring* says that it is a question of 'reaching the Cool' (the cool – that is how she translates *nibbana* in Pali, Sanskrit *nirvana*). It takes energy (*viriya*), hard striving (*padhana*), and a determination to go right to the end of the road (*advanah param*), until 'you' become *That*.

'Monks', says Gotama in the *Samyutta*, 'I have seen an ancient way, an ancient road, traversed by the Wholly Awakened Ones of ancient times. The Cool exists, the way to it exists, I myself exist as an adviser. Yet, although some of my disciples, advised and instructed by me, succeed in attaining to the Cool, some do not. What can I do about that?'

When Rechungpa, Milarepa's disciple, wanted to set out travelling, so as to further his experience of Realization, Milarepa at first advised him to stay, but when he saw how determined the younger man had become, he at least wanted to make sure that he knew how to travel. 'How will you walk on your way?', he asked, and Rechungpa answered:

> Using the Dharma as a metaphor
> I'll move forward in the Void
> With no thought of Idealism or Realism, I'll walk ahead
> Following the path, I'll go straight on...

He's going to use all he's ever learned, he's going to use the personality of his teacher, he's going to use even his own personality as metaphors. This kind of travelling, while knowledgeable, is outside all orthodoxy, which is why it is called 'formless yoga'. It accepts all substance, but burns it for energy, passing through it into the void-awareness, and thence back into substance, and so on. If we think in terms of writing (which is itself a yoga), there can be no plot, but deployment of energy, with *yang* moments (strong, bright, energy moments) alternating with *yin* moments (quiet, reposeful moments).

Which brings us to the *tao* (one stroke *yang*, one stroke *yin*, remember?).

9

The word *tao*, 'way', is written in Chinese with two root characters, the one representing 'feet', the other 'head'. Taoism, then, could mean something like 'how to move with your head' or 'how to make headway'.

There are two types of *tao*, or two interpretations of *tao*: High Sky *tao* and Do Good *tao*. Or, to put that in another way (Taoism loves ringing the changes and all kinds of verbal jookery-pookery): Roaming *tao* and Rectifying *tao*, Natural *tao* and Social *tao*. The best representative of High Sky *tao* (with Lao-tzu coming close second, and Li-tzu a pretty good third) is Chuang-tzu; the best representative of Social *tao* is old Confucius-he-say.

The most comprehensive *tao* is High Sky *tao*.

The first chapter in the *Chuang-tzu* tells about a fish: 'In the Northern darkness there is a fish. This fish changes into a bird.' It flies up, this bird, to a height of ninety thousand *li*. Right up into the blue: 'Wavering heat, bits of dust, living things blown about – the sky looks very blue. Is that its real colour, or is it because it's so far away and has no end? When the bird looks up, about and down, all he sees is blue.'

Meanwhile, down in the flatlands, a little quail, who can make it up into the air about thirty feet and thinks that is the extent of the real, a little quail is saying: 'Who does he think he is? Where does he think he's going?'

High Sky *tao* is one of the most beautiful conceptions in the whole desperate history of thought.

I say thought, not philosophy.

Taoism (High Sky *tao*) makes fun of philosophy.

Here's a hilarious skit (in the *Chuang-tzu*) on the question of origins and all ontological discourse:

> There is a beginning. There is a not yet beginning to be a beginning. There is a not yet beginning to be a not yet beginning to be a beginning. There is being. There is nonbeing. There is a not yet beginning to be nonbeing. There is a not yet beginning to be a not yet beginning to be nonbeing. Suddenly there is being and nonbeing. But between this being and nonbeing, I don't really know which is being and which is nonbeing. Now, I think, I have just said something. But I don't really know if what I have said has meant something or whether it hasn't meant anything.

One day T'ien Ken (literally Heaven Root) was wandering on the sunny side of Yin Mountain. But he was worried. Worried about the world. When he met a man called Nameless, that was the question he put to him: 'How is it possible to get some order into the world?'

Nameless answered: 'What a dreary question! I'm just about to set off with the Creator. And if I get bored with him, I'll get up on the back of the Cosmic Bird and fly out way beyond the six directions. Once out there, I'll wander in the place called Nowhere-at-all and spend my days in the Endless Field.'

But T'ien Ken was really worried (all those myopic cultural officials, all those commercial crap-merchants, all those blinkered politicians, all those ironbrained militaries – they were destroying the world!), and he put the question again: 'What about the world, how to keep it in order?'

And this time Nameless answered: 'Let your mind wander, blend your spirit with the vastness, leave no room for personal views – that is the best you can do.'

That was probably when T'ien Ken started *going*. When the Ch'an master Yün-men was asked the question, 'What is the *tao*?', he answered with just that one syllable: 'go!' (*ch'ü*).

Taoist going means having superabundant virtue (in the sense of *vertu*, power) and integral capacity. It means at times being as unmoving as a man at a wake, and at other times being as changing as a dragon, at some times being as loud as thunder, and at other times being as silent as the abyss. It means moving to and fro in infinite space: free and easy wandering (*yu*).

And if you're going to be a Taoist writer, you'll have to know how to 'mount on the truths of Heaven and Earth, and ride the changes of the six breaths'. You'll have to know how to 'roll the ten thousand things into one'. You'll have to know how to find your way with 'the lamp of chaos', and see far while talking near. You'll have to know how to 'make Spring' with all kinds of materials, use 'big and useless words', to give some sense of the totality. You'll know (as an extravagant intellectual) how to theorize now and then, but you'll never engage in confused debate. And even when you're dabbling in ink, you'll always 'embody to the fullest what has no end' and keep in mind a sense of wandering 'where there is no trail'.

Nan-po Tzu-k'uei met an old woman on the beach (old, she was old all right in years, but she had a young girl's complexion), and he listened, amazed, as she told him about the *tao*.

'Where did you get all that?', he asked her.

And she answered: 'I heard it from the son of Aided-by-Ink, and Aided-by-Ink heard it from the grandson of Repeated-Recitation, and the grandson of Repeated-Recitation heard it from Seeing-Brightly, and Seeing-Brightly heard it from Whispered-Agreement, and Whispered-Agreement heard it from Waiting-for-Use, and Waiting-for-Use heard it from Exclaimed-Wonder, and Exclaimed-Wonder heard it from Dark-Obscurity, and Dark-Obscurity heard it from Participation-in-Mystery, and Participation-in-Mystery heard it from Follow-the-Source!'

That's only a rough, wild sketch of Taoism, but rough, wild sketches are what Taoism is all about.

'A good completion takes a long time', says the *Chuang-tzu*.

10

If ever there was a country that put a value on travel, raising it into a highly developed meditative and poetic practice, it's Japan.

Like a lot else in Japanese culture, literature-of-the-road (*michiyuki-bun*) got conventionalized and miniaturized in Kyoto, but at the beginning, and every now and then at other times, with such figures as the peregrine poets Nôin ('place-crazy'), Zôki, Gyôson, Saigyo, Shinchô or, later on, Bashô, it had the whole archipelago for its scene and arose out of direct contact with the landscape.

Much more complex than 'travel-writing' in the ordinary sense of that term, the poetic road-book could bring together inner and outer landscape, geography and intellectual space, topography and the imagination. It could combine the experiential, the informative and the didactic. It could operate on several levels of time: the present (the actual movement of the traveller); the past (with references to cultural tradition, echoes, quotations); the future, with discreet allusions to the distant aim of the journey, both in physical and in mental terms; the timeless-eternal (a poem suddenly arising out of past and present prose). Archaic sensations (vapour and cloud seen as the vital forces of the cosmos, white birds flying seen as vehicles of the soul), could come up alongside the most subtle of intellectual ideas. The tempo was rapid, connections never too obvious (a basic continuity left room for a lot of surface discontinuity), the accent being on dynamic mobility. Such books are difficult to classify. Maybe, to begin with, the very idea of getting 'out on the road' was to resist classification of any kind. Maybe even at the very beginning, road-writing was the sign of a de-classification, the expression of individuals who were felt, for some reason or other, not to 'fit in' with the established scheme of things, and who were actually exiled. This sensation of being 'cast out' – on to dangerous roads, into unknown territory – was to remain in the road-books, but if, early on, this 'exile' was a subject for lamentation and nostalgia, it came gradually to be seen, largely thanks to the arrival of Buddhism, as an opportunity for seeing into a larger scheme of things. Exile was transmuted into initiation.

In the twelfth century, the travelling poet-monk Saigyo set out on the road, and he was to become *the* symbolic representative of this way of life. Nijô, in the *Towazu-gatari*, tells how much he himself was inspired by the example of Saigyo:

> At the age of nine or thereabouts, I saw a picture illustrating an edition of Saigyo's *Ascetic Peregrinations* in which he was shown standing on the banks of a stream, with deep mountains at the side, watching cherry flowers falling into the water of the stream, and reciting this poem:

Writing the Road

At every breath of wind
waves of white flowers
cover the rocks
I hesitate to cross
this mountain stream!

Ever since I saw that picture, I wanted to do as he had done.

When Bashô wrote his *Oku no hosomichi*, variously translated into European languages as 'The narrow road to the deep North', 'A trip to the distant provinces', or 'The path to the end of the world', he was thinking of these predecessors.

And others after him were going to put on the *tabi-goromo*, the travelling robe, and set out, especially in the Autumn, the season of the migratory birds (crane, goose, swan):

> The passing days and months are travellers in time. The years that come and go are travellers too. Life itself is a journey. As for those who spend their days upon the waters in boats, and those who grow old leading horses, their very home is the open road. Many an ancient died on that road. I myself have long been tempted out by the cloud-moving wind.

11

One of the main themes in Iranian soufism is the 'Search for the Orient'. The searcher is one who has broken with the collective, who makes no reference to the collective (except, perhaps, to remember in passing the 'city of the oppressors'). He is the Stranger, who has known 'Western exile', and who is now a *sâlik*, an itinerant mystic. The 'Orient' he seeks is not situated in any geo-physical-astronomic space (though reference will be made, symbolically, to geography, and astronomy, all along the way), it is a transcendental dimension of his own mind. To attain to it implies a passage North: 'The Orient sought by the mystic lies to the north, beyond the north' (Henry Corbin, *The Man of Light*), the North being seen as the threshold to what Corbin calls *transconscience* (outside the normal dualism of conscious-unconscious). All along the road, which is at one and the same time sensual and supersensuous (Corbin talks of a *suprasensible concret*), there are little epiphanies: encounters with 'Perfect Nature' (mostly female figures) and 'angels' (bursts of light), until such time as the traveller becomes truly 'hyperborean' (Corbin: 'The Hyperborean is a man whose soul has arrived at such completion and harmony that it is without negation or shadow.') Colour symbolism is particularly important: the Sufis, for example, favour blue (that's why in Persian they are called: *kabûd-pushân*, the wearers-of-blue).

What we're concerned with, then, is a visionary geography, with the accent on the North and the East, and the travels of a soul or mind moving towards a totality of being and a 'morning knowledge' (*cognitio matutina* in Western gnostic texts, *'ilm ishrâqi*, oriental knowledge, in Arabic) which is an ecstasy and an illumination.

Two of the best examples of these 'mind-travel' books are *The Tale of the Bird* (the bird flies into more and more subtle skies, bluer and bluer) and *The Story of Western Exile* (an explicit account of the gnostic path). Confronted by these books, and trying to describe them, Corbin has a problem of nomenclature. Refusing such designations as 'mystical allegories' or 'philosophical tales', he tries 'spiritual novels', and finally opts for 'visionary narratives' or 'initiation stories'.

To my mind, they are predecessors, like the other examples quoted, of what I call the 'waybook'.

And what I've been suggesting in these short accounts of the waybook as it exists in various traditions is that these books can serve as models and references for a kind of writing necessary for us today.

Along the Atlantic Coast

His brain must have been a perfect warehouse of shapes of
obscure coasts, aspects of innumerable islands, images of
headlands.

(Joseph Conrad)

1

In 1847, during the expedition 'over field and shore' he made in
the company of Maxime du Camp, Gustave Flaubert, on a halt
at a lighthouse near Brest, which is to say at the finisterrian tip
of Brittany, wrote this:

> This is where the old world ends: this is its most advanced
> point, its extreme limit. Behind you lies all Europe, all Asia; in
> front of you, it's all sea. However big areas may seem to our
> eyes, aren't they always a bit hemmed-in once we know they're
> not limitless? From a French beach, looking across the Channel,
> you can't help seeing the pavements of Brighton. And from any
> stony little village in Provence you can embrace the whole of
> the Mediterranean, like a great pool of blue water surrounded
> by rocks, with its promontories littered with ruined marble, its
> yellow sands, its drooping palms, its curving gulfs. But here the
> eye sees no limit at all. In this place, thought can travel as fast
> as the wind. From wave to wave it can spread, expand and lose
> itself in the air. Maybe, yes, away over there, on the dream
> horizon, looms some vague America, a cluster of nameless
> islands, countries full of crimson fruit, hummingbirds and
> savages. Or yet again, the silent twilight of the poles, the vapour
> of spouting whales, great cities lit by coloured lanterns, Japan
> with its porcelain roofs, China with its golden-belled pagodas.

There you have a limit-situation, which is a possibility. And at
the same time a commentary on the human mind, which
almost immediately forecloses that possibility. In the face of
the opening, the emptiness that's just been evoked, the human
mind, according to Flaubert, will block it up, fill it up with
civilizational paraphernalia, more or less fantastical imaginings.
A few days earlier, at the Pointe du Raz, that jagged promontory jutting out into the Atlantic, facing the 'satanic hole' of
the raging waters below and the 'indescribable colour of the

111

submerged rocks', Flaubert had come to the conclusion that 'man can't live in such a context, he can't bear Nature to such a high degree'.

Which leaves a lot of questions in the air.

Might it be that man or, let's say, an anthropological type different from the one familiar to Flaubert, could learn to live if not in, at least with, such an 'inhuman' context? Is it possible to conceive of an (oceanic) vision of emptiness? Is it possible to live in such an area?

Since the end of the nineteenth century, numerous (well, not so very numerous, but enough to form a kind of constellation) have been the figures, the body-minds occupying 'lookout posts' analogous to that of Flaubert at the Brest lighthouse.

I'm thinking of Nietzsche, outside all the norms, conventions and categories, on the plateau of the Engadine in the Alps, 'six thousand feet above humanity and the age', describing himself now as 'philosopher-artist' now as 'a poet at the limit of the word'.

Then there's Rimbaud, rejecting most of the cultural artefacts he saw around him as 'foolish', saying that real poetry would always be 'out ahead', going all out himself to reach it via 'a confusion of all the senses', evoking 'new theories penetrating into secret places', crossing Europe, passing through Indonesia, and ending up on the high plateau of Ogaden in Abyssinia, writing reports from that arid, burning, austere and ascetic area: 'The central region of the country, Ogaden, lying at 2700 feet, is a steppe-land. After the thin rains that fall in their season, it's a sea of grass interrupted here and there by fields of stones.'

Think too of Herman Melville, isolated in America, his mind full of images of the Pacific with its 'unknown archipelagoes and impenetrable Japans' and, deeper still perhaps, of a sensation discovered in the Galapagos, the Encantadas: 'Little but reptile life is here found: tortoises, lizards, immense spiders, snakes, and that strangest anomaly of outlandish nature, the iguana. No voice, no low, no howl is heard; the chief sound of life here is a hiss.'

Also that writer who called himself Lautréamont – Lautréamont in his little room in Paris, at 7 Rue du Faubourg-Montmartre, invoking 'ancient Ocean', seeing tempests, mountains of tumultuous water, swarms of monstrosities, working out a high-energy poetics that leaps from metaphor to metamorphosis and goes way out beyond the frontiers of humanity.

At a lesser degree of intensity, less in touch with actual place, less physically present, less intense poetically, but with undeniable graphic and intellectual force, come to mind also in this context two writers: Spengler when, in Munich, he wrote his apocalyptical 'sketch of a morphology of world history', *The Decline of the West* ('historical perspectives', 'origin and landscape'); and Toynbee when, in the cloisters of Cambridge or thereabouts, in the last pages of his *Study of History*, he evoked, outside all the wastelands, the future navigation of Western minds on the waters of time, along the shores of the world.

Such are the perspectives of this essay.

2

In the seventies and eighties of the twentieth century, the author of these lines was living in the Pyrenees (the Atlantic Pyrenees), having left a country, Great Britain, which, in the late 1960s, was passing through the final stages of the industrial revolution. The wastelands I referred to in the previous section sprawled miserably, plaintively, sullenly on all sides. If the factories still belched out greasy expressionistic smoke – black, yellow or red – the cranes in the shipyards were already turning more slowly. On every street corner, up every side street, you could hear the rock 'n' roll of hysterical despair. The humanism of the old school was in agony. Pathology, more or less picturesque, was in the air. Wandering the streets and the thoroughfares, navigating in my mind the fog-bound river, I went through Glasgow from no-place to no-place in a kind of supernihilistic transcendentalism, or stood, pensive, on the Suspension Bridge, on Atlantic Quay.

Journey to the end of night...

Then I decided to move out, breaking my bridges, burning my boat.

I wanted out of a civilization that was only marking time.

I wanted more space – and the poetics of that space: a poetics that would go away out beyond personal poetry, beyond art as mere reflection of a state-of-things, and yet would not be pure abstraction.

It was unlikely to be an easy undertaking.

There would probably be more than a few fracture zones.

But I didn't see anything else really worth doing.

My new 'outlook post' was a studio in a tower on the edge of the town of Pau, down there in the south-west, near the Spanish border (paleolithic caves on every hand, their walls covered with signs). Right there in front, filling the windows, the range of the Pyrenees: a line, broken and complex, uprisen from a field of force, with changing lights. Without writing it on the wall or shouting it over the rooftops (to go far you have to know how to keep silent), I thought of that studio as 'the five mountain hermitage' or 'the studio of depths and heights'.

The hermit of the Tower, an *aficionado* of poetry and philosophy, had studied the morphology of mountains in Scotland: all those glacial valleys, all those lava flows, all those plateaus inhabited only by the wind, all those ridges of gneiss. He continued these studies in the Pyrenees, starting off with books such as Élie de Beaumont's *Leçons de géologie pratique* and Ramond de Carbonières' *Observations faites dans les Pyrénées.* He loved those eighteenth-century books where not only did science and thought go hand in hand, but the investigating, searching mind allowed itself aesthetic perspectives and poetic projections. Sure, the thought was often theological (genesis, providence, finality). But at least there was, in addition to information, another dimension. And the hermit of the Tower was after an analogous dimension, something that was completely missing in the more modern monographs marked by pure technicality.

The question was: how to be up to, how to measure with, such massivity, such height, such space? How to get at the totality of the mountain, the plenitude of the landscape? How to transform intelligence into light on a rock, how to transfer wind on a high ridge into intelligence?

One attempt that our 'hermit' found particularly interesting was that of Franz Schrader. Schrader was out to renew and develop the basic approach laid down by Ramond. With this in mind, he invented two instruments, the *orographe* and the *tachéographe*, for sighting and delineating the 'character' and the 'physiognomy' of the rocks. It wasn't just a general panorama he was after, but a formal vision of the landscape lines that would have aesthetic value: 'The nature of these mountains was already quite well known, but only the vaguest notions prevailed concerning their precise form, and there was no exact map.' Schrader drew up his extraordinary map of the Mont Perdu in 1874. And then gradually, from topography he moved on to something else. Landscape, he realized, was made up as much of light as of lines – and there was something even more undefinable than light: 'atmosphere'.

There was an approach in that work of all that's involved in the creation of a significant, radiant line.

I find it impossible to separate in my mind the line made by a range of mountains or a sea-tide from a line of writing or a line drawn in a painting. I see analogous forces at work, resulting in similar forms. The literature and the visual art that interest me have always something of this order. What I'm looking for in literature and art is a sensation of space, a tentative exploration, and a reduction to the essential. This goes away beyond story-telling. On the heights, on a stormy sea, you don't tell stories – there are more urgent and more necessary things to be done. The art and literature of the heights can of course carry stories with them, like flotsam and jetsam on the ocean. But the essential is elsewhere, and it's not an 'essence'. If I was moving farther and farther away from thick, heavy literature (of which 'light literature' is only the corollary), it was in no way to enclose myself in any essentialist poetics.

'I don't paint being', wrote Montaigne (and to 'being' we can add correlated words like 'essence' and 'identity'), 'I paint passages.'

It was in order to paint those 'passages' (from state of mind to state of mind, from feeling to feeling, from attitude to attitude, from mind to place and thing), that Montaigne, master of the floating world, at ease in the relative (which implies a relationship), invented the essay, a form, a way of writing, that allowed him to follow all the meanders of his thought. Élisée Reclus speaks of the 'hydrographic complex' of the Aquitanian coast (writing these words, I see in my mind's eye certain maps of the Cape Breton rift and the thalwegs of the Gulf of

Gascony) – that's what Montaigne's essays are, or rather, that's their configuration.

If I go now from Montaigne to Saint-John Perse, some will say that I'm not only jumping centuries, I'm jumping categories. But I'm not out to do anything like the history of literature or art (with its false continuities), nor anything like comparative literature or art (with its enforced juxtapositions), I'm travelling from island to island, in a field of energy, according to a kind of quantic map.

In 1899, the Saint-Leger Leger family, from Guadeloupe, settled in Pau, where the young Alexis, a pupil at the local lyceum, met up with 'a world of exile and legend: Latin or Russian emigrants, Austrian music-lovers and German philosophers, English eccentrics, explorers from Africa'. It was all there in Pau, in that cosmopolitan, exotic, secret, little city. Early on he made the acquaintance of the old Irish mountaineer, Henry Russell, who gave him the key to a hermitage he had on the Vignemale. It was up there on the Vignemale that the young man who was later to be the poet Saint-John Perse saw one day a rare and solitary bird, the 'Rose-of-the-Mountains' that he would never see again but which left him with the sensation of having been in touch with, initiated into, the secret life of the earth. It was in a house in the Ossau Valley that he began writing his book *Éloges* ('praises'), which, stylistically high-toned, is an attempt to write poetry 'above oneself', outside the psycho-social complex of the person, able to measure up to, to be adequate to, the universe. He reads *The Face of the Earth* of the Austrian geologist Edward Suess, whose revolutionary conceptions haunt his mind. And from the mountains he looks out to the ocean, the Atlantic: 'The Atlantic, that open sea, was never the "cradle" of any particular civilization, it was a place of formation. It has always been the least closed site of humanity. Here, man was uncircumscribed.'

A non-circumscription, an opening – but not quite the absolute endlessness Fernando Pessoa evokes when one of his characters, standing at the extreme limit of Portugal, 'looks out over the Atlantic and salutes the Infinite'.

The Infinite can be such a blinder. It can annihilate the mind. If I like abstraction in the verbal sense (the act of abstracting), if I like to push sensation up to an abstract crest, I don't go totally for 'the abstract'.

3

Before trying to move out farther, it will be useful to take a closer look at the general pathology I evoked at the start of these latitudinous passages, a pathology which lies at the base of the great mass of what we call 'culture'. One has to analyse this pathology in order to see the possible paths out of it, and to prevent these paths from being overgrown, encumbered. It's so easy to enclose the really new in old categories, including that of 'the new' (in the sense of mere novelty).

'For too long the Earth was an insane asylum', writes Nietzsche in *The Genealogy of Morality*, half of his work consisting in the study of this asylum, to see how it was built up, the other half consisting in the attempt to open up a new field. On the other side of the Atlantic, in the essays that accompanied his 'open road' poems, Walt Whitman talked of 'this disease called humanity' and commented on the symptoms of this disease as he saw them around him: a shrivelled, stifled psyche; a taste for the bizarre and the morbid; an excessive interest in technicality; and the neglect of what is 'permanent and democratic: the body, the earth, the sea'.

But the best known study of the pathology in question is of course Freud's *Civilization and its Discontents*.

Most of the time, psychoanalysis smells musty, but in the *Discontents* book, while analysing civilization as a perpetual state of neurosis, while insisting on the fact that happiness was less and less a part of culture (the times of ersatz and simulacrum were at hand), Freud allows himself some lateral perspectives that give at least a glimpse of a context outside the curtained closet, the family album and socio-personal history. It's the case notably with what he calls 'the oceanic feeling' (*das ozeanische Gefühl*). 'In the beginning', he writes, 'the self includes all, later it excludes the exterior world. As a result, our present sensation of the self is nothing more than the shrivelled residue of a vaster sensation, so vast that it contained all, based on a more deeply felt relationship, indeed union, between self and environment.'

Freud does not dwell on this 'oceanic feeling', and hardly considers it as a real existential possibility in the present state of civilization. But the question can be posed, the perspectives opened farther. Might it not be said that all the great poets, all the great artists, all the great thinkers, all those whose work gives the sensation of an open world, allowing 'being' to breathe better, have known something of this kind? I'm thinking of Heraclitus, in that book of his on Nature, of Walt Whitman 'ebbing with the ocean of life', of Hokusaï when he painted the Great Wave.

It's this point of view that Marcuse develops in *Eros and Civilization*. Starting out from Freud's 'primary feeling', Marcuse envisages the possibility of 'a larger biological instinct, not just an extension of sexuality'. We're not talking about a sublimation of sexuality, and certainly not of its repression, but of the expansion, the deployment of a deep biological need concentrated in sexuality but which can move out into a larger existential field.

The proposition could find support in Bergson ('creative evolution') and in Bachelard ('the experience of space', 'the poetics of day-dreaming').

But rather than seeing the proposal, the possibility, getting paraphrased in philosophy, confounded with and reduced to socio-revolutionary praxis, or lost in an anthology of flowery images that sound more like the scientist's Sunday evening than a real existential (and poetic, artistic) dawn, I prefer to come back to the tough initial field.

I'm out to follow firm lines, keeping close to physicality and plasticity.

That's why, from Freud's 'oceanic feeling', I turn to Sandor Ferenczi's *Thalassa*.

Ferenczi goes from psychoanalysis to biology, from the disease in civilization to a desire for, shall we say, oceanization. Discovering what he calls 'the biological unconscious', deeper than the psychological unconscious, deeper also than normal biology (he speaks of 'depth biology'), Ferenczi feels that he is 'on the shores of a new science', 'a science of primal things'. In the evolution of the human species, the earliest traumatism came from a drying-up of the oceans: it's the loss of a marine mode of life. The deepest desire of the human being is to recover that state of life. It's not that famous 'return to the mother's breast', or to the ventral cavity, psychoanalysis dwells on (Dylan Thomas' 'womb with a view'), it's a re-inhabitation of oceanic existence. The human being will try out all kinds of methods at least to approach this (sexuality, drugs), but it ultimately depends on an 'erotic sense of reality', a *general* sense.

To this great oceano-erotic field Wilhelm Reich brings a colourful extravagance. He sees cosmic energy as blue, or blue-grey, with whitish streaks – as in a stormy sky or the aurora borealis. I don't accompany Reich right to the end of his thought: when the theorist of cosmic superposition (so far, so good) starts wanting to concentrate 'orgonomic' energy in boxes, I go away for a walk along the shore. But I admit I've always had a liking for blue-grey atmospheres with white lines...

It was with these studies in mind, as well as certain experiences of my own, that I began to think in terms of 'erotic logic' and to develop a theory of biocosmopoetics.

Later, the theory of open systems, translated from thermodynamics into biology, seemed to give weight and impetus to this tendency. An open system (the planet Earth is one, a human being *can* be one) is characterized by its capacity to receive energy and transform it. An open system integrates differences, lives and thrives on change, knows alternate rhythms of expansion and concentration.

4

I've always delighted in the reading of old geographers and explorers. You feel in their texts the first tentative steps, see the earliest visions, register the initial astonishment at the appearance of the world in all its phenomenal strangeness.

So with this Atlantic coast.

Strabo in his *Geography* speaks of 'the paroceanic region of Aquitania'. In his *Descriptions of the Earth*, Pomponius Mela says that, as from Hispania, the coast follows a straight line (it's the line that goes from Biarritz to the Pointe de Graves) before curving away to the west (that's the great curve that goes from Royan to the Pointe Saint-Mathieu). Ptolemy for his part, in that section of his *Treatise on Geography* devoted to the

'Aquitanian ocean', dwells on the phenomenon of tides: that eternally changing line between earth and sea – unusual, indeed uncanny, for an eastern Mediterranean mind of that time.

Alongside these ancient cartographies, I read with assiduity the texts of early literary and poetic writers.

In this Atlantic context, there was, for example, Seneca, exiled from Rome on Corsica, in the far western Mediterranean, undergoing an initiation into space and silence, away from the courts of commerce, speaking prophetically of future times when the ocean (*Oceanus*), would loosen 'the bonds of things' (*vincula rerum*), when both earth and sea would be of huge extent, in a world in which no Thule would be the ultimate Thule. This was fourteen centuries before Christopher Columbus, nineteen centuries before Einstein.

Then there was Festus Avienus, that Roman functionary of the fourth century who, for some reason or another, by some stroke of luck or another, had access to Carthaginian records that even the great historico-geographical investigator, Herodotus of Halicarnassus, knew nothing of and who, in his *Ora Maritima* ('the shores of the sea'), sketches a fast but fascinating picture of all the lands laved by the Atlantic from Spain to Scotland. The start-off place is Massilia (Marseilles), from where we move to Callipolis (Barcelona) and the island of Gymnesia (Majorca). We meet up with the Tartessians of Cadiz, those travellers of the tin-road between Spain, France and Cornwall. We go out beyond the Pillars of Hercules, out into the monstrous, wonderful Atlantic, passing the Island of the Moon, the Galactic Gulf, the Sacred Promontory, the Pelagian Isles, Cape Venus... Unknown coastlines, strange topographies, hitherto unseen traces.

There's an emptiness in these cartographies: great spaces left blank, only occasional features highlighted. It's an emptiness that speaks to us today, not as a lack, but as a possibility. And it's still there in the landscape, behind all the constructions, still there, with its latent logic.

'The Atlantic out beyond the Gulf of Gascony is a desert', writes Élisée Reclus in his *Universal Geography*. Years later, another geographer, Le Lannou, was to speak of 'a negative destiny'.

In these Atlantic margins, on the arenaceous ground we are

travelling over and surveying, not only has history not greatly marked the area, but the few traces it did leave have faded. On many a map of the sixteenth century, one reads phrases like this: 'Here was once a Parish, now covered with sand.'

We're on the south-western edge of Europe, facing the Open, facing, perhaps, a 'new world' – but without conquistadorian ideology, without moral utopianism, without promethean planification.

Forgotten movements, ghosts...

Here's Guillaume d'Aquitaine, the troubadour (that is, 'the finder') who sang of distant love (*amor lontana*), where it's not the ocean that symbolizes the woman, it's the woman that symbolizes the ocean: the body is volatilized, the mind expands.

Here's the erratic son of Alienor of Aquitaine, who bore the name of Landless John, Jean-sans-Terre.

Here's Echaid, the first man, say the Basques, to discover the new lands, later called 'America', to the west.

Here's Sebastian El Cano, who sailed wide-eyed with Magellan round the world and came back to tell of what he'd seen.

Here's Champlain, Champlain of Brouage (a harbour there on the coast, now silted up), who sailed first to the Isles of America (la Désirade, the Virgins), then made for Canada, where he mapped the long coast with a keen eye and a loving hand.

Here's Jean Lafitte, from Dax, a pirate to his trade, who plied up and down the Gulf of Mexico before financing (there's a kind of paradoxical logic in it) the Communist Manifesto of one Karl Marx.

5

For years, mostly in the Summers, but also at other seasons, I went up and down that celtogalatian coast (I forget in which old text I found that lovely, expansive word).

My first stop would be at the Museum of the Sea in Biarritz, situated on a spot that was a watchpoint in the old whaling days, and, before that, a lookout post on the Phoenician route. I'd salute the whales, study the birds and fishes: an orgy of morphology.

Then it would be Cape Breton, Mimizan, Biscarosse – villages of bleached, silvered wood, and, everywhere, sand.

Farther up still, the Cordouan lighthouse, like a great white exclamation mark in the sultry blue emptiness.

La Tremblade, Brouage, Rochefort, Oléron.

The Pertuis d'Antioche.

Over there on the horizon, the Île de Ré.

These peregrinations along the sand-country always ended at La Rochelle, where there was another museum, the Museum of the Americas. La Rochelle was at that time my northernmost point.

There I'd turn back.

It was only later, years later, that I was to take up residence in another 'lookout post', further north, on the coast of Brittany.

In Jules Michelet's book *The Sea* (it's significant that this writer of epic history – *The French Revolution* – turned at a certain moment in his career to the mountain and the ocean), one reads this:

> The advantage of cliffs is that, at their base, much more than anywhere else, you can feel the breathing, ay, the very pulse of the sea. In the Mediterranean, you're hardly aware of the tide – here, it's a main feature. The ocean breathes as I do, corresponds to my inner movement [...]. It's a constant reminder of the world's movement and how I share in it [...]. If I were asked what ocean coast provides the highest impression, I would say: that of Brittany, thinking in particular of those wild and sublime granite promontories that constitute the old world's finisterras...

In what I was going to think of as my 'Atlantic workshop', I gathered together not only books scattered over many places: an apartment in Pau, a house in Scotland, other places in the Ardèche, in Champagne and in Burgundy, but also all kinds of objects picked up in various spots around the world: a little Ainu totem, a battered old compass from a Japanese fishing-boat, a sea-chart of the coast of Maine, 'truth bells' from a Thai temple, the shoulder bone of a caribou from northern Canada, a piece of whalebone from the Grenadines, and bits of rock I liked the look and feel of from everywhere. To objects such as these were added, from the Breton coast, some Neptune maps of the Atlantic, a nautical instrument or two, as well as pieces of flotsam and jetsam: enough for a period of prolonged cosmo-poetical contemplation.

If my 'Atlantic workshop' was first and foremost a place of concentration, it was also a place of resistance. I don't mean a tense, tightjawed resistance – I mean a *laughing* resistance, the kind of *gai savoir* one finds in Cercamon, Rabelais and Nietzsche.

I'm talking about resistance – resistance to what?

To the marketplace and the fairground; to the great mass of hollow show, inept image accompanied by stupid noise that constitutes our pseudo-culture; to demagogy and triviality.

In his book, *Epochs of Chinese and Japanese Art*, Ernest Fenollosa evokes the figure of Michael Angelo, 'holding back, single-handed, like a grand promontory half-submerged by storms, the mediocrity due to a flippant and corrupt *cinque-cento*'.

If, given the pedestals on which 'classical' art has been placed, the reference to Michael Angelo sounds grandiose, let me make it clear that in this Atlantic context, there is no desire whatever for pedestalization, pantheonization, or any other phoney glorification. What I mean by an 'Atlantic attitude', if I can sum it up in a definition, is an attitude of mind that is high without being lofty, ample without being floppy, open without being gaping.

6

Atlantic space, the west coast of Europe, is characterized in the first instance by fragmentation: the ocean has roamed over and eroded the land for millennia, and the result is a multitude, a proliferation of islands and peninsulas separated by difficult waters. It is a territory of dispersion and precariousness – but each fragment is exact in itself, there is no confusion in this plurality. In a word, unity is not something given, to be taken for granted, it has to be *composed*.

This is where poetics comes in, a poetics both ample and exact, both open and definite, which will erode all unitary symbolism and be able to carry a great deal of elements in a complex movement.

It's possible to see the preludes, the premises to this in late modernity. When, for example, in a poem written at Cape Ann, on the Atlantic coast of America (part V of 'Landscapes'), T. S. Eliot writes: '... resign this land at the end, resign it/To its true owner, the tough one, the sea-gull./The palaver is finished.' This kind of silent radicality is extremely rare in Eliot, who, after wandering discursively, even rhetorically, in the waste-land, was going to have recourse to orthodox unities of both a political and a religious order. For him, the palaver was not over – not by a long way.

Ezra Pound, less reverential of establishments, though with a political fascination that led him deliriously up a blind alley, is more relevant. His erratic periplus ('no Aquinas map'), moving from one luminous focal point to another in history, is an attempt to get out of hell. The empty beach on which he was left with a few broken phrases was no paradise – it looks rather like the shipwreck of Ulysses as evoked by Dante. But it was radical ground, close to the cold shore Yeats also came down to.

With Eliot and Pound in the same late-modern context there was Gerard Manley Hopkins, who, over against a civilization that produced wastelands, praised the wilderness: 'What would the world be, once bereft/of wet and of wildness? Let them be left,/O let them be left, wildness and wet;/Long live the weeds and the wilderness yet.' But the tone, enthu-siastic, tended to become hysterical, and the wilderness context was wrapped in theology.

There's a certain atlanticity in James Joyce. If for long he was a kind of sordid Ulysses of the streets, he moves out into an open sea of linguistics in *Finnegans Wake*. It's all too linguis-tical, but it might have been the prelude to a final book he envisaged, which he never got round to, the book of the ocean.

A major reference for my multifocal and complex use of the word 'atlantic' was that compendium of mental meteorology and oceanic meditation written by Leonardo da Vinci and known, appropriately, as the *Codex Atlanticus*. It's full of marine observations: 'A wave results from percussion and its size depends on the force of the percussion. A wave is never alone, there will be all the more of them if the place is irregular.' It's direct perception moving up, via description, into graphic thought: a language of earth and sea dynamics. And there are recommendations in the *Codex Atlanticus* which amount to a poetics: 'In the first place, talk of movement. Then of the weight that comes from movement. Thereafter of the force that comes from weight and movement. Finally of the percussion that is born of movement, weight and force.'

My liking goes to poets and artists who have weight without being ponderous: weight, force and movement, the overall result being a resonance, something that sounds and resounds in the mind.

We're talking about a poetics: a large, atlantic poetics. And about a context: a general context.

This opening up of a new context is much more necessary, and much more difficult, than piling up texts and artefacts within a context that is moribund or dead. Action, activism leads only to agitation, or lassitude, without a new attitude from which new acts can proceed. This goes for politics and economics as well as for poetry and art. If you write only poems, these poems will be relegated to the hold-all category of 'poetry', too confusionist and at times nonentical to be of any real validity or efficiency. The same goes for art-work. The ultimate thing is to open up a world. And in a world, poetry and art are not separated from other activities of the mind, other aspects of society, other fields of the multiverse.

Which is why, over the years, in addition to writing poems, I wrote peregrinations (outside 'literature'), and in addition to peregrinations, I wrote essays, trying to bring into one coherent field (proto-world) all that had been happening in the 'bio', 'geo' and 'cosmo' sciences, as well as in philosophy and philology since, say, the beginning of the twentieth century.

I've already mentioned my interest in certain eighteenth-century studies in which science, thought and aesthetics sometimes come together in very interesting ways. In one of them, Martin Martin's book on the Atlantic isles of Scotland, one reads this: 'There's a great change in the humour of the world, and by consequence in the way of writing.' It was true that the eighteenth century had seen a great encyclopedic beginning: new matter, new methods. It was something similar I felt myself involved in, embarked upon. Back there, however, in the eighteenth century, the fundamental argumentation (perhaps more so in Britain than in France) tended still to be theological, which is why Clarence Glacken, in his *Traces on the Rhodian Shore*, prefers to see the eighteenth century as the end of the classical period rather than as a new beginning. But I still like to think of it in terms of prelude, at least in certain areas. In a very engaging phrase, Glacken describes the ideas of Montesquieu and other French thinkers of the kind arriving like bits of driftwood on the shores of Scotland, where they were picked up by all the William Robertsons, the Adam Smiths, the David Humes, the Adam Fergusons and the Dugald Stewarts of the place. In his *History of America*, Robertson, doctor of divinity as he was (that is, with a vested interest in the theological, teleological idea) nonetheless speaks of 'a more ample field'. And David Hume in his *Dialogues* declares without hesitation or ambiguity: 'The field is the world.'

7

Is it possible, in any cogent and coherent sense, to speak nowadays of a 'new world' or, since that term has so many uncongenial theo-terroristic, ethno-terroristic and techno-terroristic connotations, what I prefer to call an 'open world'.

I have in my archives a French map of 1740: 'A Map of all the Islands known along the coasts of Zanzibar and Madagascar on the way to India'. In fact, there were several routes on the eastern run. There was the 'inner route' that hugged the coast of Mozambique, the 'outer route' that went farther down into the Indian ocean, and the 'pirates' route' that went through the Maldives. The boats left Lorient, on the Breton coast, around December–January. Three months later, they were off the Cape. A month after that, they were in the Mascarenhas. Two months more, and they touched the shores of Malabar and Coromandel. Two months again, and it was China. The boats would return between June and September, laden with Javanese pepper, nutmeg from the Moluccas, cinnamon from Ceylon.

While all this was going on (and what goes for Lorient went for Brest, Saint-Malo, Rouen, Le Havre, all the Atlantic ports), there were still politicians thinking, like the great statesman Sully in the seventeenth century, that 'faraway things' were 'not suited to the French mentality'.

126

I'm taking a French example here, because I'm writing this essay on the Breton coast. But the same would go for many another country. The general point I want to make is that there can be a disproportion, of mammoth extent, between super-structural politics and what is actually going on in the world, what is potentially emerging there.

But there are also exceptions to this state of affairs, when politics open up.

About sixty years after Sully's declaration of territorial introversion, Colbert, out to launch France on the high seas, boosted the Navy budget from the wretched sum of three hundred thousand French pounds to twelve million. To get 'distant commerce' going, he set up a shipyard on the banks of the River Scorff in Brittany. To the shipyard was added an arsenal, to the arsenal were added hangars, warehouses, workers' lodgings – that's how Lorient ('Orient Town') began.

Then came Law, John Law, a Scotsman, born 21 April 1671 at Edinburgh, who was going to bring to this nascent political economy (and, given other contributions, potential culture-space) the vigour of his genius. At the death of Louis XIV, the economic situation of France was disastrous. Law proposed a solution. In order to reduce public debt and liberate economic activity, he created paper-money and set about gathering into one vast enterprise all the companies that were doing privileged trade over the world: 'The East Company', 'The East Indies Company', 'The Moluccas Company', 'The West Indies Company', 'The China Company', 'The Senegal Company', 'The Barbary Company', 'The South Seas Company'. This one multi-focal company he called the Compagnie Perpétuelle des Indes. The immense and extraordinary project sketched out in Law's mind might have succeeded. As it turned out, owing to the pusillanimity of some, the jealousy of others, perhaps too the overbold speculation and impatient exuberance of Law himself, it came to a resounding crash. The extravagant Scot spent his last years in Venice, ruined. But the State debt had been reduced, the India Company was set up, and towns like Nantes, Rochefort, Bordeaux, along with Lorient, were thriving.

In his study of economic history from the sixteenth to the eighteenth century (*Civilisation matérielle, économie et capitalisme*), Fernand Braudel describes the state of the 'Inner Sea' in the sixteenth century, but also sketches the emergence of the world-economy of the 'Outer Sea', the Atlantic.

In *The Destiny of Civilizations*, written at a time when the Atlantic world-economy had long been active, Leo Frobenius declares that the world has known four great cultural stages: the myth stage (Africa, the Pacific), the religious stage (Asia), the philosophical stage (the Mediterranean) and the techno-economic stage (the Atlantic), and suggests that the Atlantic coast may be the focus of new beginnings, may see the emergence of another cycle.

I go with that. It's confirmation of all the 'atlanticist' work I've been into over the past few years.

A Wave and Wind Philosophy

Dawn and the great sun and the bright Moon, and Earth and
wide Ocean and the dark Night.

(Hesiod)

1

In that classic textbook for biologists, Forbes and Hanley's
Molluscs, you find the following general description of the
octopodidae:

> The cuttle-fishes of this family have mostly more or less global,
> inflated bodies. They have rather small heads, prominent eyes
> protected by eye-lids, fleshy lips to their mouths and strongly
> curved compressed beaks. Their arms are eight in number, and
> all similar though more or less unequal; they bear sessile suckers.
> The mantle is always attached to the neck. They are active
> animals, swimming and creeping with facility, but living chiefly
> among the crevices of rocky ground.

Thereafter, in a section devoted to what Lamarck called
octopus vulgaris ('the species of this genus were the *polypi* of
the ancients') you have the following details as to colour:

> Its colour is tawny grey above, with brownish spots marking
> the position of the warts. The intensity of its hues, as in other
> cuttle-fishes, is exceedingly variable and transient. The back of
> the arms and the head are similarly coloured, but beneath and
> around the head it is bluish white.

The octopus may not be the most beautiful of animals (though
some species can perform amazingly graceful movements),
indeed to some minds it may be positively repulsive, but it is
interesting. First of all, it is intelligent, very. I've heard a
biologist say that if it could exist outside the saline element it
needs, if it could live longer and had some means of commun-
icating acquired knowledge down the line, the octopus could
rival (ain't that something?) *homo sapiens* himself. And when
you see it abstracted, reduced to its geometry, as on so many
Greek pots, it has a definite fascination.

What is certain is that it fascinated the early Greeks. It was
connected in their minds with the origins of the world, and

with a certain type of thinking. In order to get into this area, I propose now we move back from modern marine biology into some of the sea-myths of ancient Greece.

2

It's Hesiod, in the *Theogony*, who tells the story, at least in its best known version: there was this woman, Metis, who knew more than anybody, whether man or god. Zeus married her, then swallowed her.

To iron this out a little: Zeus represents the principle of order, he symbolizes the attempts to move out of disorder and chaos into an organized, differentiated, hierarchized cosmos. In the beginning, Zeus needs Metis, because of all the knowledge she possesses, but it is a dangerous knowledge, connected with all that chaos and disorder it is his mission to overcome. Which is why, if Metis starts off at his side, she ends up inside him. Her knowledge and her way of being must be subordinated to Zeus' own handling of affairs. In other words, Hesiod tells a more or less straight-line story: from disorder to order, QED. It's the official version of Olympic control. The triumph of orthodoxy.

There were, however, more paradoxical minds who felt that Hesiod's version was too simple, that Zeus himself was too high-handed, and that this subordination, if not total occultation of Metis, just wouldn't do. These were the Orphics, the followers of Orpheus (the man who sang the song of the cosmos when the Argonauts set sail), and they worked out their own version of the Zeus–Metis myth.

For the Orphics, Metis is the great primordial goddess, aquatic and polymorphous, and to show that she can never be subordinated to any oversimplified Olympic control principle, they no longer present her as female but, in a male-dominated society, give her masculine status. As common noun, however, *metis* was still of feminine gender, which tended to mean that to the Greek mind Metis was both he and she. He–she transcended the opposition of male and female, just as she–he transcended the opposition of black and white so often used by the cosmogonic imagination to express the play of forces at the origin of the world: Metis is both dark and light, she rises from

130

darkness, bringing light, before plunging into darkness again. He–she represents a creative power dating from before the constitution of a precisely differentiated cosmos. With the Orphics, when Zeus swallows Metis, he goes back beyond Kronos and Ouranos (regulated time and space), to the primordial area. Over against Hesiod's straight-line story of progression, the Orphic narrative presents a cycle of expansion and contraction, dispersion and concentration.

Close to the Orphics in his vision of things was Alcman, who wrote a cosmogonic poem in Sparta, in the seventh century before our era. Again, the sea is the primordial element, and at the start of things Alcman places a marine goddess, Thetis, half-woman half-fish.

In the beginning, there was a state of total formlessness: *ten hulen panton tet aragmenen kai apoeton* ('the matter of everything was in a state of confusion and incompletion'), till Thetis, who is *phusis kai thesis tou pantos* ('nature and the disposition of all things') and *aitia euthesias* ('cause of the good disposition of the elements'), by means of a demiurgic act, created the good order of the universe: *eukosmia*.

After all that has been said of Metis and her fellow-figure Thetis, it will hardly come as a surprise to hear that the creature associated with her was the octopus, or closely related members of the same genus. It was no doubt the observation of this animal that gave rise in the first place to the myth-idea of Metis. From neolithic times, the octopus has symbolized water and the sea, its undulating movements mimetically representing the motions of that element. Then, it seems peculiarly female: because of those self-same movements, but also because of its colour, especially perhaps in a Mediterranean context where men, living outdoors, are burned by the sun, while the women, staying at home, tend (at least tended) to have paler skin. And the same animal took on mystic proportions when it was observed not only how cryptic and secretive it was, but how from its whiteness could exude blackness: it seemed to unite qualities that were usually separated, and represented therefore an earlier stage of creation. Describing a certain type of calamar, *cologo-teuthis*, Ovid, in his *Haleuticon*, says that it is *nigrum niveo portans in corpore virus* ('carrying a black strength in its white body').

131

Before leaving the figure of Metis–Thetis, we must come back to Alcman. In that poem of his, Thetis is accompanied by three other figures: Skotos, Poros and Tekmor. In order to get at their meanings, let me recount the genesis in other terms. In the beginning, there was *mega chasma*, a great abyss of darkness, a state of matter in which no ways were indicated and no signs shown, *aporon kai atekmorton*, with everything, for lack of distinguishing marks, confused in a dark fog: *adiakriton panton onton kata skotoessan omichlen*. If Skotos still accompanies Thetis, even after her demiurgic act founding the good disposition of the universe, this means that essential darkness still remains. But Tekmor is a promise of signs, just as Poros indicates the possibility of a way.

This is where we make the move back from myth to methodology.

3

Greek thought, as it has come down to us from Plato and Aristotle, invites the mind to think of reality in terms of two levels, two distinct categories.

On the one hand, you have the realm of ideas, the domain of the One, of all that is immutable and eternal. This is the region of philosophy, metaphysics of being, a logic of identity, and science (exact calculation and rigorous reasoning). On the other hand, you have the world of becoming, the world of multiplicity, of all that is unstable, erratic, ephemeral. This is outside the domain of philosophy and science, outside the domain of real knowledge, *episteme*. If the mind can be active in this area also, its activity, for Plato, can only be of a low epistemological order: partly mere floating opinion, partly a type of thinking which is called *metis* (the name of our fishy sea-goddess). This type of thinking is described as *pantoie* (multiple), *poikile* (multi-coloured), *aiole* (undulating). It is polymorphous, polyvalent, versatile. *Polumetis* is a word used to describe Ulysses, the man of a thousand tricks, who is often likened to an octopus, which Aristotle, in his treatise on nature, calls *panourgotatos*, the most cunning of fish. This 'secondary' type of thinking is in fact cunning rather than knowledge. Let's call it octopus logic, or tentacular intelligence. Ulysses has it, with his tricks, his duplicity, his deviousness and his stratagems. The politician has it. And the sophist too – the sophist, for Plato, being neither the sage, who claims he possesses wisdom, nor the philosopher, the lover and seeker of wisdom, but the man who does not take wisdom seriously and who *plays* with knowledge and rationality.

The hunter and the fisherman must have *metis* if they are to track and trap animals and catch fish. That is, confronted by a multiple, polymorphous, rapidly changing reality, they must themselves become multiple and polymorphous in order to get a hold on an almost unseizable object which never stays long enough in the one place to be contemplated like an idea.

Even more interestingly (for the hunter and the fisherman, however distractingly mobile they may be, are still concerned, like the philosopher and the scientist, with 'fixing' something), the navigator must have *metis* in order to find his way in the open sea. He must know tides and stars, he must be attentive to time, season, sky and winds, all changing elements. He must have a many-sided intelligence, *gnome poluboulos*.

The Greeks had their city, a citadel of philosophy and science. They also had their known sea: *thalassa*, *pelagos*, *kuma*. But while they did not 'have' it or 'know' it, they also had wind of another sea: *pontos*, the open sea, with no well-known coasts in sight, no signs, the kind of sea the Argonauts got lost in: a panic area. That was what the Black Sea was: *Pontos Axeinos* (*axeinos*, from a Scythico-Iranian word meaning 'dark'), which inspired so much fear its name was euphemistically changed to *Pontos Euxeinos*.

Now, to a poet, who is not exactly *persona grata* in the city, and who is never quite at home there, to a poetical mind, this open sea, this *pontos*, might seem a pretty good analogy for life (non-constricted, non-codified life), and he might begin to try and think (can it be admitted that a poet might wish to think?) in terms of a life-thinking, a kind of thinking concerned with a way-of-life (*poros biou*), a sort of wave-and-wind thinking, a chaos-cosmic thinking... Oh, it would be vague enough at first. But it would be something more than lyrical enthusiasm, something more than emotive effusion, and a lot more than versified commentary.

He might go back to Plato, who is after all the most articulate of his fellow-citizens, and the one against whom, eventually, he may have to argue his case. Perusing once again the texts he studied in the Academy (because our poet was, and still is, a scholar) he'd find that for Plato, Metis, our famous sea-goddess, is the mother of Poros (*poros*: a way out), who lives with Penia (*penia*: need, necessity), and from these two is born Eros. For Plato, the philosopher par excellence, Eros is not a god (*theos*), but a demon (*daimon*). From Metis and Poros, he inherits a very alert mind that enables him to procure in a hard world what he wants, which is, ultimately: knowledge, beauty.

Our scholar–poet, who finds similar notions in Parmenides, begins to think in terms of 'erotic logic', and to invent extravagant words like *biocosmopoetics, chaoticism*...

He is still talking Greek, our poet–scholar–thinker, but it is disconcerting Greek. The philosophers will refuse to take him seriously, the lyrical poets will consider him a renegade to speculation, the defenders of the ideal will consider him a dangerous nihilist and confusionist, while the mentally flat-footed will shun him as pretentious. On all sides, he will be accused of something or other. Which is why he may choose to leave his native city-state for a while. He may go away out beyond the pale and live with barbarians, like Ovid during his exile on the Black Sea. Or else, he may travel over sundry lands, picking up signs here and there, and thinking wildly to himself.

Oh yes, he is an extravagant fellow, this poet we are gradually getting to know.

4

It was Eratosthenes – poet, grammarian, philosopher, mathematician, geographer, and for long years head of the library of Alexandria – who made fun of the Greeks for dividing the world neatly into two sections: Greeks, that is, civilized folk, and Barbarians. The world, for him, was wider and more complex than most civilized minds cared to think.

For Strabo, by no means the most limited intelligence in Athens, the world ended towards the west at Cape Sagres, on the ocean coast of Iberia; towards the east, at the Taurus mountains; towards the south, at the island of Taproban (south of India); and towards the north, at Ireland. 'From Celtica', he said, 'the farthest you can go north is the island of Iern, which is situated well beyond Britain, and where the cold is so intense that only a mean and wretched life is possible.' Yet three centuries before him, Pytheas of Marseilles had spoken of an island still farther to the north which he called Thule. Strabo simply refused to believe it: it was scientifically impossible.

We can imagine the poet–scholar we met up with on the barbarian coast reading Strabo and comparing him with Pytheas who'd actually *travelled* north. We can imagine him taking out his Homer and reading about all those peoples that lived on the Bosphorus and beyond, peoples with no distinct name, referred to globally as 'Hyperboreans'. We can imagine him travelling round the seaboard of the Barbary States, or the shores of the Black Sea, or the ocean coast of Celtica.

He might see strange patterns engraved on stones, strangely undulating and whirling patterns unlike the angular geometry he had learned in school – though he might remember the representations of octopuses on Greek vases, as well as old stories about Typhon, the spiralling, labyrinthine, manifold (*poluplokos*) Typhon, the son of Tartarus, the underworld and Gaea, the earth.

After contemplating the tumulus at New Grange, the pillar at Pfalzfeld, a stone or two in Gotland and the flowing lines of the great stones on the island of Gavrinis, in Brittany, our scholar–poet–thinker, with a head full of swirling, whorling, writhing forms, might travel east.

On the way, for he has studied linguistics and grammar, he might think of certain etymologies. He might take the vedic word *panthah*, meaning a path not traced out in advance, the crossing of an unknown region, the road to be opened where none exists and where no road, in any all-too-heavy sense of the word, *can* exist. And he might connect it in his head with the Greek *pontos*. Studying old Chinese, he might come across a definition of 'intellectual' congruent with his own feeling of the word: 'wind-and-lightning man'. He might actually come to China and hear about Tao, the watercourse way: 'The Tao of the heavens operates mysteriously and secretly. It has no fixed shape. It follows no definite rules. It is so great that you can never come to the end of it. It is so deep that you can never fathom it.' He might even come, this wandering poet, to a certain temple in Japan where the god of healing is depicted riding the waves of the sea on the back of an octopus.

He is finding more and more living confirmation of what were at the outset tentative intuitions of his awakening intellect: that erotic logic, those biocosmopoetics. He is more and more convinced that the sharp division in Greek thought between being and becoming, feeling and intelligence, however fine its achievements, however much the West has depended on it in practically all fields, is fundamentally invalid.

He is out on another way.

And he will be out on his own a long, a very long time.

5

But by the second half of the twentieth century, science, or maybe rather the philosophy of science, seemed to be giving some kind of confirmation to the tentative apprehensions of our traveller–poet.

Certainly the times were ambiguous, as times often are. On the one hand, they resembled closely the fifth-century Western Empire as described by Whitehead in *Adventures of Ideas*: 'In the Western Empire, there was no pursuit. Its remnants of irritability were devoid of transcendent aim.' Irritabilities were rampant, but mostly confused, and often stupid. What transcendent activity and talk there was tended to be hollow. But in the margin and on 'islands', there were moves towards an enlarged epistemology and a more vibrant cosmology, with a new sense of creative life. Certainly, there too was much frothy discourse – but something was in the air, there was a *ripple* of something in the mental atmosphere. Thought was moving out from its established divisions and connections into a larger space, a larger and more *breathing* space.

'In order to understand the essence of thought', wrote Alfred North Whitehead in *Modes of Thought*, 'we must study its relation to the ripples amid which it emerges.' And in *Adventures of Ideas*, there was a similar sense of complex relation and oceanic being, seen this time not from the point of view of philosophy, but from that of physics:

136

Modern physics has abandoned the doctrine of Simple Location [...]. There is a focal region, which in common speech is where the thing is. But its influence streams away from it with infinite velocity throughout the utmost recesses of space and time. [...] For physics, the thing itself is what it does, and what it does is this divergent stream of influence. Again the focal region cannot be separated from the external stream. It obstinately refuses to be conceived of as an instantaneous fact. It is a state of agitation, only differing from the so-called external stream by its superior dominance within the focal region. [...] Thus if we endeavour to conceive a complete instance of the existence of the physical thing in question, we cannot confine ourselves to one part of space or to one moment of time.

It was in statements such as that one that the traveller–poet and wandering scholar whose tracks we picked up a short time ago found confirmation of his intuitions and justification of his nomadic activity. And he found further confirmations when he read Popper's *Open Universe*, Schwenk's *Sensitive Chaos*, or Atlan's *Between Crystal and Smoke*. On all sides, in all fields, there was vagrant questioning. In fact, a new field seemed to be opening.

Whitehead had attributed the abandonment of the doctrine of Simple Location to '*modern* physics'. But early on in the same book (*Adventures of Ideas*), he had defined *modern* epistemology, *modern* cosmology in the following terms, which represented a previous (Cartesian–Newtonian) state of things: 'The universe is shivered into a multitude of disconnected substantial things, each thing in its own way exemplifying its private bundle of abstract characters which have found a common home in its substantial individuality.' The use of the same word *modern* to designate two radically different visions of the world could only lead to confusion. It seemed advisable to restrict the term 'modern' to the Cartesian–Newtonian system, which coincided with the rise of the 'modern world' out of the Middle Ages, and find a new word to designate the new 'field', the new world-in-emergence. The first word to present itself was, or course, *post*-modern. In the general confusion of the pseudo-culture, it was likely to be picked up and indiscriminately mouthed on all sides by superficial minds, but it would still be useful as a global, transitional term until a more precise vocabulary became current.

If the proliferation of neologisms can become a lexical disease, there is no doubt that at some point, they are necessary: 'At any moment', says Whitehead again (*Adventures of Ideas*), 'twenty new terms may be required by some advance in the subtlety of logical theory', and any outcry against them is 'a measure of unconscious dogmatism'. We have already seen our scholar–traveller–poet advancing concepts like 'erotic logic', 'biocosmopoetics', 'supernihilism', 'chaoticism'... He considered these as laxative concepts, meant to loosen up the functioning of the mind, but what really interested him, beyond all the -logies, was a new sense of the *logos*. That meant, in the final instance, a new poetics.

Most of the poetry that had come the traveller's way in 'modern times' left him totally indifferent. It all came out of the context described by Whitehead: 'The universe is shivered into a multitude of disconnected substantial things, each thing in its own way exemplifying its private bundle.' So you had private bundles of this or that nature (mostly sad sacks), a modernistic glee in incoherence, various types of simple location as exhibited by lawnmower poets, back-alley poets, national poets (etc.), or else wild wailings and noble nostalgias for lost ideals and coherences past. Which is why, in his search for a new world-poetics, our traveller–scholar–poet preferred to the latest volume by X, Y or Z studies in geomorphology, biogeography, oceanology.

Dwelling in isolated places here and there, walking the whispering shores of the world, though also at times moving through cities, he was trying to work it out, trying to work his way into what he conceived of as a complete logos-life.

Living the tides and the multiple spaces.

Thinking.

Trying to say it.

The Complex Field

Disintegrating the image, turning meaning into movement.
(Ossip Mandelstam)

1

The wind's howling round my study: 'Hebrides, Minches, Baillie. South-west backing south-east 6 to gale 8 decreasing 4 for a time. Rain showers. Good becoming poor for a time. Fair Isle, Faroes. Westerly severe gale 9 decreasing 4 backing south-east 6 to gale 8 later...'

If there's anything I listen to with pleasure on the radio, it's the marine weather report. With very few exceptions, the rest of the news is just the story of never-ending human imbecility. Joyce wanted to waken up from the nightmare. Hegel thought he saw a logic in it and he wrote the *Phenomenology of the Mind* in order to demonstrate the fact. In my more philosophical moments, I'm tempted to compose a *Meteorology of the Mind*, but I've come to want to leave the -logies alone and work closer in to the landscape, in an intellectual context still in the defining. I've been calling it for some time now geopoetics, and consider it as aiming at a new mental geography and a new language of communication (a wavelength our culture hasn't yet tuned into).

That's what I've come to work at here in Brittany.

2

Paul Valéry evokes somewhere those monks of the western rim of Europe who, at one point in our history, 'isolated themselves, in order to write huge poems – for nobody'. In his history of books and book-production, Fernand Cuvelier describes them in some more detail:

Along with that anxiety-ridden period of emptiness between two civilizations came a renewal of human expression in the form of written texts [...]. There was an early burst of activity about the third and fourth centuries [...]. A second burst came between the seventh and ninth centuries [...]. Strange characters,

139

travelling monks, started moving all over Europe. The historians tell us their heads were partially shaven, that their eyelids
were painted with vermilion, and that they spoke a rough,
guttural language [...]. After a nomadic period, those monks
chose a place to stay and settled down. [...] The monasteries
saved all that could be saved [...]. The Scots influence was to be
predominant for centuries.

My head isn't shaven and my eyelids aren't daubed with
vermilion, but there's more than one analogy between the
situation of those monks and mine, between what they did and
what I try to do.

It's probable that we also are going through, more or less
consciously, a passage between two cultures. Just as those
monks and others of their age were leaving paganism for
Christianity, we today are leaving humanism (self-centred man
as the measure of things in the world) for another field. But if I
refer to those monks, if I do a little cultural history in this way,
what is certain is that it's not to situate myself in a tradition, it's
not to adopt any historicist standpoint, it's simply to sharpen
my sense of intellectual and cultural movement, and, perhaps,
to draw up my historical accounts in order to feel free to
enter... a geography.

3

These last few weeks, I've been re-reading Hölderlin, who
talks of the *free usage* of what is native and national (this 'free
usage' implying a move through other cultures) and who, in a
beautiful letter of 1802 to his friend Böhlendorff, evokes a
sense of nature and a notion of poetic activity which is
germane to what I'm trying to get at:

> The more I study nature's manifestations here in my native
> country, the more deeply I am moved by them. Storm, seen [...]
> as power and figure among the other forms in the sky; light, by
> its effects, giving national shape, light as a principle, almost as a
> destiny, something sacred for us, the intensity of its coming and
> going; the particular shape of the woods here; the coming
> together in one region of different aspects of nature, so that all
> the sacred places of the earth can foregather at one place; and
> the philosophical light at my window all that gives me great
> joy in living at this moment. I hope I'll be able to stay on the

path that brought me here! [...] Dear friend, I think we shall
spend no more time commenting on the poetry of the past. The
art of poetry is about to change radically. And if we are not
quite up to it yet, it's because, since the Greeks, we're the first
to make a new beginning.

There's no need nowadays to share Hölderlin's idealism, or his
romantic pathos, or his poetic nationalism, and the word
'sacred' can quietly drop from our vocabulary, like so many
other over-connoted terms of the same order. But what can
inspire us in Hölderlin is this deep sensation of circumambient
context, allied to the notion of 'philosophical light'.

4

Before trying to get farther into the space of the *work in
progress*, let's take a look at the landscape out there, the landscape, for me at this moment, of the north coast of Brittany. I'll
do this by means of three quotations, which will be like so
many prologues.

Here first of all is Eugenio d'Ors, in his book on the baroque:

Land's ends. Ireland, Brittany, Spanish Galicia, Portugal, the
first islands of the Ocean... At the pit of their soul, panic. Panic,
a heritage from the times when those lands lay at the edge of a
sea whose bounds were unknown. You cannot occupy a box in
the theatre of mystery and come away unscathed.

Here's Eugen Fink, in the seminar he directed, along with
Heidegger, on Heraclitus, whose cosmo-poetic thought can
make the mind reel:

The sea turns partly into earth and partly into fiery breath.
Then it is said that the earth is spread out like a sea. Whether
the fiery breath turns into something else, and how it does it,
that the fragment does not say. With the fiery breath, the
process is over. There is only mention of the process by which
fire turns into sea and from sea partly into earth and partly into
fiery breath and from earth finally turns into sea. Fire turns into
sea, the sea deposits itself as earth and transforms itself into
fiery breath, and the earth comes back partly into the sea. [...]
The contrary terms of a known difference turn about in such a
way that one passes over into the other. The differences
between sea, earth and fiery breath are related to a common

origin, to a genesis, but *we still know nothing about the nature of the genesis.* [My emphasis.]

The third quotation (those voices, those phrases and others like them are part of the *rumour* that surrounds me on this coast) is from Élie Faure:

> Seismic upheavals that change the shapes of the mountains, with tidal waves, sudden mists that modify the appearance of the valleys, concealing with their mobile veil or revealing through its rents unexpected sites, fleeting shadows moving over a soil where crops, forests, fruit-trees cover with black and with green, with red and pink and white, an earth humped and twisted by ancient throes of the earth's crust...

That last quotation in fact concerns Japan, but who doesn't recognize also Brittany? All places in one place...

When, to conclude this series of preludes, I read this, in Heidegger's *On the Way to Living Language*: 'A West such as this is more ancient, closer to the dawn and therefore of greater promise than the Platonic or Christian West', I think of my situation here, out on the Armorican promontory. I think of the approaches to a possible 'primal space' where what would be relevant and prevalent would be, not the platonic world of ideas, nor the Christian salvation of the soul, nor Conquest and Progress, but simply *enlightened earthly situation.*

What is moving on the horizon is a poetics of the earth.

5

What an extravagant claim for poetry, it may be said. Is it not more or less established that it's science and politics that have the serious things to say about reality and the life-of-man-on-the-earth, while the gentle or wretched (or witty or goofy or wet) poet will content himself with his artistic personality, his linguistic legerdemain, his interesting fantasias, etc. for the delectation of the Friends of Poetry?

I've already said, here and there, how nauseating I find such a situation and such a reduced conception of poetic activity, and no doubt I'll have to say it again, here, there and elsewhere, but for the time being let's talk a little about politics and science.

Politics isn't concerned with 'the life of man on the earth', it's concerned with *polis*, that is, with human agglomerations animated by more or less obvious, more or less vicious power-motives (sometimes they have a little ecological sub-department on the side). So, while recognizing its massive importance on the scene and realizing that we'll have to come back to it, we can discount it for the moment as having little relevance to our fundamental question.

As to science, its aim, up to very recently at least, has never been to inhabit, as fully as possible, the planet, its aim has been to systematize the earth, to iron it out, so as to become its master and possessor. Maybe today, in its farther reaches at least (elsewhere, the scientists keep cutting and measuring, more concerned with their measures than with the world), we're witnessing a change. Here's Ilya Prigogine in *The New Alliance*:

> From now on, the sciences of nature will be describing a fragmented universe, rich in qualitative diversity and in potential surprises. What we're discovering is that the rational dialogue with nature no longer means the disenchanted survey of a lunar world, but the *exploration, always local and elective, of nature seen as complex and multiple* [...]. We no longer have the right to say that the only aim worthy of science is the discovery of the world from that exterior point of view to which access was possible only for those demonic minds that fill the classical treatises. Henceforth, the most fundamental of our theories will be defined as *the work of beings implicated in the world they explore*. In this theory, science has abandoned all theoretical extraterritoriality [...]. As an inhabitant of the world, man participates in a natural process of becoming [...]. Nature has a thousand voices, and we're only beginning to listen to them. [My emphasis.]

Prigogine speaks of 'a poetic listening-in to nature'. We can see there the effort (but no doubt there shouldn't be *too much* effort – perhaps a mixture of attention and nonchalance) to get on to the wavelength I mentioned at the beginning of this essay. But there are other aspects of the work in question, more precise, more *thought out* than most scientists can conceive of.

In a little text, *Aus der Erfahrung des Denkens* ('On the experience of thought'), published in 1954, Martin Heidegger spoke almost secretively of a new type of work-field:

> That thought be poetry is something that still lies concealed.
> Wherever it shows itself, this thinking evokes the utopia of a
> nascent poetic understanding, and it will remain utopian for a
> very long time. But the poem of thought is the topology of being.

Maybe rather than utopia (which tends to suggest hasty idealistic projections) I'd say *atopia*. But with these few indicative phrases we're entering the territory, the place of the subtlest topology.

6

Something, then, is beginning: a practice, an activity which is neither 'philosophical', 'scientific' nor 'poetic' in the banal senses of these words, but which consists in moving about in a place (space and time) and trying to say what one is aware of around oneself.

But what is this 'place', and what is that 'self'?

Already Aristotle was saying: 'It's an important thing, place, *topos*, and it's hard to grasp.'

As for the 'self', since we're concerned here with a topology of being, a way of thinking that takes place in an area situated at the exit of all metaphysics, this self can't be a metaphysical self, like the Christian soul or the *ego* of the Cartesian *cogito*. Nor can it merely be a lyrical subjectivity, which is only social sub-product. Thinking in terms of physics rather than of metaphysics, let's say we're concerned with a body: a body in movement through space. But how to speak of a body, how to let it speak? In his *Douze questions à propos de Martin Heidegger* ('Twelve questions concerning Martin Heidegger'), Jean Beauffret has the following commentary on Heidegger's thought:

> The relationship we have to the body is, according to
> Heidegger, difficult to bring to expression. 'Husserl tried', he
> told me one day, 'but almost from the start he was launched
> into kinesthesia.' To speak of the body in a language other than
> that of psycho-physiology is something that remains to be
> invented.

So, for this place and this body, a language has to be invented. Heidegger's dissatisfaction at hearing Husserl speak of kinesthesia reminds me of Niels Bohr's exasperation on hearing one of his colleagues expatiating on mathematical theories of space: 'Space is blue', retorted Bohr, 'and birds fly through it.' That doesn't mean a return to good old simple folk-talk or half-baked poetry as some naive, tired or hasty minds would no doubt like to think. What it does mean is the need, in this emergent context, for this body in this place, of a language that is more direct, more immediate, more expressive.

Which implies work, poetic work.

7

In his *Aesthetics*, Hegel, the last mind to have a global view of things, had said that, in the modern age, poetry would have a hard time of it, would, in fact, find it almost impossible to make headway. When I speak of 'poetic work', I'm thinking of those who were ready to take the time and the trouble to try to make headway, in spite of everything. Which is to say that I'm putting aside all the daily and journalistic uses of the word 'poetry', as well as most of the more sophisticated ones. So diminished and confused has the poetic field become that, for a mind that's in any way demanding, the words 'poet' and 'poetry' will seem hardly adequate as definitions of what interests him.

'For me', writes Valéry in his *Cahiers* ('Notebooks'), 'to be a poet, to be a writer was never an absorbing desire. But to be, purely and simply. [...] Nothing seemed to me more crude and less worthy of attention than the poet reduced to being a poet. [...] It's hardly worth writing if it isn't to reach the heights of being, and not just produce more art – but of course the heights of being are also the heights of art.' And Georges Bataille (*Haine de la poésie*, 'In hatred of poetry'): 'Poetry which isn't engaged in an experience going beyond poetry (distinct from it) isn't real movement, it's just the residue of agitation.'

To get out of and beyond the residues and the agitations, the confusions and the complacencies, we need, not only a new philosophy of poetry, but a new poetic anthropology.

Plato distinguished four types of man: appetitive man (the one who tries to gather everything into himself, like an infant); spirited man (the man of heart and of courage, the man of action); rational man (aiming at mastery of life and the world); and demonic man (the man who follows his *daimon*, a super-personal power linking him obscurely to what surrounds him). To this list I'd like to add one more type, close to the demonic, but nevertheless distinct from him (less inclined to frenzy and characterized more by clear energy than by obscure impulse) which I'll call: the *mondomaniac*, the man who has a mania for *mondo, mundus*, world. The poet, in the sense I accept to use the word, is a mondomaniac, who follows out his *mondomania*, that is, his desire for world. I'm thinking of Hölderlin's *Hyperion*: 'What you are looking for is a world.' I'm thinking also of Diderot, that extravagant and encyclopedic mind, who said: 'Poetry is out for something enormous.' That doesn't mean necessarily something huge and grandiose. It just means something *outside the norms*.

8

For Valéry, in his *Propos sur la poésie* ('Remarks on poetry'), the difference between the action of a poem and that of ordinary narrative is physiological: 'The poem deploys itself in a *more complex field of movement*.' (My emphasis.)

Heidegger describes himself (or the figure he projects) as *unterwegs im Wegfeld* (literally: 'on his way in the road-field'), having in mind a 'beginning thought' (*anfängliches Denken*) that will try to 'grasp' (*anfangen*) a 'beginning that begins differently' (*ein andersanfänglicher Anfang*), this thought being inseparable from a meditation which, he says, is 'a listening in to the original source in its upsurge' (*ein hörendes Wissen um den ursprunglichen Ursprung in seinem Entspringen*). Heidegger is one of the few philosophers who have worked resolutely and profoundly towards a new (poetic) thought, a thinking which would, he said, be simpler than philosophy, but precisely because of its simplicity, harder to achieve. One can share his impatience with a more 'professorial' colleague (professorial in the sense of heavy and pedantic) who was expatiating one day in his presence on Heideggerian problematics. If people didn't actually come to *see* his thought, said Heidegger, it was a waste of time, they'd still be bogged down in philosophizing discourse.

It may be that the *evidence* of thought is poetry: the poetry of those who have made headway in the field of new poetic thought.

'To think !' cries Henri Michaux in *Passages*. 'Rather work on my thinking-and-being machine in order to find myself in a position where I can think differently, know the possibility of really new thought.'

And 'thought' may not be the final word.

Biocosmography.

Geopoetics.

'In our day', said Mandelstam (*Zametki o poezii*), 'there is no really salubrious poetry.' But, there in Russia, he saw signs of it at least in Pasternak:

> With eyes wide open, with nerves taut and ready to perceive the most subtle details, with mind *astonished*, Pasternak gropes his way forward in this world [...]. In his pages we have a sense of the first day of Creation [...]. This primordial freshness is particularly obvious in his landscapes. [...] The horizons are wet and smell of rain. Storms, cloud and showers rush and roar over the land, mist and foam and spray unexpectedly flood his verses and the words gleam like grass under white frost. [...] To read the poetry of Pasternak is to clear one's throat, strengthen one's breathing, renew one's lungs.

All of this (that landscape, that *breathing space*) brings me back to this north coast of Brittany where I now live, work and have my being.

9

To conclude, provisionally, this poetic and philosophical divagation, I'd like to speak of one particular spot on this coast that I often visit. It's what the geologists call a 'centred complex', that was formed roughly as follows: first of all, there were granitic magmas that moved in a whirling or laminated way till they crystallized; then there was a cataclysm that fractured the central and southern zones of the rough-grained granite, putting in place a second group of fine-grained granite, diversely coloured (pink, ochre, violet-grey), that cemented the blocks of rough red stone; finally, there was a further collapse at the centre of the complex, liberating a volume of matter in which the third and last group of granite, fine-grained and white, came to crystallize.

That geological phenomenon, with its mass and its movement, is a pretty good analogy of the complete work in progress.

Elements of a New Cartography

As intelligence and language, thought and the signs of thought,
are united by secret and indissoluble links, so in like manner,
and almost without our being conscious of it, the external world
and our ideas and feelings.

(Alexander von Humboldt)

1

'In each age of the world distinguished by high activity', says
Whitehead in *Adventures of Ideas,* 'there will be found at its
culmination, and among the agencies leading to that culmination, some profound cosmological outlook, implicitly accepted,
impressing its own type upon the current springs of action.'

If we're willing to admit the hypothesis that there exist, in
the present age, at least some fields of 'high activity', it may be
interesting to see what 'cosmological thought' is in the air,
giving its shape to our mental space.

In his studies on the spiritual crisis and revolution of the
seventeenth century *(From the Closed World to the Infinite
Universe)* Alexander Koyré reduces the changes made at that
time in the conception of the world to two main elements: the
destruction of the notion of cosmos and the geometrization of
space. This new cosmology set aside the geocentric world of
the Greeks (the original *kosmos*), and the anthropocentrically
structured world of the Middle Ages, replacing them with the
decentred world of modernity. The consequences of such a
fundamental transformation were many, two of the main ones
being the displacement of the mind from contemplation and
teleological philosophy to the mechanistic mastery over nature,
and the rise of modern subjectivity accompanied by a sense,
more or less vague, of having somehow lost the world. The
poet of the crisis is John Donne, a sharp and subtle mind, who
declares: ''Tis all in pieces, all coherence gone, all just supply
and all relation.' The typical writer of the new age, swimming
sceptically in the waters of his (learned) ignorance, enjoying,
despite everything, the divagations of his floating personality,
is Montaigne.

It's difficult to say exactly when modernity comes to an end, and when something else begins (by signs here and there), but a useful date is 1917, the year of Einstein's *Cosmological Considerations*. There you have a cosmology which is no longer modern, in the sense I've defined (that so many artists should still be floundering about in what they call 'modernity' is neither here nor there). And the notion of 'cosmos' returns: 'It appeared', writes Jacques Merleau-Ponty in *Cosmology of the Twentieth Century*, 'that cosmological thought was again feasible, that the universe was susceptible to thinking, not only to dreaming, and that this thinking was grounded in the most general of physical theories. Astronomy and the Theory of Relativity brought back the desire for intellectual possession of nature, and brought to life again the Greek passion for cosmic contemplation.'

Let it be said in passing that the use of the word 'possession' in this text is a hangover from modernist vocabulary and that if cosmic contemplation was eminently practised by the Greeks, it was by no means restricted to them. Other contemplations, other types of space-poetics, can attract and interest us today.

But what is certain is that, if this cosmology has not yet entered the mores (intellectual, existential, industrial), if the fairly simple consequences to be drawn from it are rarely made, it is this new cosmic thinking that informs and inspires certain areas of high activity in these times.

I've mentioned the year 1917, and a particularly significant formulation. But you can see it, at the intuitive stage, in Chateaubriand, when, in the *Mémoires*, he talks of a 'kind of confusion, or, if you like, a kind of undefinable unity'. You can see it in the anarcho-poetic thought, the 'chaotico-practical' thought (as Henri Birault says), of Nietzsche: 'You must bear within yourself a chaos in order to give birth to a dancing star.' It's present in, it presides over, René Thom's 'theory of catastrophes' and Benoît Mandelbrot's 'fractal objects'. It is the theme of the book *Order in Chaos* by Berge, Pomeau and Vidal. Likewise in the interviews of those (Hubert Reeves, Richard Schaeffer, Pierre Fayet...) who took part in the colloquium 'Scientific perspectives' of 1985, interviews collected under the title *Chaos and Cosmos*. And an aesthetic illustration is provided of it in Theodor Schwenk's *Sensitive Chaos*.

Manuel de Diéguez *(Science and Nescience)* speaks of a 'cosmology of energy'. Given the mobility of this cosmos, and the disparity, the diversity of its localizations, given also the frequency of the word 'chaos' in the above-mentioned titles, I feel justified in having used for some time now, among other concepts I found it necessary to invent, neologisms like chaosmos, for the cosmological entity, and chaoticism, for the notion of order in disorder, disorder in order.

What we're concerned with is a new world-sensation.

3

It's this sensation that it's important to get across today.

That can mean piling up information about hot stars and cold stars, about hyperdense stars and rarefied stars, about variable stars and cosmic clouds, plasmas, nebula; it can mean all that, of course, but, more, it means becoming aware of the expansion and the singularization of our universe-multiverse, it means a sensation of immensity and incommensurability, it means a sense of relativity and topology. It means, globally, a heightened sensitivity towards the environment in which we try to live.

In a society which is betting everything on quantitative information, it will be necessary to stress the importance of qualitative *en*formation and, further, the notion of *ex*formation: direct contact with the outside, the acquiring of a nonpanic, poetic sense of dispersion, disaggregation, dissolution.

This will mean moving out of a certain scientistic terrorism that has long prevailed and re-discovering something like what used to be called natural philosophy, as well as something we might call cosmo-aesthetics. We should, for example, be able to talk of 'space' without specifying and formulating what mathematical approach we are using. These mathematical lines, these angles, exist, others, many others, might also exist, but beyond them all, is... space that can be directly apprehended and immediately appreciated.

'It'll take many years of patient teaching in a thousand open-air schools...', said Harry Martinson, in his *Aimless Travels*, referring to initiation into the new space-field.

Let's look at some elements of what we might call planetary pedagogy.

It's been said, and it had to be said (Korzybski was the first), that the map is not the territory. But if you want an initial and initiating sense of the world, what's better than a map? Who doesn't remember the first maps he saw as a child? Robert Louis Stevenson found it hard to believe that anybody could fail to be interested in maps. So do I.

If maps provide information as to the shape of the earth, the absolute beauty of some of them can go so far as to illuminate the mind. I'm thinking, in no particular order, of the magnificent Çurat-al-Ard (image of the world) by Muh'ammad Ibn Mûsâ al-Khuwârizmî, of a certain Spanish map of the coast of California and the Gran Apacheria, of Kuwagata Keisai's Nihon Ezu (Japan like a dragon coiled in a green dawn...), of a Chinese map of the Yellow River, of a Dutch map of the Gulf of Gascony, which is the Bay of Biscay (De Spaensche Zee) by Lucas Jansz Waghenaer... And from the maps themselves, I go to the map-makers and the travellers: those who worked in the House of Wisdom, at Baghdad, in the eighth century; Muquddasî (tenth century) who went about questioning old sailors (they'd draw on the sand the coasts they knew around Arabia – gulfs, creeks, capes) and who then drew up his map, tracing itineraries in red, sand in yellow, the sea in green, rivers in blue, and mountains in grey. Then there was Ibn Bat't'ît'a, who worked at Idrîsi's map-shop on Corsica. And the Casa da India in Lisbon, the Casa de Contratacion in Sevilla, the Map School in Dieppe, all working feverishly after the Portuguese, those 'geographers with the wind in their sails', as Lucien Febvre called them, had launched out into the Atlantic from Cape Sagres. And then finally there are the texts: Marcian of Heraclea's *Periplum of the Outward Sea*, Denys the Periegetic's *The Stadiosmos of the Great Sea* ('there's a rock fifteen stadiums from land, a high rock, like a falcon'), Gautier of Metz's *Image of the World* ('a philosopher once there was/who travelled many earths and lands/looking for knowledge every-where/ and on many a good book put his hands...'). And there are even individual phrases, just simple phrases, that are enough to set the scalp tingling, for example this one, from the Saintonge pilot, Jean Alfonce: 'I have sailed over all the seas over eight and forty years, and I've had space to see a lot of experiences' (*J'ay eu espace d'avoir veu beaucoup d'expériences...'*). He had space. To 'have space', isn't that a pre-requisite for any kind of decent living and cogent thinking?

5

It will be said perhaps at this point, either in a tone of lamentation or with a cynical snigger, that there is less and less of space, and that this sense-of-space I have been evoking, this earth-discovery, is a thing of the past. Our space, our earth-space, has been filled up, cemented up, and it will be more filled up, more cemented up, with every passing decade.

In this physical and mental context, there are two principal attitudes, adopted more or less consciously: get what fun you can in the noisy, crowded circus, or at least try to convince yourself you're getting fun. Or else bet on some other kind of living in interstellar space. I can't share either of these atti-tudes. While being well aware of the process of filling-up and cementing-up, I say, let's start slowing down this process, let's try to work out other tactics. I'm aware of cosmic space, I like contemplating the starry heavens, but I don't fancy living on the moon, and I'd hate to have the space between me and it full of bip-bip-bipping. Living on the earth, with a cosmic sense, but living on the earth. I like this place, I love this place. I don't think we know it yet. I think if we evolved a bit more, we'd know better, we'd love better. It's that evolution that interests me. Towards a finer earth-living.

In *A Grammar for the Living,* David Cooper asks if, given all the encumbrances of our world, given the opaque screen of conditioning everywhere, which no light ever penetrates, is it worthwhile continuing to live at all? It's a question more and more people will ask – unless, of course, thinking and feeling also become obsolete practices. Less existentially, less suicidally than Cooper, in *Naked Man,* Claude Lévi-Strauss protests against the exclusive attention paid to Man in our civilization, Man, 'this unbearably spoilt child who has been too long on the scene, preventing all serious work'.

Where find a little disencumbered space? Where, far from invading cacophony, find a locus of serious work? How to effect in one's-self a disengagement and an expansion?

That is for the individual, it will be said.

Yes, these are immediate tactics, for the individual – but also for the production of a language, a grammar that may have an influence on the general. Politics will also, eventually, have something to do with the process. But politics itself needs a concept of living, a grounding, that only the single, complex living intelligence can provide.

And try to spread, by example, by teaching, by propagation.

6

A few years ago, Fernand Deligny left for the mountains of the Cévennes with a group of psychotic children. What he wanted for those children, as a therapeutic, was 'a livable environment', so he settled with them 'in the waves and among the eroded rocks of the hercynian chain'. There, 'in linguistic vacancy', they would follow out 'lines of errancy' (*lignes d'erre*), work out a system of co-ordinates between themselves and the landscape, gradually establish a network. Along with the errancy in the territory went the drawing-up of maps, which Deligny considers not as 'instruments of observation', but as 'instruments of evacuation': evacuation of anxiety, evacuation of false language. But if this cartography is an evacuation process, out of it, at the same time, rises a new topology, a topology of places called, with terms invented for the occasion: 'tangle points', 'black blooms', 'white prints'.

Deligny comes to the conclusion that what is happening there, without there ever having been any precise aim, any pre-scribed methodology, is the resurrection of 'ancient harmonies'.

It may be said (while following out, and tracing out, my subjectivities, convinced that what is important is no fixed objective, but the subjectivity that opens most space, I am also trying to answer objections), it may be said that what is good, perhaps, for psychotic children, has no relevance to the life of normal adults. But who can define what is normal, and who can claim to be so? Are not those autistic children, lacking in 'livable space' and with no adequate language, the revealed image of modern humanity? Isn't schizophrenia, of some degree, one of the marks of our civilization? Showing a hiatus between our minds, our inmost needs, and that civilization?

After criticizing the modern-traditional attitudes to schizophrenia in *The Anti-Oedipus*, Gilles Deleuze and Felix Guattari, in *A Thousand Plateaux*, proposed a schizo-analysis: 'Over against psychoanalysis, and psychoanalytic know-how, which clamps every desire, every statement on to a genetic axis or a super-codifying structure, schizo-analysis refuses every kind of reproduced fatality, whatever name be given it: divine, anagogical, historical, economic, structural, hereditary or syntagmatic.' To the psychoanalyst's couch, where everything gets reduced to the dimensions of a family photo, the schizo-analyst prefers an open-air walk: 'The schizophrenic's walk is a better model than the neurotic lying out on a couch. Let's have a little open air, some kind of relationship to the outside.' The new self that gradually emerges from such perambulations and peregrinations is 'a strange subject, with no fixed identity', which 'moves along the rim of a circle whose centre has been deserted'.

From this ex-centric field, David Cooper, who shares the same aversion for psychoanalysis ('a lifebuoy jacket for the normal world'), takes a leap into ecstasy:

> By ex-stasy, I mean the fact of being outside one's 'self' after passing through an anoia (loss of the normal subject) – a liberation from our conditioned 'minds'. Once outside, you let things be, you let go ('letting be' isn't a psychological context, it's an ontological one), and you retrieve a topological presence. The 'I' which is no longer 'myself' resides in spaces that are no longer mere places, mere localities, but in such a way that particularity is not lost – there is an 'incarnation'.

It's this notion of 'topology of being' that we find in Heidegger. Beyond subject and object, the 'being' is thrown into an ex-static presence (a *Dasein*), in which it knows a 'tuning' (*Stimmung*) which isn't just an internal psychic event, but is a liberated way of being in the world. In Rainer Schürmann's reading of Heidegger (*The Principle of Anarchy*), identity, here, consists only in 'directive traits'.

By various routes, by various channels, a certain type of identity that has marked Western civilization for centuries, is in the process of disappearing: 'The image of man is breaking up' – says the biophysician Henri Atlan in an essay 'Man as open system', and he goes on, seeing in this disappearance no cause for lamentation, on the contrary: 'It's not because Man is being effaced "like a face made of sand at the edge of the tide", as Foucault says, that we have any cause to shed tears or bemoan our fate. This "Man" that is disappearing is not us, it's a fiction of the imagination which has played its part... This man is being replaced by things, but we can recognize ourselves in those things because they can speak to us...'

Atlan finally evokes the possibility of a 'unified existence'. In his more highly idiosyncratic vocabulary, Heidegger speaks of 'the co-originary revelation of the world and of existence'. And in *The Anti-Oedipus* by Deleuze and Guattari, we find this: 'The day a human being will be able to behave like intentionless phenomena – that day, a new creature will proclaim the integrity of existence.'

To trace what I like to call the biocosmographic way from the conditioned self to open system, ex-static existence, is not easy. To find live words with which to proclaim 'the integrity of existence' is not easy either. At every turn, we come up against problems of language.

7

Practically everything, in 'our' age, is against the possibility of a clear and powerful language, able to say a presence and a clarity.

'Unlike discourse', writes Henri Lefebvre in *Language and Society*, 'speech is initial and unique'. But today, we live under the dictatorship of discourse: political, commercial discourse, journalistic discourse, edifying discourse... If one adds to that the flood of insignificant images and the mass of mechanical noises that daily besiege the brain, one readily understands that speech, far from being initial and initiating, far from being unique and unified, gives way to inane chatter and incoherent palavering.

In such a context, art will be considered all the more 'artistic' the more it is incoherent, inane, incomprehensible. Or else, in reaction to this state of affairs, and nostalgic for some past dignity, it takes refuge in some kind of over-refined rhetoric.

Finding a language that is at once open and effective, re-discovering one's 'expressive self' (Deleuze, in his book on Spinoza: 'Leibniz's monad and Spinoza's mode both mean the individual as expressive centre') implies a practice which will for long be isolated, clandestine and 'inhuman', a multiple and complex practice going beyond not only psychoanalysis and linguistics, but also 'philosophy' and 'poetry'.

In every grammar, there's a logic, and in every logic, there's a metaphysics. To renew a language takes more than verbal jugglery, all kinds of 'innovatory' permutations and combinations within a given system, it means moving right up (or right down) to the level of metaphysics. This can be done in two ways: either by archaeo-logical work on a language, or by an 'exotic' recourse to other languages with different metaphysics, different initial fictions.

Heidegger belongs principally to the first category:

'Our Western languages', he writes in *Identity and Difference*, 'are, each in its own way, languages of metaphysical thought. Is the essence of Western languages definitively impregnated with onto-theology? Or can those languages reveal other ways of speaking?'

Is it possible for a mind (Cooper, in his *Grammar for the Living*: 'Unlike certain tribes, we can't yet do without words such as 'mind', 'self', etc.'), to unlearn the grammar of dictatorial principles which have made the West – not in order to enclose oneself in an autism or in some neutral 'literary space', but in order to speak a language freed of principial structure, a language simpler, more direct, closer to the 'physics' of the universe?

I'm trying to talk about the physics of speech...

Before looking for a primordial tongue, Heidegger establishes the primordiality of language. Our consciences are full of notions, according to one of which man thinks and, then, 'dresses up' his thought in language. Heidegger reverses the process: for him, language doesn't 'dress up' thought, thought is rooted and develops in language. We leave the notion of a person thinking in his 'inner self' and who thereafter 'expresses' that self for the speech of a world. We leave the idea of a representation of the world for a presence in the world, which is the *Dasein* (literally, 'being there'). 'The *Dasein*', writes Heidegger in *Being and Time*, 'doesn't emerge from some inner sphere, its primordial way of being means being always outside.'

To this primordial way of being corresponds a primordial way of speaking which the West no longer knows: 'Once, at the beginning of Western thought', we read in Heidegger's volume *Essays and Lectures*, 'the essence of language flashed like a stroke of lightning in the light of being.'

It might be said that, for Heidegger, ancient Greek is a pre-text that permits him to get closer to a primal world-text, but his obsessive archaeo-logy (his etymologizing), and his obsession of a 'poem of being' irritates more mobile minds, such as that of Gaston Bachelard: 'Metaphysics', he writes in *The Poetics of Space,* 'has nothing to gain from pouring its thought into fossil linguistic moulds. It should make full use of the extreme mobility of modern languages, while however remaining true to the homogeneity of a mother-tongue, according to the habit of all real poets.'

As a refugee from science, Bachelard is more indulgent to poetry than is the philosopher (and, let it be said, any fundamental poet). Where the philosopher is looking for being (and in most poetry would find only fantasy and psychology), the scientist, trying to rid himself of a reductive rationalism, is less radical and has pleasure in finding himself in an atmosphere of sensitive intimacy, replete with ambiguous complication and imaginative flights. Wary of any adamant notion of 'being there', Bachelard favours a kind of inbetween-being that knows alternate moments of opening and closing: 'One should hesitate before talking of "being there". Enclosed in being, one has to get out. Once out, one has to get back in. In being, you have circuits, tours and detours, courses and discourses, refrains of couplets without end...'

Refrains of couplets without end... To describe the poetry he likes, in which he feels at ease, Bachelard uses an expression that a mind poetically more demanding might use to designate the kind of poetry he can well do without.

If Heidegger's studies concerning the poem of being can appear obsessional and logomachic, Bachelard's anthological commentaries can seem too disgustingly facile. To find a satisfying poetry and poetics, it looks as if we have to go beyond the purist radicality of the one and the poetical complacency of the other.

But are 'poetry' and 'poetics' still useful words for the work-field whose contours are beginning to emerge?

'Sometimes', says Cooper in *A Grammar for the Living*, 'a kind of poetry seems to be the most appropriate form of discourse.' Sometimes... a kind of... While Lefebvre, in *Language and Society*, has this: 'What we want is a poïesis or creative word', taking care to use the Greek word so as to differentiate what he envisages, what he would like to hear, from mere 'poetry'. He makes this even more clear when he mentions Nietzsche (surely no self-satisfied poetaster), saying that in *Thus Spake Zarathustra* we witness 'the upsurge of a Word which is out to be poïetic and is only poetic'. The poïesis which is lacking in so much poetry is a 'poem-act that tries to appropriate the world'. In *The Principle of Anarchy* (sub-title: 'Heidegger and the question of action'), Reiner Schürmann comments on the famous phrase of Heidegger's in *The Experience of Thought*: 'That thought is poetry is something which has not yet been revealed. Where it manifests itself, this characteristic of thought evokes a utopia of poetic understanding. But the poem of thought is in truth the topology of being. It's topology of being that says the place where the poem can deploy its power.' Schürmann, like the others quoted, takes care to distinguish the German *Dichtung* from 'poetry': 'The "poïetic" characteristic of presence is what Heidegger calls *Dichtung* (poetry)... Needless to say, this has nothing to do with the art of composing verse, nor even with human language. The poïetic nature of thought is only the echo of the poïetic nature of presence.'

When he says all this has nothing to do with human language, Schürmann is exaggerating – Heidegger looked into the work of poets (some poets), and wrote poems himself. But most of the restrictions listed above can be accepted. What we are trying to delineate is a field of presence and activity which has poïetic characteristics, but which has little in common with what is habitually known as 'poetry'.

Around the end of the seventies, I began talking about

'geopoetics'. It seemed a good word for what, vaguely enough at the beginning, I felt I was 'into to' and 'after'. It had something to do with geography, certainly – maybe a new type of geography. That I'd felt already when, in the Ardèche, at the house Gourgounel, where I wrote my first prose book, I'd read Henri Pourrat's *Vent de Mars* ('The Wind of March') which contains this fine page on geography: 'Geography, as we now see it, draws itself up to its full height in the sun, with the wind blowing through its hair, a little farther forward than geology and history. It is geology and history, it's even a kind of novel, but in a more serious way. It is the great investigation of man in action, action allied to the Creation, from the grain of wheat to the amazing nebula.' It had geography behind it, as well as cosmology and philosophy such as I've outlined in the previous pages. But while the concept was growing in my mind, like a coral reef, I was also looking for actual writing. Working at it in my own writing, but also searching for hints, directions, maybe at times corroborations in other writers. Of that quotation from Henri Pourrat, I said it was a fine page. So it is. It's in the right space, if I may say – but it's all too metaphorical, anthropocentric, humanist, theological. I wanted something else.

I took up my Whitman again, the first poet who had ever really meant anything to me, and I looked through the *Leaves of Grass* for signs of geopoetics. I found them. Take, for example, these lines written (1881) in Platte Cañon, Colorado:

Spirit that form'd this scene,
These tumbled rock-piles grim and red,
These reckless heaven-ambitious peaks,
These gorges, turbulent-clear streams, this naked freshness,
These formless wild arrays, for reasons of their own,
I know thee, savage spirit – we have communed together,
Mine too such wild arrays, for reasons of their own;
Was't charged against my chants they had forgotten art?
To fuse within themselves its rules precise and delicatesse?
The lyrist's measur'd beat, the wrought-out temple's grace –
    column and polish'd arch forgot?
But thou that revelest here – spirit that form'd this scene,
They have remember'd thee.

There you have almost pure geopoetics. I say 'almost pure', for that 'spirit' is probably too much, but it hardly matters. What matters is what's actually there. It's in the contact between the mind and those rock-piles that the poetics lie: the basis of another art. Continuing my investigation, in those *Notes and Fragments* brought together by Richard Bucke and published in Canada (for private distribution) in 1899, I came across this curious meditation which Whitman recommends, and which he must, I imagine, have to some extent practised:

> To you. First of all prepare for study by the following self-teaching exercises. Abstract yourself from this book: realize where you are at present located, the point you stand on that is now to you the centre of all. Look up overhead, think of space stretching out, think of all the unnumbered orbs wheeling safely there, invisible to us by day, some visible by night; think of the sun around which the earth revolves; the moon revolving round the earth, and accompanying it; think of the different planets belonging to our system. Spend some minutes faithfully in this exercise. Then again realize yourself upon the earth, at the particular point you now occupy. Which way stretches the north, and what country, seas etc.? Which way the south? Which way the east? Which way the west? Seize these firmly with your mind, pass freely over immense distances. Turn your face a moment thither. Fix definitely the direction and the idea of the distances of separate sections of your own country, also of England, the Mediterranean sea, Cape Horn, the North Pole and such like distinct places.

And then, to cap it all, in the same book, I came across this note on style: 'Rules for composition – a perfectly transparent plate-glassy style, artless, with no ornaments, or attempts at ornaments for their own sake... Clearness, simplicity, no twistified or foggy sentences at all – the most translucid clearness without variation.'

I was beginning to feel quite excited. I felt that we were very definitely going places. There was a line that had not been seen, and that I was now able to trace.

Looking still farther afield for confirmatory elements, I'd turned to Victor Segalen's *Journal des Iles*. Under the date 10 January 1905, I found the following note, which refers to Arthur Rimbaud: 'On the strength of the few documents that have come to light, I'm trying to imagine the nature of the explorer in him. Others have spoken of the poet. And might it ever be possible to reconcile those two beings, so distant the one from the other? Or maybe those two sides of the paradox can be subsumed into an ever higher unity that hasn't yet shown itself?'

Poetry, geography – and a higher unity: geopoetics...

As is well enough known by this time, Arthur Rimbaud's last published texts were geographic reports sent to the Société de Géographie. I have by heart the report he wrote on the Somali coast about 1883, and have it often in mind. 'According to Sottaro, the central region of the country, Ogaden, whose average level is 2700 feet, is a vast stretch of steppe land; after the light rains prevalent in this area, it is a sea of tall grass interspersed, here and there, with stony fields...'

One can well understand Rimbaud preferring a text such as this to so much 'poetry'. And this meeting in his movement of the poet and the geographer was for me a sign of things to come. I remember seeing, in the Rimbaud museum at Charleville – and it was a moment of some emotion – the poet's travelling trunk, and in it two maps: one of Vienna, the other of Abyssinia (*Justus Perthus' Afrika Sektion Abessinien...*)

But, if already there are vagrant signs, it is not finally in Rimbaud that we can see realized that 'higher unity' Segalen speaks of. Rimbaud goes, without transition, without dialectics and without hesitation, from an explosive transcendentalism to a positivistic professionalism, in a way that Spengler, who came to the same conclusions, would have approved: the 'knuckling down to business' seen as the only means of survival in an age of decline.

Segalen himself is in fact a better example, who left Europe first for Polynesia, then for China, and achieves that 'higher unity' when he travels down the 'great river', the Yangtse-kiang, or when he approaches the frontiers of Tibet.

To come back to Europe, and to Spengler's analysis of the situation. According to Frobenius, if Spengler's analysis is unsatisfactory, shortsighted, unable to discover latent possibilities in what he peremptorily called 'decline', it was because he lacked what Frobenius called 'the cartographic method'. All he saw was the end of a history. The cultural cartography inaugurated by Frobenius remains to be developed, as well as the cultural programme he lays out at the end of *The Destiny of Civilizations*. I recapitulate the four great cultural periods he defines: the mythological, which flourished on the shores of the Pacific and Indian oceans; the religious, whose domain is western Asia; the philosophical, which began in the western Mediterranean before spreading throughout Europe; and the techno-economist, whose domain is the Atlantic, and which was initiated by French rationalism, English realism and North-American materialism. This age is now coming to its end, and the time has come to move towards and into another cultural space. Since a world-economy is now, more or less, in place, this culture must be a world-culture, and it will have two main characteristics: on the one hand, it will mean the orchestration of all cultures, an original synthesis; and on the other, the ability to move away from the 'slavery of fact' to the 'liberty of the real', which means a disengaging of the mind from rationalism, realism and materialism, and an openness to direct apprehension.

Traces of a cartography and a programme such as this can be found at least sporadically in writers round the world.

Here's Harry Martinson, in his *Aimless Travels*, moving between Stockholm, Montevideo and Cape Farewell: 'In what unheard of intimacy of exchange does man live on earth! And how the earth breathes through him! My own travels have been too accidental, too much the movements of a will-o'-the-wisp, to provide anything more than chaotic impressions. But I know at least a bit about multiple life on earth.'

Rambling also from harbour to harbour, Pierre MacOrlan practises what I'd call picturesque geopoetics. Blaise Cendrars' geopoetics are more energetic, more projective, but the tough guy with the million-dollar deals tends to take over from the intellectual nomad. There are aspects of geopoetics also in Saint-John Perse, Ezra Pound, T.S. Eliot, René Char, Charles Olson, Rainer Maria Rilke, Henri Michaux, and many others. But, after readings and re-readings, one dreams of a Whitman free of naïve progressivism and less burdened with Spirit and Self; of a Saint-John Perse with less rhetoric; of a more extroverted Michaux; of a Pound out of history and ego; of a T.S. Eliot out of the wasteland without enclosing himself in religious structures; of a René Char less knotted; of a more coherent Olson; of a Rilke who's moved beyond the elegiac, etc.

In short, as MacOrlan says in *The Little Bell of the Sorbonne*: 'Poetic geography is still in the making.'

That's what I've been working at. That's what geopoetics is all about.

9

'Production as process cannot be contained in ideal categories', declare Deleuze and Guattari in *The Anti-Oedipus*. And in *A Thousand Plateaux*, a whole sequence of phrases attempts to define a 'nomadic' type of writing: 'writing has nothing to do with meaning, but everything to do with serpentine movement and cartography'; 'a book has no object and no subject, it is made up of variously formed matters, written at different times, at different speeds. If you attribute a book to a subject, you're neglecting this work in its matter and its exterior nature. You set up a Lord God in the place of geological movements'; 'writing will never be done enough in the name of the Outside. The Outside has no image, no meaning, no subjectivity'; 'establish relations in the heterogeneous'; 'to augment one's territory by deterritorialisation, to prolong the line of flight till it becomes an abstract machine extending over the whole plane of consistency'; 'to produce the most tortuous and the most abstract line, with n dimensions and broken directions'...

This is exciting, and if a certain hypermodern feverishness may attach to it, in its haste to get out of what Nietzsche called 'corpse-books', this can be tempered through recourse to cultural spaces outwith the hypermodern West, where a similar kind of writing was practised, but without fever-heat.

In *The Spirit of Tao*, Jean Grenier evokes 'the loose texture' of the Indian epic and, especially, 'the literary form adopted by the great taoïsts', which makes fun of heavy logic, moves rapidly through multiple spaces and mixes up all the genres. What I'm suggesting is that a passage through 'the exotic' (with no attachment to any exotic orthodoxy) might help the post-hasteness of the post-modern not to fall over its own feet.

Then, there's the question of residence. For Deleuze and Guattari, as for Baudrillard, this is not a question: concerned with flight from constrictions, stifling enclosures, and with a line of flight anxious only to flee farther and farther, beyond all

164

emplacement, into a dimensionless abstract, they are like men who leave a motel to hop onto a jet. Heidegger is the opposite. He is much concerned with residence, dwelling, with quiet paths of thought around a well-felt place, which can border on localist pietism and *Heimat* ideology.

Might it be possible to conceive of a 'great residence' that would reconcile movements and things, removing and remaining, stravaiging and staying?

That's what I think I see in the twentieth chapter of the *Chuang-tzu*, where we hear of someone who 'can stretch out like a dragon and remain folded in himself like a snake'. And in Rinzai's text concerning the real man without situation: 'He's on the road, yet he hasn't left the house. He's in the house, yet he hasn't left the road.'

10

Very often, in this house on the Breton coast, I take a trip on a snowboat.

I'm referring to the landscape-scroll painted by Sesshu (literally: snowboat) in 1486. The original is about seventeen metres long, but I read it in a reduced version put out by Tuttle of Tokyo.

I like that name 'snow-boat'. According to the story, Sesshu got it when he left China, where, while buying up Chinese paintings for Japan, he had been engaged in various studies for the pursuit of his own work. When departure time came, so many people on the pier threw farewell poems on to his boat that it was as though 'covered in snow'. That's the story, but if Sesshu kept that name, I think it's because he had other things in mind. 'Snow-boat' – the word evokes one who moves at ease in a turmoil, one who is at home in a moving white space. Doesn't every artist, every writer with some sense of a high dimension, live in a snow-boat that sails among white flakes, I mean white sheets of paper, knowing one day he'll disappear into a white ocean of silence? But this is divagation. Let's come back to the actual scroll.

An inscription at the beginning states: 'This scroll was painted by old Toyo Sesshu, who once held the First Chair at the Tendo temple, one quiet day of his sixty-seventh year.'

It's difficult to believe that Sesshu really painted those seventeen metres in one day. Maybe we should think of a 'great day', one of those lengths of concentrated work that last more than twelve or twenty-four hours.

The journey begins in Spring: abrupt rocks, trees clinging to a cliff, temples bathed in mist. On the road, a baggage-carrier and a travelling monk. Between this scene and the next, a flood of misty whiteness. Then more trees, twisted, eccentric, useless for anything, just marvellously there. And another meditative monk, followed by his disciple or his servant. They're skirting a turbulent mountain-stream, maybe about to cross it. If anyone is tempted to speak of Zen, let him hold his tongue. We are travelling. Here's a harbour. It's a beautiful Summer morning: fine-lined boats, the undulation of waves, and the open sea, white and empty. Over there beneath the willow, an inn where we can drink tea or sake together. And then we go back into the white space, till we come to steep cliffs and pine trees dancing on the edge of nothingness. A Chinese pagoda there. And then more rocks, trees, temples, and two people meeting on the road, and two others sitting in a roadside kiosk looking at the landscape. Emptiness again, then, for a few miles, a few days. And we plunge into Autumn: fantastic rocks, all kinds of foliage, and boats, but quieter now, less animated. We cross a bridge, alongside two monks and a baggage-carrier, see more rocks, more trees, more temples - and an inn, a popular inn where (a flag-advertisement proclaims it) they sell good wine. After which we go back into the solitude: misty forests, and the first snows, the first of the great snows that will finally cover the entire landscape. It is Winter, it is silence, it is, at last, the Great Residence.

Ahhh...

PART III

A Cultural Project

The White Bag of Books

A lamp in the dark, a compass for the longest journey.
(Mongol definition of a book)

1

At the age of fourteen, my favourite poem was Matthew Arnold's 'The Scholar Gypsy', of which I'll quote just one stanza out of the twenty-five:

> And once, in winter, on the causeway chill
> Where home through flooded fields foot-travellers go,
> Have I not pass'd thee on the wooden bridge
> Wrapt in thy cloak and battling with the snow,
> Thy face towards Hinksey and its wintry ridge?
> And thou hast climb'd the hill,
> And gain'd the white brow of the Cumner range,
> Turn'd once to watch, while thick the snow-flakes fall,
> The line of festal light in Christ-Church hall –
> Then sought thy straw in some sequester'd grange.

The setting of that poem is Oxfordshire, but it took no great effort for me to translate it into my own Ayrshire context: it was important enough for me to want to import it. Thus, when I read 'Cumner', I thought 'Cumnock'. 'Hinksey and its wintry ridge', was, for me, the Kaim Hill, rising up there over Fairlie, maybe the piled-up remains of a glacier's edge. As for Christ-Church, it was the parish church of St Paul's, down there at the foot of the Craigie.

Not only was my topography taking on poetic density, something which I consider fundamental for anything like a well-founded life, a well-grounded culture, but my mind was expanding, with that kind of expansion, expansiveness, which is the characteristic of any live, open, radiating mindscape.

I'm talking about a 'well-grounded culture', no easy notion, and one which, in the present amorphous context, may seem anachronistic: too radical for relevance, the kind of question nobody dare broach any more. But around 1870 in Britain, it was *the* question, and Matthew Arnold (along with Carlyle and Ruskin in Britain, Nietzsche in Germany) was in the forefront

169

of the debate, with essay-books such as *Essays in Criticism* (1865), *Culture and Anarchy* (1869), *Literature and Dogma* (1873), and individual essays with wide-ranging themes such as 'Hebraism and Hellenism', or 'Barbarians, Philistines, Populace'.

It was Arnold who introduced the word 'philistine' to the English language, borrowing it from the German, saying that, if there was no word for this attitude of mind in Britain, it was because philistinism there was not something to be remarked on, and designated, it was ingrained, endemic.

If 'philistine', in Arnold's vocabulary, was a general term, it applied in particular to the Middle Class, flanked on one side by the Aristocrats (those Arnold called 'Barbarians') and on the other by the Proletariat (those he called 'the Populace'). Arnold had no admiration for the Barbarians, no truck with the Philistines, and no liking (though perhaps some sympathy) for the Populace. Under a general slogan of Prosperity and Liberty, terms not in themselves repugnant, the whole context was given over to money-grabbing and an ethos of do-as-you-like. On this population marked by ruthless greed, bumptious complacency, self-satisfied knownothingism, brutal uncouthness were dumped every day tons of commonplace and triviality thanks to the *Daily Drivel* and other such products emanating from Fleet Street and Grub Street institutions.

What could be done, what world could emerge, from such a huge, lumpy, mushy mess?

Before this massification took place, two cultural currents had had an enlivening, enlightening force on civilization: the Hebraic and the Hellenic. But if the Reformation had meant moral energy and a moral superiority over a decadent Catholicism, it had lost on the intellectual plane, and had degenerated into mindless Bible-thumping and pathetic soul-saving, not to speak of all kinds of psychological perversion and moral hypocrisy. If the Renaissance had meant a return to Greece, it was mostly mythology and trappings it had taken over, all the quick, keen flexibility of the Greek mind as manifested by the Dorian tribes of Hellas or the Asiatic Greeks of Ionia becoming a stucco kind of aesthetic idealism, destined for the façades of banks.

Arnold looked in the final instance to individuals – individuals who would emerge from all the classes. They would carry with them a wider intellectual horizon, a whole new range of thought and feeling, and convey some notion of harmonious development. But if they were to have *world-*effect, they would have to be backed up by education – an education for value rather than simply use. And education would have to be backed up by politics – a politics that would be more than simply representation followed up by accommodation, followed by... well, you know the way it so often goes.

That was what I got, in my own intellectual translation, from Arnold's essays as I read them on the top of the Craigie Rock in Fairlie, my favourite vantage-point.

With an addendum concerning the people to whom I belonged. When Arnold spoke of 'the Populace', I didn't hear 'the people'. A populace is a people bludgeoned into insensibility by circumstance. I'd read enough to know that a people, as people, can be demanding. In the old days, in Scotland, a bad harper playing among the clachans would be invited to go away and cut his nails, stop plucking cacophonous hell out of an innocent instrument. And when John Francis Campbell was gathering his popular tales of the West Highlands in the mid-nineteenth century, he met an old man with sharp wits and a fine sense of things who told him that, when the old tales had been turned into novelistic literature, they had lost all their quickness and depth. That old man was speaking of a people that hadn't lost its genius.

The examples I've just quoted are from Scoto-Celtic culture. And I must note in the present context that Arnold's essay on Celtic poetry was one of my first initiations into that field, which I have explored pretty thoroughly since.

But to come back to 'The Scholar Gypsy'.

A few years later than my Craigie Rock days, in an essay on Arnold's poem by G. Wilson Knight, I saw it described as 'the greatest educational document in the language'. I could go a long way with that, it was certainly true in my own itinerary. Wilson Knight specified its significance by saying that it 'confronts our Western tradition with suggestions of a wisdom, lore or magic of oriental affinities or origin'. I found Wilson Knight's vocabulary ('wisdom, lore, magic') more than a bit specious – it was going to take me many more years to work out my own. But there were lines there to follow up.

Matthew Arnold's 'Scholar Gypsy' led me to George Borrow's *Lavengro* (gypsy for 'Word Master'), which I picked up at a bookshop in the white-walled, west-windy town of Largs. When I say 'led me to', I don't mean anything like direct reference. But once the mind begins to drift in a certain way, it finds appropriate ports of call, the right things turn up. Borrow, for me, was one of them.

George Borrow was born, 1803, in Norfolk, his father a Cornishman, his mother of French descent. As a soldier in the West Norfolk Militia, Borrow's father was stationed for a while in Edinburgh, where George was at school (Edinburgh High) from the age of 10 to 12. He early on showed a love of languages and by his twenties had a good knowledge, not only of Latin, Greek and Hebrew, but of Welsh, Irish, French, Italian, Spanish, Portuguese, German, Danish – and Romani, which he had picked up, after his escape from a solicitor's firm, as he travelled with gypsies around England and along the margins of wild Wales. By the early thirties, he was in southern Europe, working for the Bible Society. Around 1832, he was in Russia, where, of course, he picked up Russian, but also a good smattering of Manchu. By 1842, he was back on the Iberian Peninsula, from where he published *The Bible in Spain*, which was a big success (because of the Bible). *Lavengro*, a finer book, came out in 1851, and sank like a stone, being too far out of the habitual context. Feeling more and more estranged from the established literary scene and the normal culture-world, Borrow spent his last days (he died in 1881) wandering about Cornwall and Wales, before holing up in a cottage near Lowestoft, surrounded by a polyglot library, from which passers-by would hear him chanting poems to himself in all kinds of languages.

Borrow's *Lavengro* awoke in me a latent propensity for the exploration of language – and of all kinds of logic.

It's never been my ambition to be able to say: 'Please give me a cup of tea' in ninety-nine languages. That kind of enterprise reminds me of Napoleon's remark after a meeting with the foremost linguist of his day: 'There goes a fifty-tongued fool.' But the depth-exploration of language, the attempt to get at fundamental structures, fascinates me.

I'll adduce here only one example of what I mean.

At one point in *Lavengro*, Borrow reports a conversation with a gypsy-woman: 'She told me the word for leaf was *patteran*, which our people [the gypsies] use now for 'trail', having forgotten the true meaning. She said that the trail was called *patteran* because the gypsies of old were in the habit of making the marks with the leaves of branches and trees, placed in a certain manner.'

When I looked up the word *patteran* in John Sampson's Romani dictionary (found on a book-barrow in Buchanan Street, Glasgow – it cost me a few weeks' pocket money), where it's listed as *patrin*, I learned that it came from the sanskrit *pattra*, meaning 'wing, feather, leaf'.

Leaf-strewn paths began to take on a great deal more significance for me. And from leaf-trail I went on to a field of fluttering signs, from *patteran* as trail to 'pattern'.

Moving from field to field, I was following out paths, looking for a *pattern*, that is, an organization that avoids two things: a floppy incoherence on the one hand, and a constrictive cohesion on the other.

There's a poetics there (pattern, poetry – cognates?), an aesthetics, a method of thought, a principle of organization.

It's the image of a world.

Out of that original territory, and from territory to territory, it's always world I'm trying to get at, to work my way into. World, that is, an area beyond the person, beyond the social context: a space of general being.

It was this preoccupation with 'world' that led me to 'New World' writing. There in Ayrshire, at school, I was fed on Burns. I did not dislike Burns. I must have written about fifty imitations of him. But Burns never meant so much to me as Whitman, Emerson, or Thoreau. They corresponded to my context at a deeper level.

On my father's bookshelves stood a small book bound in leaf-green leather, again bought off a book-barrow in Glasgow. This was volume III of a five-volume edition of the works of Ralph Waldo Emerson, containing essays such as 'The American Scholar', 'Society and Solitude', 'The Method of Nature'. They allowed me to become more articulate on certain specific points, provided me with a larger frame of reference, and gave some contour to my gradually enlargening sense of things.

Protestant to the core, I suppose (and pushing the Protestant urge to its logical conclusion: a protest against Protestantism), I was moving out from my Scottish-Protestant background, and Transcendentalism, among other things, was that kind of moving-out. Intellectually, morally and aesthetically, it meant the passing of boundaries, the breaking out of a system of relations that had become too fixed and narrow, with an unlimited faith in human possibilities – 'we have never seen a man', said Emerson. With no rules to respect, no religion to adhere to, no society to hem it in, Transcendentalism is largely the monologue of an ecstatic soul, a soul expanded to cosmic dimensions – which is what Emerson called the Oversoul. The question for these 'come-outers', was to realize the 'Oversoul' in oneself. This realization was the transcendental experience.

If Transcendentalism supplied me with a whole cosmos of ideas, the man who concentrated that cosmos in his person ('seldom has a head circumscribed so much of the sense and core of cosmos as this footed intelligence', wrote Amos Alcott of him), and carried it with him while he followed the Indian trails through the woods, or watched the ice melt on Walden pond, was Henry Thoreau. Again, seminal phrases, like voluntaries or preludes indicating an activity of the whole being which I still only vaguely apprehended, but which attracted me and filled me with exaltation: 'The landscape, when it is truly seen, reacts on the life of the seer. How to live. How to get the most life.'

As to Walt Whitman, the other American much read at this time, the Hegel of Manhattan, the contemplator of chaos in Colorado, the poet ready to discard all the trappings of poetry in order to express 'the undulation of a wave', he gave me not only a tremendous sense of liberation, but an increased sensation of the world, as in 'Song of Myself':

> *The wild gander leads his flock through the cool night,*
> Ya-honk *he says, and sounds it down to me like an invitation,*
> *The pert may suppose it meaningless, but I listening close,*
> *Find its purpose and place up there toward the wintry sky.*

We might say that with Emerson I found a world of ideas, the central idea being that of ecstatic, or enstatic unity; with Thoreau, a man following his own absolute way, living an utterly uncluttered life; and with Whitman, an open road and the poetry of the cosmos.

And it was all linked to my direct experience up there in the back-country of Fairlie: starting from the hawthorn-lined path by the Craigie Rock, then across the fields, through the woods, over the moors, up by the Kaim, away towards Blaeloch Hill. Up there on the Fairlie moors, I sometimes felt totally out of time, as much as on the steppes of Tartary. There would be a wind blowing. Maybe the single cry of a bird. A great space, a great silence. My presence in it was unwonted, maybe, I felt at times, unwanted. I just kept following those paths, listening in to the many and the one. I wasn't projecting imagination on to it, I wasn't trying to translate it into what I already knew. I was trying to translate myself into its undefined being, its archaic newness.

2

I came up to Glasgow, the University of Glasgow, with great expectations and great demands. I had in mind Whitman's injunction in his poem 'By Blue Ontario's Shore' to one who would be 'a poet and teacher':

Have you studied out the land, its idioms and men?
Have you learn'd the physiology, phrenology, politics, geography,
*   pride, freedom, friendship of the land? its substratums and*
*   objects?*

I'm always grateful to anyone who can teach me anything, but I soon realized that, for the essential as I saw it, I was going to be more or less on my own.

I did a lot of lone-wolfing in Glasgow. I don't think anyone ever did more lone-wolfing in Glasgow than myself. I wandered about Glasgow the way, shall we say, Rimbaud wandered about Paris, the way Herman Hesse wandered about Munich, the way Rilke wandered about Prague.

In the area of the Trongate, Glasgow, there used to be a café called The White Tower. Around 1954, there could be seen a young fellow sitting in there, reading *Sartor Resartus*. It was me.

Carlyle's grim grotesquerie, after his reading of the 'Signs of the Times', was a good counterweight to the more vapid flights of Emersonian idealism. If he also was a transcendentalist (American Transcendentalism, indeed American literature, grew largely out of Carlyle's correspondence with Emerson, who'd read his translations of the German Romantics), he insisted also, as did Herman Melville, on the necessity for an effective transcendentalist of a good dose of descendentalism. I went with that.

I know all that can be said against Carlyle. I know that, exasperated by the cultural confusion he saw around him, he turned himself at times into an apologist of the most ferocious authoritarianism. But he did speak of the 'man of letters' as a hero ('writing and teaching heroes' – Melville spoke of 'onto-logical heroes'), and I liked the transcendental humour of that caricature of the intellectual in the Modern Age, Teufelsdröckh, professor of 'all kinds of things' in the University of God-knows-where, whom he'd created after six years of concen-trated sequestration at Craigenputtock, of which he wrote in a letter to John Stuart Mill saying that no philosopher in the world was leading an existence like his: he'd walk for miles along the Glaister Hillside, from where he had a view over the granite lands of Galloway and over into Ayrshire. It was an austere vision. But desolation and solitude were the most eternal things, and in such a Patmos a man could write an Apocalypse.

Wandering about the streets of Glasgow, 'like a wild Ishmaelite' (as Carlyle describes the really radical and per-spectivist writer), I felt a bit apocalyptical myself, and Carlyle's description of Teufelsdröckh's study in the 'street of illusions' coincided pretty well with my Glasgow lodgings: 'To dwell here. These fringes of lamplight, struggling up through smoke... Oh, under that hideous coverlet of vapors, and putrefactions, and inimaginable gases, what a fermenting vat lies simmering and hid!'

It was as a student in Glasgow that I began to think of writing, and the figure that bulked largest on my immediate literary horizon then was that of James Joyce. I wrote a couple of manuscripts at that time situated somewhere between *Dubliners* and *Portrait of the Artist*. But the two books that really raised future-orientated questions in my mind were *Ulysses* and *Finnegans Wake*.

Everybody here will remember the opening of *Ulysses*, in that Martello tower overlooking Dublin Bay. Amid evocations of snot and bile, which give a glaucous, slimy, acidy green tone to the whole context, Stephen Daedalus, with the winged name, who, like some migratory bird, would like to fly off into some space beyond the nightmare of history, is in conversation with Buck Mulligan. Mulligan looks to a Greek-based Renaissance in Ireland, hoping for some Plato of the pubs, some Aeschylus of the bogs. Stephen is, to say the least, sceptical. Later they are joined by Haines, the Englishman. Haines has a bee in his Eirophile bonnet about Gaelic, which he is busily learning, looking forward to a Celtic Renaissance based on ethnic piety and picturesque folksiness rather than on anything like intellectual, poetic or cultural energy. Stephen is, understandably, even more sceptical.

In then come Bloom and his wife Molly. With Stephen, they constitute a trio that reduplicates Joseph, Mary and Jesus Christ. So you have a Christian paradigm, with Dublin as Bethlehem (let's say: Bedleyham), presiding over a Greek periplus (all the episodes in the book, it will be remembered, correspond to episodes in the *Odyssey*), which makes it all a scholarly, goliardy, music-hall caricature of Western civilization.

With *Finnegans Wake*, we don't go farther, but we go, vertiginously, deeper.

Finnegans Wake is a mytheological, metafuzzical, foolosophical compendium. Written by and for a myopic, microscopical insomniac, it's a babeldom that puts all noveldom in the shade, that puts culture, with a sardonic laugh, in a cul-de-sac.

A lot of Joyce I later put aside as intestinal rather than inspirational. I saw his work more as a summing-up than as anything like a pathfinding. Joyce's 'funferal' (funereal fun-for-all) of culture was of culture as it had been till then: based on myth, religion, metaphysics, history. Might it be possible to get outside of all those, without falling into the platitudinous, redundant, numbly nihilistic reproductions of a blasted social reality, or mere fantasy?

Work, evolve from another ground?

Was it possible to do anything more than work with tail-ends, scraps, leftovers, 'spiced', shall we say, with more and more snot and bile; can 'begin again' (Finnegan's final message) mean something more than just a re-cycling of the same old stuff?

That was the question I'd put to myself as I'd walk some Saturday or other from my digs in Scotstoun, crossing the Clyde on the Whiteinch ferry, down to Fairlie via the Kilbirnie road and over the moors, with, on my mind, those last words of *Finnegans Wake*: 'A gull. Gulls. Far calls. Coming, far! End here. Us then. Finn, again!.. The keys to. Given. A way a lone a last a loved a long the...'

By my second year at Glasgow University, it was in the work of Nietzsche I was plunged. The movement may seem haphazard, the connections not obvious, but (I realize it with hindsight more and more) there was a hidden logic to it all. In a letter written towards the end of his life, Nietzsche says the only writer he could read any more was Emerson, and he had read Carlyle thoroughly: Nietzsche's 'Overman' is a development of Carlyle's 'Hero' – but although he sometimes expressed them in a brutally provocative way, Nietzsche's conceptions are finer.

'We want to be the poets of our life!' Nietzsche had cried, and I was listening. It was after a breakaway from regular civic life that Nietzsche – moving from room to room, from place to place (southern France, the Ligurian coast of Italy, the Engadine plateau in Switzerland) – wrote his books, those books of essays, attempts, trials, trying to get right back into the ground of existence, and from there open up new space.

3

Concerning the existential strategy, the social tactics of the really radical writer and intellectual, Joyce said it was a question of silence, exile and cunning. That's pretty well how I've lived.

My stance may seem highly individualistic. It is. I submit that it's with individuals (individuals who have concentrated in their work-field the maximum of general energies and elements) that the really significant developments begin. It's the individual who has taken the time and the pains to develop his/her life and thought who has, in the long run, on the long view, in the last analysis, the most to offer society in general.

As to the specific literary-cultural scene, it is, to say the least, confused. I don't want to waste time characterizing, far less criticizing, the various types of glit-lit or shit-lit that go the commercial rounds. Space is devoted in our 'cultural' journals to the relative merits of X and Y, where, in an even slightly more demanding scale, neither would be seen as meriting attention at all.

At a time when more clarity and precision was demanded, and current, in this field, Virgil the Grammarian (Virgilius Maro Grammaticus), born in France, maybe at Toulouse, but who spent a good deal of his working life in Ireland, laid out, in the seventh century, a list of the 'arts' as they were practised in 'our tradition of learning'. That list went from *geometria* to *poema*, via *rhetoria*, *grama*, *leporia* and *dialecta*. The meaning of most of these Latin terms is more or less self-evident – except maybe for *leporia*. This was a kind of mixed prose, with a very complex interweaving of language, involving several idioms: Celtic (Brythonic or Gaelic), Latin, Greek and Hebrew. Called 'Asianism', this practice was first developed in Africa before it came out of the Mediterranean, worked its way round Spain and then along the west coast of Britain. A lot of it was done on Iona. The *Altus prosator* attributed to Columba may be said to belong to this tradition. The texts composed in seventh-century Ireland called the *Hisperica famina* certainly do. These were intricate scholarly exercises (*Finnegans Wake* I see as a hypermodernist version of them) performed at the ultimate stage of a scholar's education, just before learning (*filosofia*, in the vocabulary of Isidorus of Seville, another mind to my liking) turned into poetry. Here's an example, a hisperic text on the sea where a pearly poetry is palpable in the contorted, multi-levelled, oysterish Latin:

> *hoc spumans mundanas obvallat pelagus oras*
> *terrestres anniosis fluctibus cudit margines*
> *saxeas undosis molibus irruit aulonias*

which, Englished, would give something like this:

> the spuming sea spirals round the shores of the world
> it pounds its ancient tides against the edge of the land
> it rushes piles of water into every rocky pool

A text such as this, like the *Altus Prosator*, tied in both with my early experiences on the moors and the coast of Ayrshire, and also contained elements (elementary force, linguistic flexibility) I would use in my own work, with other perspectives.

Before going on, a word as to my reference to seventh-century Scoto-Celtic culture, as elsewhere to Greek thought of the fifth century BC, or Chinese poetics of the thirteenth century. No writer of any scope nowadays is restricted to contemporaneity, is strictly contemporary. For the first time in the history of humanity, we have practically the whole of world-culture at our disposal. Very little use is made of it, except in terms of erudition and cultural history programmes, but it is there, for the intellectual nomad, for the world-poet, as a field of reference, as a hoard of elements, to be recomposed, reactualized.

To come back to Virgil the Grammarian and others like him, the satchel in which the travelling monks carried their books was described as 'the white bag that gleams' (*alborea taberna*). Maybe it's appropriate for me now to talk a bit about the books I've been bringing back, after long peregrinations and investigations, in my own 'white bag', and about the type of writing they contain.

The writing has its basis in a relationship to what the Greeks called *phusis*, what Aristotle in his *Metaphysics* calls 'what is present in presence' and what John Scot Erigena in his *Periphyseon* describes as 'all that is and all that is not'. That last phrase is startling, setting the great field of things in the even greater space of the void. I consider that without this fundamental relationship not only is intellection limited, but the mind is mutilated.

Thereafter, it's open system writing (open world writing, if you like), working on a triple expansion process of *eros* (energy in movement), *logos* (gathering together what's there, finding adequate language) and *cosmos* (the composition of unities).

This writing takes place in three types of books: poem-books, a kind of prose-book I call waybook (neither novel, nor 'travel-writing'), and essay-books.

The poetry is cosmo-poetic, based on a sensation of space, working out configuration in space. The waybooks follow paths and roads – as well as pursuing territorial investigation, they constitute an *itinerarium mentis* (an intellectual path). As to the essays, they are cartography.

When a poet writes prose, this doesn't imply a slackening of mental energy, nor does it mean 'poetic prose' (something I personally loathe) – what you'll get in the best cases is a style with more liveliness and audacity, more breaks, opening, projections than you find in ordinary prose. Likewise, when a poet's poetry and prose are at all significant, they will tend to push his essay-writing into the shade. But I consider Milton's *Areopagitica* to be every bit as important as his *Lycidas*. And there are poet's essays that, in their philosophical import, go beyond the philosophy of the philosophers.

It is possible to advance on the poetry front, the prose front and the thought front at one and the same time, ranging over a wide, composite field.

That's exactly what I have tried to do.

The New Europe

We are beginning to discover the deepest antinomy of all. It looks as if we're going to see a conflict between the model and the way. This conflict will be theoretical and practical, philosophical and political.

(Henri Lefebvre)

1

What I want to do in the first place is present a general outline of the *idea* of Europe, and of the various ways that idea has been carried throughout European history.

It is not perhaps totally useless to linger a while by the original myth, as recounted, say, by Ovid in his *Metamorphoses*.

According to this story, Europa was a Phoenician princess, daughter of the King of Tyre, who was carried off by Zeus in the guise of a white bull to Crete, where she became the mother of Minos. What the story, with its abduction and journey from East to West is saying, is, first, how much Europe (Minoan civilization, in Crete, to start with, later Mycenean and the others) owes to Asia (Europa's brother Cadmus, who went over the wide world in search of her is said to have brought the art of writing to Greece) and at the same time how much it wants to start out anew. What we have too in the image of the white bull, the sea-journey, and the fluttering of the girl's dress in the sun and the wind (*tremulae sinuantur flamine vestes*) is a combination of earth-power, world movement and mental agitation. Without wanting to read *too* much into it, I'd suggest that a good few of the characteristics we might call European are contained in that image. Fundamental European energy is a mix of *eros*, *logos* and *cosmos*.

After a Greek start, in an open archipelago, then in city-states, Europe was Roman.

Here we go from legend to legions, for, in its beginnings at least, the *orbis romanus* was a question of military power – unity, if it was to come, had to come through violence. Military marches, military camps, military roads extended the empire from Rome outwards, pushing the frontier farther and farther

182

forward. When Agricola, who was from Fréjus (*Forum Julii*) in the south of Gaul, invaded Britain, he had with him four full legions: the 2nd Augusta, the 14th Gemina Martia, the 20th Valeria Victrix and the 9th Hispania, along with a good number of auxiliaries, making for something like 40,000 troops in all. The campaign was efficient and ruthless. One Celtic chief (Calgacus) commented: 'They make a desert and call it peace.' But there were benefits: books, wine, baths – and a language that could be understood from land to land, across all borders. It might take some time for the Caledonians looking at the line of forts between the Forth and Clyde, the Roman Empire's north-west frontier, to be convinced of this, but they were there.

If the first attempt at European unity was military, the second was mystic and religious. That was Christianity, which equated Europe with Christendom. Again, although there are obviously non-Christian strands in what can be called European culture (a pre-Christian substratum, and the Renaissance was rumbustiously neo-pagan), although, since at least the eighteenth century, many if not most of the best minds in Europe have been totally atheistic, nobody will easily reject the value of Christianity-Christendom, the *res publica christiana*. For many, even when gone, it will be a nostalgia and a reference. I'm thinking there, for example of Novalis' essay of 1799, *Die Christenheit oder Europa* ('Christianity or Europe'), which begins, splendidly, thus:

> Those were beautiful, brilliant times, when Europe was a Christian land, when this continent of humanity was infused by one single Christianity. One great common interest bound together the farthest-flung provinces of this wide spiritual empire.

Then in a duller, more repetitive way, but with the same ideological, historico-cultural emphasis, there are T. S. Eliot's *Notes towards the Definition of Culture* (1948):

> To our Christian heritage we owe many things beside religious faith. Through it we trace the evolution of our arts, through it we have our conception of Roman Law which has done so much to shape the Western World, through it we have our conceptions of private and public morality. And through it we

have our common standards of literature, in the literatures of
Greece and Rome. The Western World has its unity in this
heritage, in Christianity and in the ancient civilizations of
Greece, Rome and Israel, from which, owing to two thousand
years of Christianity, we trace our descent.

Before moving to a more paradoxical field and to the paths of
what we might call *erratic* Europe, mention must be made at
least in passing to the two most recent attempts at massive,
monolithic unification. I'm referring here of course to Fascism
and Communism. Whether it was Mussolini's dream of a new
Roman Empire, or Hitler's Third Reich, the New Order had
plans for a *Nation Europa* that would have made Agricola look
like a gentleman farmer or a tourist in a khaki toga. As to
Communism, if it started out with a ferociously intelligent
criticism of ideology (the 'decomposition of the absolute'), an
investigation into the dialectics of nature, and a generous social
vision, it pretty soon degenerated into the most formidable
man and mind killing machine that Europe has ever known.

2

I come now to what I've called erratic Europe and the
paradoxical field.

This begins with that period in European culture-history,
between, roughly, 1680 and 1715, that Paul Hazard, in his book
of 1935, calls 'the crisis in the European mind' (*La crise de la
conscience européenne*). The writers concerned (*héros de l'esprit*,
Hazard calls them, 'intellectual heroes') are Spinoza, Locke,
Leibniz, Fénelon, Malebranche, Fontenelle, Bayle. We've left
the sophisticated formalities and the perfectionist formalisms
of the Classical Age and haven't yet entered into the systematic
Enlightenment. It's an 'ill-defined, uncertain zone', full of
masses of ideas in movement being noted down and composed
at lightning speed. The accent is on variety and diversity (think
of Fontenelle's *Entretien sur la pluralité des mondes*, 'Essay on
the plurality of worlds'), but always with a tendency towards
some as yet undefined unity: *utique delectat nos varietas, sed
reducta in unitatem* ('variety delights us, but we must compose
it into unity'), writes Leibniz. Leibniz travels (through Germany,
France, England, Holland, Italy), studies, meditates, writes

and writes and writes – always with a paradoxical unity in mind: the unity of Europe (*status Europae incipiente novo saeculo*, 'the status of Europe at the start of the new century'), but also a unity of thought such as Aristotle knew but in an infinitely more complex context. Historical and critical dictionaries abound, essays on the workings of the human mind, as well as books of travel (*ce genre littéraire aux frontières indécises*, says Hazard, 'a type of literature with fluctuant boundaries'), as though what was sought after was a new mental geography.

None of all this was uniquely French, but it was concentrated in France, and from France it radiated out all over Europe. Which is why in 1776 Caracciolo, an Italian, could bring out a book entitled *L'Europe française*. Europe was French, France was considered the incarnation of European culture, from the final years of the seventeenth century up to 1815. That year saw the French wave waterloo'd. It may be a pity. Napoleon's attempt, applauded by such deep and wide-ranging minds as Goethe and, later, Nietzsche, was France's endeavour to unite Europe (including Russia), politically and culturally, *militari manu*. It failed. The great wave built up by the Crisis, by Enlightenment, by the Revolution of '89, receded, leaving Europe like a great stretch of deserted sand. But that wave did not die – it only faded, shall we say, into the intellectual-poetic sphere. I have no truck with Franco-French nationalistic chauvinism, I have no sympathy with French cultural complacency, but, as a Scot, as an erratic European, as a cosmological (an erotocosmological) poet, a chord in me vibrates deeply in relation to a French line that goes, shall we say, from Montaigne, through Diderot, to Rimbaud.

It's not a French historian, it's not a Euro-Franco-Scottish poet, but an *English* historian (Norman Davies, *A History of Europe*, Oxford University Press, 1996) who describes the culture of France as 'the most influential and the most universal culture of the continent'.

That's why, as a European Scot, I chose to work from that context.

3

The collapse of the Roman Empire meant the incursion on to the cultural map of Europe of all those barbarian peoples – Celts, Scythians, Sarmatians – stravaiging over plain and mountain at the north-eastern, north-western frontiers of the Greco-Roman world, subsumed generally under the name 'Hyperboreans'. The break-up of the Holy Roman-Catholic Empire meant the rise of the modern nation-states, all quarrelling and bickering, ready to go to noisy and bloody war at the flickering of the slightest rag of a flag.

There was every reason to despair.

And yet.

Summing up his book on 'the crisis in the European mind', and trying to answer the question: 'What is Europe?' Paul Hazard draws up a list of definitions concerning context and concept: 'Neighbours ready to fly at one another on the slightest provocation' (*un acharnement de voisins qui se battent*), 'tormented territories, areas of discord and jealousy' (*terres tourmentées, terres de discordes et de jalousies*), 'a form full of contradiction, both strict and uncertain' (*une forme contradictoire, à la fois stricte et incertaine*), 'a power of thought never content' (*une pensée qui ne se contente jamais*). He then concludes by saying that if there are some peoples on earth who are content to live without asking questions, without thinking, others with no inventive power who simply copy, imitate, reproduce, what distinguishes Europe is its unceasing research, its unending curiosity. And Hazard quotes Fontenelle: 'There's a certain genius, which has never existed anywhere but in Europe.' (*Il y a un certain génie qui n'a point encore été hors de notre Europe*).

From now on, Europe has no mythical or metaphysical foundation, no religious connotation, no canon and no cannon, it is only (only?) a drifting genius.

4

Intellectual investigation, ideological debate, hypothetical projection went on, sometimes in flurries, at a rapid rate, at other times in a more spaced-out kind of way.

In the absence of an Absolute Ideal (that of Christendom), there was a great deal of idealism and even theological tele- ology. I'm thinking there of Guizot's series of lectures at the Sorbonne (1828–1830), *Histoire de la civilisation en Europe*, where we are told that 'European civilization has entered into the realm of eternal truth and is firmly set on the plane of Providence.' It was too much. To this metaphysics, I prefer by far the notion put forward as early as 1767 by Mercier de la Rivière in his *L'ordre naturel et essentiel des sociétés*: that the unity of Europe is not part of a Grand Design, not an idealistic programme, but 'a physical necessity'.

On the more strictly defined political sphere, there was Aristide Briand, an ardent spokesman for European union, saying this before the General Assembly of the League of Nations, at Geneva, on 5 September 1929: 'I think that among peoples constituting geographical groups, such as the peoples of Europe, there should be some kind of federal bond. Obviously, this association will be primarily economic, for that is the most urgent aspect of the question. Still, I am convinced that this federal link might also be operative politically and socially, and without affecting the sovereignty of the nations belonging to the association...' Politically, the question of national sovereignty, as Briand well knew, was the rub – how many nations would be willing to give it up in the interests of European associationism? For years, from congress to congress, from debate to debate, politicians would skirt round the problem, and whenever any general resolution was arrived at, it would be weighed down with so many subsidiary clauses and loop-holed in so many ways that any effective implemen- tation was practically impossible. Close to Aristide Briand, but coming out a bit more into the open, there was Jean Monnet (1888–1970) with his 'functionalism': the transference of more and more national and international business to supranational organization and supervision.

After yet another hot world war and the beginning of a cold one, the question of European unity became more urgent, the move to create a Euro-community speeded up, and the institutional map of Europe was complexified. In 1947, at Montreux, there was the meeting of the Union Fédéraliste Européenne. At the Hague, in 1948, at the Congress of Europe, the notion of 'supra-nationality' was to the fore. In 1949, at Strasburg, there was the Council of Europe. And then, in 1956, came the EEC.

5

In all this politico-economic busyness, the question of culture tended to be left aside. Not that it was entirely forgotten. Lip-service would be paid to it, at intervals some kind of oecumenical orchestration or international cultural festival would be organized, and the strictly politico-economic discourse was often leavened by one more 'spiritual' in intent: Marc Sangnier talked of the need for *un nouvel état d'âme international* ('a new international state of mind'), and Jacques Delors, president of the European Commission at Brussels, spoke of 'a soul for Europe'. None of this, however well-meant, was very convincing or very inspiring. But more fundamental work had been going on, and still was.

Vidal de la Blache, the founder of human geography, was bringing new elements into that science, and, by his teaching and example, he'd sent social historians like Lucien Febvre and Marc Bloch, founders of the *Annales d'histoire*, out to comb the countryside for vestiges and sources that could open up new perspectives. Henri Berr had set up the Centre international de synthèse, bringing out a series of books on the evolution of humanity, inspired by the notion of unity.

All this work was centred in Europe, but it was not Eurocentric.

Now and then, especially in recent times, you would hear a Eurocentric, a Euro-defensive discourse. That would be in protest, say, at the disneyfication and mcdonaldization of Europe, at the arrival *en masse* in Europe of all kinds of mindless trash, and of an American version of Western civilization (suffered in silence by many Americans, or refused by others in various ways), or in disgust at the move within Stanford University to throw out of its general programme Virgil, Cicero, Tacitus, Dante, Aquinas, Luther, More, Galileo, Locke and Mill as 'dead white Europeans'. In fact, there's no saying just how far the 'New World' (in fact, an agglomeration of the most obscurantist elements of the 'Old World') will go in its rush towards not only the most simplistic of ideologies, but total cultural nonentity. The signs, however, are already there.

Whatever Eurocentric discourse there has been is as nothing compared with the fundamental work going on. This was looking at Europe, but as a part of the world. European does not mean closed, it means open – but that doesn't mean open to anything.

With decolonization, energies were released from colonial ties, able to think in terms of an integrated Europe. With the opening of the frontiers in 1991, open-mindedness increased.

In all the drifting since the collapse of the Roman Empire and the break-up of Christendom, *something* has emerged. It is something that has moved between identity and intention, between diversity and unity. It is dynamic, rather than idealistic or formalistic. It is more in the nature of a correspondence than of an essence. With the changing of the politico-economic landscape has come a change in mindscape.

Except here and there.

6

On 20 September 1988, addressing the College of Europe in Bruges, Margaret Thatcher, Britain's then Prime Minister, spoke out passionately against the, for her, appalling prospect of a 'European superstate' and 'an identikit European personality'.

All the Little Englanders (*not* all English people) applauded – so did a lot of Americans (I insist, not *all* Americans), worried at a possible threat to US world-hegemony and the potential 'anti-American activity' of a rising United States of Europe.

I don't think any Scot with the slightest sense of Scotland's cultural geography could have applauded – but I'll come back to that later.

This wasn't the first time Britain (a Britain identified with a certain England) had vetoed the European idea. In fact there's a deepset bred-in-the-bone, lurking-in-the-guts hiatus between Britain (a certain Britain) and the Continent that it's going to take more than a Channel tunnel to heal. When Winston Churchill, not the most unenglish of Englishmen, spoke in 1946 at Zurich about 'a kind of United States of Europe', *The Times* dismissed the idea as an 'outrageous proposition'. In a 1950 Labour Party pamphlet, it was adamantly stated that 'no iota of British sovereignty' was negotiable. When the European Coal and Steel Commission was set up in 1951, a reasonable and in fact successful project, Britain held aloof. When there was talk in 1962 of Britain's entry into the EEC, Hugh Gaitskell, toeing the old line and committing a monstrous historical howler while he was at it, declared that such a step would mean 'the end of a thousand years of British history' (every Scottish school pupil at least knowing that Britain only started up in 1707). For years, political Britain was to be hovering between a kind of 'Holy Anglo-Saxon Alliance' represented by NATO and the Atlantic Pact, and the EEC, which meant hobnobbing with all those foreigners. The blockage in politics had of course its counterpart in the intellectual sphere. Asked recently (see Bryan Magee, *Modern British Philosophy*, Secker & Warburg, 1971) why British linguistic philosophy (Ayer, Austin, Moore) was so little thought of on the Continent, an Oxford professor of philosophy had this to say: 'I'm inevitably rather guessing about this *because philosophy outside the English-speaking world is a field in which I'm not particularly well informed*' (my emphasis, and no comment).

It's not that Britain is insular. If it were really insular, I'd be interested, we'd have a theme for discussion, and could get on to the subject of archipelagism. But Britain isn't insular – it's just English, the Englishness in question being compounded of narrow outlook, cultural complacency, and abysmal ignorance, including ignorance of the very island. Writing (1993) in the *Transactions of the Royal Historical Society*, Jenny Wormald says without hesitation or ambiguity that 'the ingrained reluctance to ask fundamental questions about the nature of Britain remains constant'.

London, flanked by Oxford and Cambridge, walks with heavy feet – hardly helped on by visionary poetics such as those of Blake, in 'Europe: a prophecy' (1794). In that poem, we hear of 'Albion's angels' going silent 'along the infinite shores of Thames', seeing 'Urizen on the Atlantic'. It's Blake, so there's some power in it. But it's a good example of those gnarled mythologies English poets tend to get into when they're not content, as so many are, to mow their primly circumscribed lawns.

Given all the parochial Johnbullism I've just evoked, it's a relief to hear, coming from London, another voice.

Here's Hugh Seton-Watson, Professor of Russian History at the School of Slavonic and East European Studies, talking in a lecture ('What is Europe, where is Europe?') delivered, in 1984, at the Royal Institute of International Affairs:

> Let us not underrate the need for a positive common cause, for something more exciting than the price of butter, more constructive than the allocation of defence contracts – a need for an European *mystique* [...]. The European cultural community includes the peoples living beyond Germany and Italy [...]. To these peoples, the idea of Europe is that of a community of cultures to which the specific culture or sub-culture of each belongs [...]. The unity of European culture is simply the end-product of 3000 years of labour by our diverse ancestors.

I don't share Seton-Watson's vocabulary ('mystique'). I think we must try to go beyond the conception of a cultural mosaic, but here at the very least, and it is a necessary basis, we have a sense of the whole map, large perspectives and a travelled intelligence.

Now, Seton-Watson, as he was always at pains to make clear, was a Scot.

7

I think it little open to argument that, always of course with exceptions, the Scot is more continental, more European than the Englishman, and have, elsewhere (*On Scottish Ground*), piled up a considerable amount of evidence to that effect. Let me just allude here rapidly to the medieval figure of the *Scotus vagans*, wandering all over the Continent; to Duns Scot, born (1266) near Edinburgh, moving from Scotland to Oxford, from Oxford to France, from France to Germany; to all those Renaissance students (Walter de Scotia, Jacobus de Scotia, Simon de Scotia...) to be found at Paris, Orleans, Avignon, Louvain, Cologne, Bologna, Padua; to all those Scottish teachers, poets, philosophers you would come across in Renaissance times all over France: George Buchanan in Paris and Bordeaux, Michael Scott in Paris, Robert Pittiloch in Gascony, James Kidd in Toulouse, Adam Abernethy in Montpellier,

John Gordon at Avignon. On up to David Hume, Robert Louis Stevenson, Patrick Geddes.

Much of all this continentalism, wide-ranging existence, extravagant thinking and writing has been forgotten in Scotland – marginalized, occulted – but it is once again becoming common knowledge, and the consequences may be immense.

The last great influence Scotland as a whole exercised on Europe (but don't let's forget the darker grey wave of *Ossian*) was with its Enlightenment.

A few years back, and it may still be the case, it was possible, in the antiquarian bookshops of Paris, to come across the translations of books by Thomas Reid or Dugald Stewart that were basic philosophical texts in the lyceums and universities of France around the middle of the nineteenth century. That was how, in the very early sixties, in the rue St-André-des-Arts, I came across three little brown-stained volumes entitled *Éléments de la philosophie de l'esprit humain* by Dugald Stewart, published by Charpentier Éditeur, Paris, 1845. This was the revised translation by L. Peisse of Stewart's *Elements of the Philosophy of the Human Mind* that had originally appeared in London, 1792, and the first translation of which, by P. Prévost, had come out at Geneva, in 1808.

As I've demonstrated elsewhere, including other chapters in this book, I don't think Common Sense philosophy is the brightest, sharpest movement in thought. But the Scottish Enlightenment wasn't all 'commonsensical'. It was a moment that gathered in a lot of various energies. In its later phases I think of it as the culture-moment capable of bringing out such magnificent and far-reaching productions as Audubon's *Birds* and Johnson's *Atlas*.

The presence of the Enlightenment in France (which had itself inspired its beginnings) was strong.

But it was not restricted to France. Recently I was in Poland, in some sense Europe's stricken heartland, and I was able to pick up traces of it there too, notably in Poznan. Here's Jan Sniadecki, describing, in a letter of 1821, the 'Edinburgh School' as 'a seat of true philosophy, cleansed of misconceptions and preconceptions'. Here's Michal Wiszniewski, in a book, *Human Mental Characters*, of 1837:

The Scots note subtle differences and in this arduous way arrive at the clear understanding of a problem. They have an all-embracing, sagacious intellect. Theological disputes, in which they willingly participate to this day, have sharpened their wits. In a crofter's cottage on an isolated island, one can find, lying beside a pair of shears, a book, or even a diary, of theological disputes about which this nation reads with such delight.

Coming back to British shores, here's a real English philosopher, Alfred North Whitehead, in *Adventures of Ideas*, commenting on Scottish Enlightenment thought:

Adam Smith and Hume are two of the last great Scotchmen who mark the traditional affiliation of Scotland with France, which had survived from the earlier centuries of joint antagonism to England. At their date the intellectual life of Edinburgh and Glasgow is not to be assimilated with that of England. Throughout the greater part of the eighteenth century, during its central portion, the intellectual life of England, so far as concerns any originative energy, is negligible. Indeed, one of the reasons for the separation of America from England was that the particular circumstances of English life were not applicable to America, and that England was not fermenting with any universal ideas capable of specialization for American conditions. English influence survived, it is true, in the Common Law; but, apart from that exception, the mentality of men like Jefferson and Franklin was French. There was the homeland of their thoughts.

Having spoken against English complacency, I would not want to offer the slightest suspicion that I could fall into anything like a Scottish complacency.

Scotland can afford also to be strong in self-criticism.

If, as Wiszniewski suggests, Protestantism with its theological disputes sharpened wits, it also brought about a macadamical moralism, and, as Novalis says in his essay, a 'desiccation of the senses', an 'atony of the higher organs'. There is, too, prevalent yet in Scotland, a reductionism, an almost vindicatory reductivism allied to a superficially conceived democratism that makes for an unwillingness to recognize individual value. If the original ground as I see it is quick, flashing and radiant, there are also great areas of opaque puddingstone. As to so much literature called Scottish, like so much art produced within the nations, on inadequate ground, I am reminded of an old Gaelic poem that describes a flotilla of chamber pots bobbing down the Minch.

Some of those ruts and blockages are endemic, self-engendered, others stem from Scotland's relegated position since 1707, its provincialization. Most indigenous reactions (localist literature, the narrower brands of nationalism) are primary attempts to cope with that provincialism, deal with that subordinate situation.

What I have wanted to do in this section is emphasize the increasing awareness of *pre*-provincial forces, and the emergence of a new field.

The new Europe should, naturally (geographically), concern the island as a whole. But if Anglo-Britain continues to be so obstinately ignorant and so complacently myopic, then Scotland may quite simply secede from Britain, and not out of nationalism, but out of Europeanism.

8

At the end of the nineteenth century, with his mind on *Realpolitik*, Bismarck dismissed Europe as a mere 'geographical notion'. At the end of the twentieth century, after all kinds of historical upheaval, it's to geography we're coming back: trying to get back down to basics and start out again from there.

In his *Study of History*, Toynbee places at the genesis of civilization man's response to 'the challenge of the environment'. I think in fact that any attempt at real residence depends on a reading of the land. We tend, in times of stress and distress, when looking for roots or identity, to think only in terms of the human patrimony. But it's even more radical, even more necessary, to think in terms of the natural patrimony.

So, in this open conclusion, let's try to get a sense of European space.

Here, first of all, to use an old text (some of those old texts have a density often lacking in more modern ones, and are at times close to poems), and tie in with some references made earlier, is a description of the continent by John of Trevisa, in a fourteenth-century encyclopedia: 'Europe is said to be a third of the whole world, and has its name from Europa, daughter of Agenor, King of Libya. Jupiter ravished this Europa, and brought her to Crete... Europe begins on the River Don and stretches all along the Northern Ocean to the end of Spain. The East and South part rises from the Black Sea, is joined to the Mediterranean, and ends at Cadiz.'

The presentation is succinct, it is naive, but it has all the firm freshness of a medieval miniature.

In any case, Europe was to expand, and with the enlargement of space went a deepening of the concept. It was a Swedish officer in the Russian army who suggested that the boundaries of Europe should be set at the Urals. Hence the definition of Europe, first made official in Volger's *Handbuch der Geographie* of 1833, as 'from the Atlantic to the Urals'.

It's varied country. The Atlantic keeps pounding at its coastline, making for gulfs and promontories, with many islands offshore. Its mountains range over the old rocks of Caledonia through the Pyrenees and the Alps. A great plain starts in Champagne and runs through the basin of the Danube, foretelling the steppes of Eurasia.

To come now closer to the Atlantic coast.

Speaking of the 'virtues of adversity', Toynbee in his *Study* says that it's 'dour environments' (he evokes the Roman Campagna, the desert of Judah, the moors of Brandenburg...) that have provoked the most vigorous response. I think it's safe to say that Scotland is a *dour* environment (indeed, we've adopted that French word as one of our very own) and with it the whole Celto-Atlantic region.

I speak of 'region'. To make my meaning more precise, I'll say Euroregion. It could well be that the nation-state as fashioned by centuries of history is no longer the best ground for a coherent and radiant Europe. It's been said that the nations as constituted are too small to cope with the big issues and too big to cope with the small ones. So it may be useful to think in terms of a different configuration, a different cartography. This has to some extent already happened. Belgium, the Netherlands and Luxemburg came together as the Benelux. Denmark, Sweden, Norway, Finland and Iceland have formed the Nordic Council. A Baltic Region brings together Germany and Poland.

Maybe Europe has to be perpetually created. Its changing frontiers have been likened to tidelines. Maybe it is a tidal area.

In my Scoto-European 'house of tides', on the coast of Brittany, I often think in terms of that Celto-Atlantic region I've just evoked.

It's the space I work in.

9

The townhall, the *mairie*, of the little village on the north coast of Brittany where I live has been displaying over the past few years three flags: the French tricolour, the *gwen y du* (the black and white flag of Brittany) and the flag of Europe with its golden stars on a deep blue background. It is a sign of the times, it connotes also a sense of space and connection.

On these shores, about fourteen centuries ago, arrived boat after boat of monks – from Ireland, from the Hebrides, from mainland Scotland: St Brandan, St Malo (in Rouen called St Maclou), St Clement, St Pol, St Renan... Eric of Auxerre evokes in a Burgundian manuscript 'all those Scotic philosophers landing on our shores', adding that 'the more intelligent and learned they are, the more they want to travel'. Centuries later, Ernest Renan was to refer to them as 'bold thinkers, teachers of language and literature to the whole West'.

This was the first great Scotic influence on the Continent, and it's the one that remains deepest in my mind.

In fact the image is so strong that I sometimes imagine myself as living in something like the continental equivalent of St Ninian's *candida casa*: a Scottish outpost, a far-flung house of Alba, a focus of Scotland in Europe.

The Re-mapping of Scotland

To bring light to the country.

(Ancient Egyptian poem)

1

The other day in Italy I was talking with a highly placed official in the Italian Ministry of Foreign Affairs. 'You Scots are an amazing people', he said. 'There are only about five million of you, and you're all over the place, always in the forefront.' It was heady stuff. To keep from swooning in sheer self-satisfaction, I felt, in typical Scottish fashion, that I had to bring in a dose of scepticism if not downright cynicism. 'Oh, we're great fellows once we get a chance', I said, 'but the country's been checked for a long time; clogged up with crap – imported cosmopolitan crap, and home-made Scottish crap. We're just beginning to work our way out of it all again.'

There, in that little exchange, you have the theme of this essay.

Scotland, which I'm considering here as a region of Europe, as an example of the work to be done, is at this moment in a transitional stage. At surface level, it's a question of politics. At a deeper level, it's a question of poetics. I don't neglect the politics, but I'm more concerned with the poetics. If you get politics and poetics coming together, you can begin to think you've got something like a live, lasting culture.

A culture – something which no country in the world has today, the very notion of which, in any demanding sense, is absent from our world-thinking.

The last time that the culture-question was raised, publicly, in a radical way, in Britain, was at the end of the nineteenth century. At the head of the debate, on the advancing contours of the field, were three Scots: Thomas Carlyle, John Ruskin and John Stuart Mill. I don't intend here to go into a presentation or an analysis of their thought and policy – I've done that elsewhere (for example, in the book *On Scottish Ground*). I mention their names simply to indicate a high line of interest, and maybe a genealogy.

Coming closer to our own times and the specific field I engage in myself, the radical culture-question was taken up again by Arnold Toynbee, in his *A Study of History*, written at the end of the Second World War, particularly in its volume 9, in which he considers 'The prospects of Western Civilization'. These prospects are, to say the least, unpromising. Toynbee speaks of a loss of intellectual energy, of a creeping existential triviality, of a sterilization of politics, to which one might add a domestication of social thinking and a general infantilization. I go with most of Toynbee's analysis of the end-phase of modernity. It's when he begins to outline a possible *post*-modernity (he invents the concept) that I begin to differ. After surveying all the renaissances which civilization has attempted (renaissances of political ideas, renaissances of languages and literatures), all of which are always 'interesting', but often ultimately unconvincing, the very idea of 'renaissance' becoming more and more timeworn and shop-soiled, Toynbee finds a haven only in some kind of religiosity. When I first read this, as a desperado kind of student in Glasgow, I found it not only disappointing, but flaccid. I preferred to stay with those whom Toynbee evoked as 'wanderers in the Western wilderness', Atlantean navigators. That was how I was to live and work in the years to come. That was why I defended, in Paris, an extra-vagant thesis on 'intellectual nomadism' (it was considered as opening a whole new field of writing, thought and research), and why I was to write books with crazy titles like *Pilgrim of the Void*.

But let us come to a particular place in the vastity of space, and to a particular area of Europe: Scotland.

2

A country begins with a ground, a geology. When it loses contact with that, it's no longer a country at all. It's just a supermarket, a disneyland, or a madhouse.

So, in this re-mapping of Scotland that I'm attempting, which is a question of scope, scape and shape, I'm going to begin with geology and geography, from which one can hardly separate meteorology (the parameters of sensitive space: weather and light).

I take it to be common knowledge nowadays in Scotland that the country was not always where it now is, that is, hitched to England. About five hundred million years ago, Scotland was situated on the edge of a continent that linked Scandinavia, Greenland and North America. Later it was to swing down south of the Equator. Later again, about sixty million years ago, it settled into its present position, but without, geologically, forgetting its previous locations, especially that very early one, which is written into its bones. A few years ago, I wrote a book called *The Blue Road*, which leaves Montreal and starts out along the north bank of the St Lawrence river for Labrador. This might be taken as an exotic hyperborean excursion, or the extreme, freezing-point venture of an absolute individualist. In fact, it can be read (also) as an attempt to get at Scotland's original geographical affinities.

The geology of the territory is extremely complex.

In a little text that appeared in 1892, Marcel Bertrand, professor of geology in Paris, wrote this: 'The Caledonian chain is one of the most ancient, if not *the* most ancient, that it is possible to reconstitute. One is faced there by movements dating from primary times.' And he concludes his essay by saying that anyone interested in geomorphism (is it possible to imagine anyone with any sense *not* interested in geomorphism?) has to make a pilgrimage there. Eighty years later, in a study on geomorphology in north-west Scotland, the most thorough study of its kind I know, published in Strasburg (1963), Alain Godard in his preface says he could never have imagined all the morphostructural combinations the Scottish mountains contained without actually looking closely at the various locations.

In the north-west, it's old lewisian gneiss, straight out from the utmost depths of the planet. Elsewhere, the original gneiss will be overlaid at least partly with red sandstone, the residue of ancient river-systems. Nearer the centre, it will be igneous, metamorphic rock: schist, quartz, granite, folded and refolded. Further south, it's coal from the time when Scotland looked like the Florida everglades.

When I was a youngster in Ayrshire, I'd be often on Arran, which sums up a lot of Scotland. It was there, just beyond Lochranza, among strata of schist and sandstone, that James Hutton, away back in the eighteenth century, worked out one of the most interesting aspects of his theory of the earth: unconformity. Other investigators and thinkers had come to the conclusion that the world was older than anyone had ever imagined. But they thought the great work of the earth's composition was over. Hutton said it was still going on. The Earth wasn't fixed, static, it was moving and dynamic: *geostrophic*.

I drew lessons in poetics from all that.

As to climate, anybody who has lived at all in Scotland soon suspects that we belong to what used to be beautifully called, for example, in Johnson's *Physical Atlas of Natural Phenomena* (Edinburgh, 1850), 'The Province of the Autumn Rains'. More than any other region in Western Europe, we're open to the movements of the Atlantic. The mass of North-Atlantic sea-air perturbed by the wind makes for a changing sky, with frequent rainfalls. That can mean series of dreich days (propitious for meditation!), it also means symphonies in black and grey, broken by strange illuminations and sometimes extraordinary enlightenments.

In any re-mapping of Scotland, that's the basic zone. Various systems, metaphysico-religious and socio-political, have tended to push it into a neglected background. But for any reconstitution of the full Scottish mind, contact with, consciousness of, that basic zone, is, I submit, fundamental.

3

I come now to what I'm going to call the middle zone, concerning history, identity and culture.

In his novel, *Les Misérables* ('The Wretched of the Earth'), Victor Hugo has a description of the battle of Waterloo. After a wide panorama, he zooms in on a man, standing amid the murderous din of history, playing music, in his eye a vision of mountain and forest. This man is, as you've guessed, a Scottish piper. It's the kind of image that gets our heart-strings throbbing and our tear-ducts working overtime. Let's try to look at it coolly.

Remembering a landscape, concerned with an art, this man, involved in a history not of his own making (for how many of us is it ever otherwise?), is ensconced in solitude. Although he's on the winning side, he's lost his real ground, and he knows it.

That's been the predicament of the Scottish people for a long time, since at least 1707.

That's where the identity question arises, that's where identity ideology begins, it's in that context a lot of literature has been written, it's there a lot of cultural thinking has been done – and all of it can never be more than a half-way house.

The identity question is paramount and obsessive when a field of energy has been lost and is not yet regained.

When a child of two looks in a mirror and says 'that's me', everybody's happy: he or she is achieving identity. 'Thank God, Charlie's normal'. At five or six, the 'me, me, me' is a damn nuisance, but it's excused, it's even expected. If at forty, you're still saying 'me, me, me', if the only thing you can see all over the place is a reflection of yourself, you're in a state of arrested development. When a whole people is in that state, it's a case of historico-cultural paralysis.

Before going on, a little more identity-analysis. When the Manchus took over China, they forced the Chinese to wear pigtails, as a sign of servitude. Later, when it was suggested to the Chinese that they modernize a bit and get their hair cut, they stuck for long to their pigtails, as a sign of identity. In other words, you can get so used to your subjection (not just physical, but ideological, imaginative) that you take it as the sign of your very self. Identity can be the mask of deep set alienation.

To come back to history, and the beginning of the alienation, the paralysis.

At the end of the seventeenth century, Scotland was a poor country, almost famished. But it wasn't finished. There was still a lot of brisk foreign trade: Leith, Dundee, Aberdeen, Glasgow were negotiating with Norway, Sweden, Danzig, the Low Countries, France, Portugal and Spain. The Scots were always the last to cross the Skaggerak before the Winter ice set in. Scottish pedlars, the *skottars*, could be seen roaming all round the Baltic, more well-off merchants were townsfolk in Stockholm, Warsaw, St Petersburg. There was a Scottish network. And attempts were made to extend it, deepen it: I'm referring to the projects, systematically put down by England, for a Scottish Africa Company and for a trading counter in Darien. The country was poor, but it had energy. And history has seen poor countries with energy physical and intellectual achieve amazing things. Italy was half-asleep after the fall of the Roman Empire, then, in the ninth century, the little poverty-stricken town of Amalfi woke up. In no time at all, with the Amalfi Tables, it was legislating for the whole of the Mediterranean and was playing its destiny hundreds of miles from its immediate locality. What was Venice, gateway to the East, wed to the oceans of the world, at the start but a handful of salt-logged islands?

With 1707, there were, sure, advantages for Scotland. But it lost its field of indigenous energy. It became to all intents and purposes an English province, a recruitment zone, a pictures-que periphery, destined to produce beef for the British Navy, the land-use accent being on stock rather than on a varied agriculture, on plutocratic landowning rather than on democratic workfields. The roving Scot ('Thus do they live as rovers and defy, this or that place, rags of geography', wrote an English poet) continued to prowl around the world, notably in the lost lands on the borders of Canada and America, where the Scots were particularly adventurous, moving away out farther ahead than most, living like Indians, but a lot more Scottish in the deployment of their energies than, for example, the Scottish director of a London bank eager to send his son to Eton and Oxford.

Within the confines of the country (and confines is the word, not contour or frontiers), you had conventicles in the kailyard, folk keeking out from windows in Thrums or going off their rocker behind green shutters, all kinds of parochial palaver – the whole caboodle wrapped up in a horrible type of psycho-logical introversion marked by a singular talent for denigration and belittling (if you weren't hemmed in, you were un-Scottish); when it wasn't pathetic, it was pathological.

Then came the nationalist explosion, with drunk men gazing at thistles or jitterbugging under the eildon tree. A meta-physical delirium joined forces with a sometimes ruthless and reckless, sometimes innocent and naive brand of political idealism. A Scottish soviet was to extend from the Solway Firth to Cape Wrath, from Polmadie to Plockton, with every-body talking Lallans, before graduating to Gaelic. It was ten times better than what had gone before, and there were radiations from it (visions from a raised beach) that pointed to something else. But was it not a great, tottering superstructure raised on inadequate ground?

After that confused utopian outburst, Scotland got hip and joined the mainstream. But what mainstream? Yesterday's mainstream. That meant a spate of sub-Zola social realism. And when flat realism began to look like the remains of last night's fish-supper, it was sauced up into sordid naturalism. Along with that went various local re-makes of cosmopolitan art that had taken place in New York twenty years before and in Paris thirty years before that.

So that, while the start-up promoters and culture-biz professionals frothed about 'the revival of Scottish literature', while the universities set up courses on 'The Scottish novel since 1945' or 'Scottish poetry in the 80s' (after abandoning a classical corpus, many universities have gone contemporary, in a nose-to-the-grindstone kind of way), the country remained, fundamentally, culture-less, with less and less awareness in the air of its primal energy field, less and less knowledge of the great intellectual and poetic, potentially cultural, outcroppings that have occurred over the centuries, less and less capacity to draw significant lines together.

Till you get to a stage which is already today's, but which may be more and more tomorrow's, where you have an anthropological type you might call the self-made nitwit, the smart semi-educated nonentity, moneyed without being mannered, with an anything-that-sells-is-good mentality, who thinks values are made on the stock exchange, who's never without lap-top and portable (he's an important guy) and who, being proud of his Scottish identity, gets married in a kilt.

The real work has hardly begun (though it has, here and there). Is it possible to accomplish it? I'm not sure. But I think it's worth while to try.

4

I come now to the third zone of my re-mapping, what one might call the head zone, which involves philosophy (I prefer to say: ground-thinking) and poetics (a term which in my usage carries both prose and verse).

This may seem a very abstract (and, of course, as they say, elitist) way of talking about a country's culture. But for a country to have lasting power, it has to be essentialized. There has to be an idea in the air – like salt in the sea, like that salty, smoky, seaweediness you can get in some of the finest whiskies. An abstract idea can create a spatial dynamics, and there's no notion-state, no territorial entity of any significance, that can do without such an element. And if there is going to be a culture-field with coherence and cogency, that is, something more than the mere sociological accumulation of this and that, it has to have a radiant centre.

Let's come back on the example of Duns Scot already presented in this book, active in the thirteenth century. It was, you will recall, the time when Wallace and Bruce were trying to liberate Scotland from political oppression. Duns Scot has his own ideas about liberation, but he doesn't act in the theatre of history: he considers that the liberation of the mind is more important – otherwise, even the most well-meant reforms will lead inevitably to dead ends. After early schooling in Scotland, Duns Scot studied at a Franciscan college in England, from where he went, avid for more, to Paris, later ending up in Cologne. He has that moving spirit I've often referred to, calling himself a peregrine, a passer-by. As to thinking, he didn't much like 'the philosophers' – they were too heavy-footed for him. He has in his thinking a *quickness* which I take to be a characteristic of the Scoto-Celtic mind at its best. I've seen his thought referred to as a 'metaphysics of exodus'. It's a nice phrase, but I don't think 'metaphysics' is the appropriate word. I'd call it simply a way out: a way out of heaviness and confusion. The poet Gerard Manley Hopkins called him 'of realty the rarest-veinèd unraveller'. Moving freely in an open mental landscape, he sees the things of the earth as extraordinarily *there*. He doesn't ask of a thing *what* it is (to identify it and insert it into some category), he looks at its *isness*, doesn't define it, leaves it in the openness. The thing may be a stone, or a moment of whiteness: hawthorn blossom, a breaking wave, cloud, snow on the heights. What we have there is an *ultima Thule* of intelligence, and at the same time a complete presence in the world. Scotism has all the rocky outlines, all the light-filled stillness, of the Corrie of the Snows in the Cairngorms.

So I'm putting Duns Scot back on the culture-map of Scotland. And if I've chosen the example of Duns Scot, it's because I consider him, both as individual mind, and as potential cultural momentum, more significant than those considered hitherto as the country's mainstays – Robert Burns and Walter Scott – and as a signpost in another direction.

I'm making distinctions here, and I know that distinctions are what some people don't want. They'll even say it's undemocratic. Let me make it plain that I'm neither utopian nor idealist. I know there will always be a load of, shall we say, less essential literature around. I don't at all envisage bookshops in Scotland, or anywhere else, divided, say, into two sections: the Crap section and the Real Stuff section. What I would look to (via a regrounded educational system, value-orientated information, enlightened and perspectivist cultural politics) is more and more individuals going into a bookshop and able, at a glance, at a whiff, to make the difference. A demanding democracy, for me, is a society of developing, developed individuals. Otherwise, all you've got, in the name of democracy, is a mixture of populism and demagogy, in other words: mediocracy.

After such re-centring as I've indicated, I'd recommend a wide-ranging reconnaissance implying a re-reading of significant works with extrapolation, updating, according to new perspectives. Thus avoiding two interconnected cultural pitfalls: musty piling up of historical patrimony on the one hand, and the mere mugging about in contemporaneity on the other. A culture needs reference, co-ordinates, a sense of salience.

I come now to actual writing. What has generally characterized vanguard writing since, say, the end of the eighteenth century, is the move from monument to movement, from model and ideal – not into putrefaction or positivism, nihilism or nitwittery (a concomitant socio-cultural phenomenon) – out on to *way*. I'm talking about writing as itinerary and as cartography, a tracking and a tracing, out to delineate new space, carrying with it the enlargement of mental categories and an increasing sense of world. If I say that writing has more to do with a flight of migratory birds than with the psychology of Joe Mc Donald, the contorted fantasia of Malcolm Gibb, or the sociology of Auchtermuchty, will you think I'm off my head? Now we've got this far, I don't think so, but maybe I'd better explain myself a bit more.

The abovementioned psychology and sociology is what you'll get mostly in the novel, along with some kind of plot. I'm talking about a writing that can pick up such elements in the bygoing, but which is fundamentally going elsewhere. I'm not prophesying the end of the novel – the novel will go on a long time yet, till television finally takes over. What I'm saying is that the novel (whether bourgeois, proletarian or slickterish) is no longer the art-form of a mind, or a culture, in evolution. Originally, the novel meant vernacular literature (over against classical Latin models), now it's vulgar literature. By vulgar I don't mean lowdown, sleazy, dark or bleak – I don't dislike some good old gutbucket stuff, and on occasion I can be as bleak as anybody ever was. I'm using the word in an aesthetic sense: by 'vulgar' I mean, for example, the exploitation of cliché-themes, intrigues in confined spaces, psycho-sociological reportage, mere smartness.

Real world-writing, including novel writing, has been trying to get outside all that for some time and go elsewhere.

Consider the book I mentioned earlier in another context. It has been said by more than one literary critic, in a demagogical kind of way, that Victor Hugo's *The Wretched of the Earth* is constructed like a detective novel. There's truth in that, up to a point. But Hugo is in fact making fun of the limited logic and narrow perspectives of the police inspector Favert. The strategy of Jean Valjean's wandering through Paris is infinitely more significant, more mind-opening. With Hugo, and with Huysmans, and others, the novel form is bursting its banks: other materials, other considerations, other strategies are just waiting their time.

It's with these other materials, other considerations, other strategies I myself have been working with, via prose, poem, and essay, all of them in a way that goes outside the established categories.

The move is, fundamentally, out of 'humanity', a concept that is outworn.

This means getting rid of inherited conceptions of the human being, and getting out of the psycho-sociological ruts they have got us into – ruts which we often interpret as roots.

in some philosophies, the self doesn't exist at all (Hume here in Scotland was pretty close to that), and recent biology conceives the human being as 'open system'.

Thereafter, it means moving out of history. This doesn't mean, as some simplistic or sensationalist minds would have it, the 'end of history', but the end of history as primal reference, and as vector towards some longed-for absolute. By extension, it means the absence of any overriding story – mythic, religious, metaphysical, socio-historical. When you've got no story left, what is there? – the nature of things. The reading of that nature is inexhaustible. It's from the nature of things that real writing emerges, not from any I–Thou dialectic. Outside the dialectics, something else takes over.

From the contact between an open self and the cosmic context can emerge a dimension on which it is difficult to put a name, on which for long I didn't care to put a name, and which I now call geopoetics.

What I've been trying to get at in this signalling, carto-graphical essay is a potential renewal of culture in Scotland on the basis of geopoetics.

I'm speaking as a poet. That word can cover a lot of things, not always very interesting. I give it more scope and more dimensions than is usually the case. I like what the poet Mandelstam said about the poet Dante: that he was more than a poet in the banal sense of the word, he was a strategian of mutation.

This country of Scotland today is in a state of mutation or, shall we say, more circumspectly, a state of *possible* mutation.

A country implies politics, economics and culture. Political space gives authority. Economic space gives autonomy. Cultural space gives aura.

My concern has been to propose a map, or at least the sketch, of a possible culture, combining these three spaces.

Aesthetic Considerations on the Calton Hill

A great art of initiation and education.
(Jules Michelet)

1

Aesthetics is a difficult word to handle. Like any other essential term, it will have been used in so many different, often confused, contexts that it needs a careening job done on it before it can move thoughtfully at all through the universe of discourse. To some, it may evoke in the first place a context of the late nineteenth century: effete individuals lolling about on purple velvet couches, devoted to the worship of Art as a divine, otherwordly domain. But let me put my own reference cards right away on the table. If I use the word aesthetics, I'm thinking, for example, of Schiller's twenty-seven letters on 'the aesthetic education of humanity', which date from 1795, or of Hegel's lectures on aesthetics at Berlin around 1830. Both of these, going way beyond idealistic definition, appreciative commentary, merely informative history, or art as a refuge, attempt to consider art from the ground up and propose its study, not as some specialist occupation, but as a general discipline for all humanity, as the fundamental grounding of a culture. I'm using the word aesthetics then to indicate the field that opens out after many paths of intelligence, analysis and work have been followed. I mean by it a *general sense of things*. So doing, I can call to my side Alfred North Whitehead declaring, in *Adventures of Ideas*, that 'the most fruitful, because the most neglected, starting-point of philosophical thought is that section of value theory which we term aesthetic', and Wallace Stevens saying, in his *Opus Posthumous*, that 'the aesthetic order includes all other orders but is not limited to them'.

For Hugh MacDiarmid, it was a discipline, a consideration, almost totally neglected in Scotland, for several reasons. Which is why, in 1950, he wrote a long essay, rather diffuse, contradictory and sometimes specious, like a lot of his work, but nonetheless provocative and perspectivist, *Aesthetics in Scotland*, only published six years after his death, in 1984. In this essay, he protested against the 'time-honoured commonplaces' prevalent in the society around him, attempted to analyse the situation, and proposed a new beginning. Let me quote from its conclusion:

> There has nowhere yet been a thorough cleansing of the Augean Stables [...]. Worst of all is the continued absence of competent modern philosophizing in Scotland, and above all the absence of aesthetic thought of any such value as might realign Scotland with other Western European countries and induce aesthetic developments based on Scottish roots and yet able to withstand comparison with the contemporary aesthetic thought of other countries. The omens are not auspicious. All we can hope for, it would seem, is, as in the past, an occasional voice crying in the wilderness.

In that conclusion is my beginning – I would like to say *our* beginning. Let me just add that, personally, I'd have less of an inferiority complex than MacDiarmid with reference to other countries. If it is true that other countries have developed aesthetic theory to an extent that Scotland has not, it is a fact that they have largely lost grip on it. A Scottish mind, and Scotland, can very well use foreign aesthetic materials that their respective countries have neglected.

What I want to explore here is the aesthetic and cultural scope of geopoetics.

2

I want to enter into the field of geopoetics in this essay by quoting from one of the most interesting essays on aesthetics ever written, the *Philosophy of Forest and Fountain*, which consists in random remarks by the Chinese painter Kuo Hsi (998–1078), taken down by his son as, over the years, they wandered together among streams and rocks, in the region of the 'Western Sea', near Hangchow:

> Wordly men can handle a brush. Technically, they paint. But they do not realize that painting is a difficult thing, requiring more than technique and talent [...]. Ku K'ai-chih of Tsin built a high-storied pavilion for his studio, so his thought would be more free [...]. Unless I dwell in a quiet house, seat myself in a

retired room with the windows open, table cleared and dusted, triviality and commonplace removed, I cannot have good feeling for painting and cannot create the *yu* [the deep and marvellous]. [...] In landscape painting [*sansui* – 'mountain and water'], there are principles and thoughts that cannot be expressed roughly and hurriedly. [...] To paint in an unprincipled, careless manner, without realizing the great idea, is like flinging dung into the wind.

This text, written towards the end of the first millennium, in the age of Northern Sung, a highly controversial and crucial period in the history of China, marks a radically new beginning in Chinese culture, opening up a spectrum of change that went all the way from poetics to politics.

This was the time when, with the creation of a democratic examination system, live and large minds of all kinds of social and regional origin could be nominated to governorships throughout the land. It was the time too of great philosophical syntheses, such as that of Wang An-shih, bringing together the best elements of Confucianism, Buddhism and Taoism. It was a time when new academies were created, notably the Academy of Art inaugurated by the emperor Hiu-tsung. A new basis was given to the whole educative and cultural framework. And back of it all, as ultimate grounding, was landscape – a deep sensation of contact between mind and land.

If I've chosen this context as a point of departure, it's because I see in it an analogy, it's because I think that something like it could take place today here in Scotland and indeed all over the world.

3

Evoking the Sung period in his *Epochs of Chinese and Japanese Art*, Ernest Fenollosa says that Europe has never known anything like it, having been built up on an entirely different basis. He says we only begin to have an inkling of it in the nineteenth century, and even then only in a sentimental, bemoralized, timidly idealistic kind of way, or as a 'fetish collection of facts'. But no 'vast vitality', no recognition that 'something characteristic and structural in every organic and inorganic form is friendly to man', no 'noble passion of interpretation'.

This is largely true, but to make the analysis so sweeping is to forget individual exceptions and to neglect entirely a whole Scoto-Celtic tradition that begins in nature poetry, moves up through pelagianism, can be seen in the *thisness* theory of Duns Scot and on, for example, to Hutton's geology and D'Arcy Thompson's studies on growth and form. This is a tradition which, for various reasons, has been marginalized, except for fragmentary emergences, not only as a strand in European culture, but in Scotland itself which, again for various reasons (politico-historical, moral-philosophical, techno-industrial) has tended to get bogged down in secondary issues, secondary discourses, mistaking identity ideology for self-action, rationalistic wrangling for live thought and all kinds of stodgy literature and petty verse for a deep and dynamic poetics.

My work as I saw it from the beginning was to recover those lost lines, bring them into relation with recent worldwide developments in science, philosophy and poetics, then open a new world-field, with renewed means of expression.

4

Just the other day I was walking through the Museum of Arte Antigua in Lisbon. As in any big city museum, many a beautiful and interesting painting or piece of sculpture has been gathered there. I stopped before a Cranach, a Dürer, a Velasquez. I lingered before medieval wooden sculptures of Compostella pilgrims, a sixteenth-century Portuguese painting of St John the Evangelist and St Vincent, and a seventeenth-century panorama by Filipe Lobo of the Belem quarter at the mouth of the Tagus, open to the Atlantic. I was particularly interested, for its masses of whiteness, in a sixteenth-century portrait of Santa Ana by Ramon Destonnets of the Catalan School, by the blue, greywhite and black tonality of a painting of three saints by Frei Carlos and of a *Lamentation of Christ* in which the figures stand or lie in an almost perfect circle – you can see pure abstraction showing through the religiously anecdotal scene. So, much to be admired, much to be interested in. You can trace, if you look closely, the whole development of Western painting from the Primitives to Abstract Lyricism via Picasso. But when I came to a painting by Gustave Courbet entitled simply *Neige* ('Snow'), 1868, it was relief I felt: relief from all that mythology and religion and metaphysics – but also more than relief: the sense of a value that went beyond artistic technique. For in that painting, there was hardly anything: just a snowy field and a few scattered firs. Yet in that 'nothing' there was something of the highest importance to me, something that resounded with a new, perhaps the highest, significance.

It's that 'snowyness' I want to explore.

5

Since its beginning, art has been carried by, or, I'd rather say, grounded in, many fields. If there is the movement of the artist's hand (technique, talent), that in itself is not sufficient for art: there must be that field, that grounding.

Over the millennia, art has been grounded in myth and magic, religion and spirituality, metaphysics and idealism. These have been the carriers of the greatest epochs of art and culture. Let me make it quite clear that, saying this, I have no nostalgia for them. I am so totally involved in the exploration of another field, in the experience of another life-vibration, and in the expression of another element, that I have no regrets. I think they are of the past, and that no great art can stem from them today. Of course they are still around – I mean actively (that is, apart from the fact that they are gathered in museums, as patrimony, as cultural heritage), but in secondary, tertiary, degraded forms. When Andy Warhol does a hyper-realistic blown-up image of Marilyn Monroe, he's tapping in on the mythological remnant in human consciousness. How poor this is as art is, I think, obvious enough, and I feel no need to belabour the point. The same goes for religion and spirituality. I remember seeing a few years back in England an exhibition of 'Spiritual Art' got up by some very earnest people – it was, to say the least, a vapid display.

But at one point, earlier here, later there, generally around the middle of the nineteenth century, we became realistic. That meant the immediate scene, fact in and for itself. In time this seemed too opaque, too thick, not quick, bright and lively enough, lacking in vibration and expansion, so we moved from

Realism to Impressionism. But very soon Impressionism seemed too pretty, too slight, lacking in force and energy. So from Impressionism, we moved to Expressionism. And from Expressionism to Surrealism, which brought in an oniric dimension. After that, it was decided to get rid of motif altogether, and we had Abstraction, geometrical or lyrical. But again, in a relatively short time, Geometrical Abstraction seemed all too technical, and Lyrical Abstraction all too slap-dashily spontaneist. The need was felt for some kind of idea, and so we got Conceptualism. But since there was no great concept around, the Conceptualism in question was mostly a series of very puny conceptules.

The picture I've drawn of the progression of art in the late-modern period is of course not complete. I had and have no intention of going into all the schools and certainly not all the 'personalities'. That I leave to the history of art. Nor am I content, as some anti-modernists are (rigid classicists, armchair nihilists, cultural vaudevillists) to make fun of this rigmarole of movements in the period under review. No, I see them all as partial attempts, as half-way houses, as segments of a whole not yet grasped.

It's that missing whole I'm after – based ultimately, as my quotation from Kuo Hsi suggested, in a relationship between mind and land, between the universe of discourse and the universe of non-human beings, things, elements.

6

Over the past few years, there has been a great deal of pre-occupation, a good deal of agitation, concerning Nature, earth, the land – and rightly so. But, in its artistic expression, it has been nowhere near the farthest reaches of poetic intuition, philosophical investigation, or scientific research. It has been almost always monstrously caricatural or pathetically inade-quate. At most, approach-work.

Although I'm all for 'thinking big', although I can imagine geopoetic centres dotted here and there over Scotland, each with a characteristic, locally inspired design, although I can conceive of one great geopoetic architectural unit, possibly out on some headland, incorporating the idea and inspiration of the country in its new phase, I don't think this can have anything in common with the kind of brutal, bulldozing interventionism, the megalomaniac monumentalism, marked by remnants of mythology and simplistic symbolism, religious or otherwise, that constitute what we can call, although not all Americans approve of it, and although it is not restricted to Americans, American Land Art. I'm thinking, for example, of Walter de Maria's 500 foot long, 100 foot broad, 5 inch deep cross of white chalk on El Mirage Dry Lake, Nevada. I'm thinking of Dennis Oppenheim's *Identity Search*, a great blow-up (300 by 1,000 feet) of two thumbprints, that of his own right hand, that of Erik Oppenheim's left hand, the line being emphasized by hot tar from a spray-truck (New York, early seventies). I'm thinking of the 300 kilos of mouldy bread wrapped in plastic spread out by Peter Hutchinson on the rim of a volcano in Mexico. I'm thinking of the fat cylinder of earth placed beside the hole of its extraction by Nabuo Sekine (Japan, 1968), entitled *Phase – Mother Earth*.

In Europe, things will tend to be on a smaller scale and it might be said that, if American Land Art works *on* Nature, European Earth Art will try to work *with* Nature. But the conceptions are just as inadequate. To show his concern for the preservation and necessary protection of life, Niels Udo will construct a nest of branches ten metres in diameter and place in it a doll, or a human figure, at times himself. A compatriot of his, Wolfgang Laib, will set up, in any place where the urge calls or where he's invited, slabs of white marble, which he calls 'Milk Stones', getting people to pour milk over them 'so as by this simple gesture to get in touch with the process of Nature'. One can only shrug and turn away. On a smaller scale still, Udo will load a chestnut leaf with bluebell flowers and launch it in a pool, while his British counterpart, Andy Golds-worthy, will stitch together iris leaves with pine needles to form an open pattern and fill the spaces with rowan berries. A certain amount of sensitivity is involved, as well as manual dexterity, a feeling for colour arrangements and delicate structure (Goldsworthy makes elegant constructions of bamboo and ice), but we're closer to pastry-making than to anything like fundamental art.

Others again will cross the territories on foot   a practice with which, in itself, I have the deepest sympathy. Hamish Fulton will cover 166 miles crossing Scotland from east to west, or 100 miles in the space of five days in the Outer Hebrides. Richard Long in the space of twelve days will visit twelve Scottish mountains. Long, in the course of his walking, will make lines and circles of stone (or other materials), which he will photograph or reproduce in more closed precincts. Fulton will bring back only photographs: snapshots as ordinary as possible. Both, to give another dimension to their work, use words. With Long, the wording will tend to be minimal – for example, sixty words ('Red, pool, reeds, gurgle, swish, reflection, skyline...) arranged in a circle to represent a sixty-minute circle walk on Dartmoor. I don't think it's necessary to insist on the poverty of the conception. With Fulton, it will be a kind of primary Zen: 'On the earth, under the sky', 'Thought silenced by bird-song', or it will be descriptive: 'Continous 25 mile walk without sleep pilgrim's way from Winchester to Canterbury'. One can be interested in the information and in the activity. But when a phrase such as this is blown up on the wall of a gallery, as art, it is meagre, very meagre. And the whole procedure has run down into ritualistic repetition.

It remains, in this context, to speak of the performance, that is, the attempt to cast people (body-minds) out of themselves, and tune them in to another dimension, by *shaking them up*. Probably the greatest adept of this in recent times was Joseph Beuys. His symptomatic performance, 'How to explain art to a dead hare', dates from 1965. In 1971, he was in Scotland, in order to experience Rannoch Moor and to awaken the Scottish people to its reality, significance and aura. To do this, he set up, in Edinburgh, the following installation: on a 25 foot long wall was projected a 16-mm film of the moor; in front of the projection wall stood a piano that was never played; farther off stood a microphone, into which Beuys would, from time to time, shout or murmur noises; and nearby stood a blackboard on which he scrawled diagrams... It is not on record how many Scots were convinced, but the intention, shall we say, was good.

Although I've shown, I think, where I differ, both in practice and in philosophy, from all that can be called Land Art, megalomaniac or minute, I have a lot in common with its fundamental desire, its general tendency and even some of its activity. I simply think that more interesting things could be done with the notions of peregrination and gathering, movement, meditation, manoeuvring and manipulation.

When I speak of fundamental desire, I'm thinking in particular of those early, exploratory years I spent on the west coast of Scotland during which I was trying to develop a poetic-and-plastic sense of things.

During long walks along the shore at Fairlie, or in the fields, woods and hills back of the village, I'd gather in stones, shells, leaves, eggs and the bones of animals plucked clean by the crows. The leaves I pasted up in patterns in large sheets, which I pinned to the walls of my skylight room, the stones and bones I laid out on my table or on the floor (I'm talking here of sympathetic, analogous practice, not of aesthetic models). That little room became a kind of cosmo-poetic laboratory, the like of which I was later to set up, with diverse developments, in various places. But if there were things, there was also the general feel of the landscape itself, from areas full of growth to the windswept emptiness of the moor. And with the moving over the landscape came the development of a mindscape.

My readings of the time took in Yeats ('Within a place of stone, be secret and exult, because of all things known, that is most difficult'), Hopkins ('long live the wet and the wilderness yet'), whose sense of inscape is germane to all this, and Hardy, particularly his evocation of the moor of Egdon in *The Return of the Native* and his statement that the future place of art and thought would be not some overhumanized context, but somewhere like the bare beach of Scheveningen. Five years after the publication of the *Native*, Van Gogh would actually be painting on Scheveningen beach – while Rimbaud was walking in the Ardennes ('If I have taste left for anything at all, it's for earth and stones'), and Nietzsche was walking on the plateau of the Engadine in Switzerland ('Brothers, remain true to the earth'). But there I'm getting ahead of my chronology. To come back to those early readings, among them were more locally orientated books, such as, for example one by William Sharp, who wrote under the pseudonym of Fiona Macleod. I must have picked up *The Winged Destiny* at some jumble-sale. For the preparation of this essay, I took it down from the shelves of my library. Some phrases I see underlined that were part of the lines I was following at the time: 'In one of the remotest islands of the Hebrides I landed on a late afternoon in October', 'a thin noiseless rain', 'the cold and barren drift of the tides.' And it was something of a jolt to me when I came across an evocation of the very place in which I have been living for the past few years: 'Those wild Breton coasts of the Tréguier headland'. And it's a funny thing: when Sharp is writing of the Hebrides, he tends to get waylaid into legend and lose himself in aery-fairy, but there in Brittany, confronted by the same fundamental landscape, but with some distance, his writing firms up and his sight clears, so that it's not 'a vision' we have, but an outlined picture, with a plastic presence: 'The grey wind of the East laboured across heavy seas, that here and there turned over green flanks, and sank in a swirling seethe, spreading idly in long ragged traceries on the grey flats and green-grey hollows.'

The first book specifically on art I ever read was *Modern Painters* by John Ruskin, that Scot who, at least in the English context, was the greatest aesthetic thinker and art theoretician of the nineteenth century. And a wild, strange book *Modern Painters* is, because it speaks just as much if not more about stones, clouds, rivers, coasts and storms than it does about painting. Before he gets to a mention of Turner's painting, 'Snowstorm', shown for the first time at the British Academy in 1842, Ruskin evokes the effect on the sea of a powerful gale: 'writhing, hanging, coiling masses, which make the air white and thick', 'utmost pitch of power, velocity, vastness', 'this chaos', 'this annihilation', and he's hardly described the painting, when he's off discoursing on political economy, the raising of silkworms, travelling in the Bernese Oberland, the Roman Campagna or the north of France, 'the white paths of winding rivers', the shape of pinetrees and flecks of orange lichen that 'reflect the sunsets of a thousand years'. That Ruskin's mind never reached the coherence it might have, that his moralities and homilies can leave one flipping through the pages fast, is true, but that an awareness of, shall we say, plant growth and the formation of glaciers can have something to do with art-practice, is a tenet which I hold myself. And it pleases me that the authority on Tintoretto and Fra Angelico should also have an eye and a thought for 'a mossy granite stone a foot broad and two leaves of lady fern'.

The first painting I ever saw 'for real', if I may say so, was in Skelmorlie Aisle, at Largs, where I used to walk at lunchtime when I was a pupil at the local school. It was the Winter scene ('Hiems') of the landscapes of the four seasons that line the chapel's walls. Seventeenth-century Scottish, it exists in my mind directly alongside Breughel's 'Hunters in the Snow'.

It will not have escaped the attention of the reader that such 'Snowscapes' constitute the leitmotiv of this essay.

We're still trying to get at all the resonances of those land-scapes, still gathering in all the elements of a geopoetic art.

Having laid out the main contours, it's 'resonance' I'm now going to talk about.

8

In 1856, in Paris, the collector Félix Bracquemond came across, in a printing shop, a volume of drawings by Hokusai. During those years too, which marked the re-opening of Japan after two and a half centuries of seclusion, Japanese woodblock prints were arriving in Europe, not quite like 'Autumn leaves on the pavement', as the Japanese phrase puts it, but in a steadily increasing stream.

To the artists, it was a revelation.

The gestures of Degas' dancers come straight from Hokusai's wrestlers. Toulouse-Lautrec's posters stem directly from the prints. The same kind of filiation could be shown in the case of many another: Bonnard, Monet, and so on. In a café on the Avenue de Clichy, a poor Dutch painter who had been collecting Dutch, Flemish and British woodblock prints for years exhibited his collection of Japanese prints, proclaiming to all and sundry that here at last was 'the real religion'.

When Van Gogh left Paris for Provence, it was in order to paint 'like the Japanese'. And if he never quite got rid of the

Biblical hangover that dogged his life (a painting like *The Sower* is too obviously a parable), he was to paint pictures so full of force and light and the sheer presence of things that they still illuminate not only the world of art but the field of consciousness. The same went for Gauguin. He also carries Biblical imagery with him (*Jacob and the Angel*), and on the Pacific islands, in an attempt to give a new lease of life to Western culture, he resorts to exotic mythology, but when he left Paris for Brittany, it was to get on to canvas 'the sound his clogs made on the granite rock', and, to bring up once more my leitmotiv, the very last picture he painted was of a Breton village under snow.

Before tracing farther the wavelength of that 'fundamental tonality' Gauguin was after, let's come back to the pervading Oriental influence.

It was Whistler the painter who brought the news from Paris to London, where he was listened to mainly by writers – those aesthetes we left a while back lolling on purple velvet, because this attitude, made up of elegance, indolence and insolence was the only opposition they'd found to the drab, dingy, squalid environment, the respectably boring, fulsomely philistine cultural context in which they found themselves. But they were not all given all the time to frivolous trifles, dainty fopperies, affectations and preciosities. Pater's *Marius the Epicurean* is a book of deep-going aesthetic research, and it was the foppiest of the fops, the most cynical of the hedonists, the flightiest of wits, Oscar Wilde, in his essay 'The English Renaissance', who found the finest and most urgent formula for what was in question and in movement: 'While the West has filled art with intellectual doubts, personal problems, and spiritual unease, the East has remained close to primary conditions.'

Primary conditions.

It was these that loners such as Gray and Collins had looked for in the eighteenth century (I'm thinking of that poem about the 'bleak Atlantic rocks' of St Kilda), it was these that Turner found during his grand tour of the Alps – I'm thinking of watercolours and gouaches such as *The Mont Blanc from Sallanches*, and *La Mer de Glace*.

There never was an English Renaissance such as Wilde

called for. There never was a Scottish Renaissance such as MacDiarmid called for.

But there has been a steady underground movement. I mean 'underground' only with regard to social manifestation, for this movement is definitely *on the ground*, while most of what is called culture is not grounded at all.

Culture most often oscillates between the real and the unreal: the heavy, opaque real on the one hand, empty invention on the other. 'There is the real and the unreal', says Montherlant somewhere (I think it's in *The Lone Traveller is a Devil*). 'Beyond both the real and the unreal, there is depth.'

9

These last few decades have been a time of questioning: questions have been raised concerning the nature of the work of art, the status of the artist in society, and the possibilities of culture. This was the social upsurge of questions put sometimes a hundred or more years earlier by farsighted individuals. It's Hegel saying that, in the Modern Age, it would be harder and harder for the real poet, the real artist, to make headway, and even harder, if not impossible, to open up a new field. It's Rimbaud, it's Nietzsche. Behind all the social flurries, I've always tried to maintain the line of these individuals, and continue it.

Most of the literature, most of the art produced was not going to be up to the questions put by these individuals, a kind of 'culture' was to go on as if the questions had never been raised, all of this being, to a demanding mind, beside the point, and of no interest.

At a higher, at least slightly higher level, there were going to be half-answers. When Walter de Maria filled the hall of a museum in Munich with earth, we can see that act as a follow-up to Nietzsche's 'Remain true to the earth', but a poor, simplistic one. Half-answers are all the more stultefying and deleterious in that they seem to be the 'new thing'. When Robert Morris, in his criticism of museums and galleries (I think myself there is still a great deal to be done with gallery space and walls), declared that the static, portable work of art conceived for an interior can only be of futile decorative value, he was going to give rise to a proliferation of installations and interventions in nature each one more futile than the other: the open-air art centres are full of them, and they disfigure, here and there, the non-art landscape (they are not all so ephemeral as often intended and as one would like). When I say they 'disfigure' the landscape, I mean that those artists impose their art on a space always liable to new and deeper readings, always susceptible of inspiring new figures, and more often than not much more interesting in its patterns than the art imposed on it.

I spoke of working outside social flurry. What I mean by 'social flurry' is this or that 'renaissance'. In the place of any renaissance (which will gather under its banner, for sheer numbers, all kinds of sub-standard work), I propose a large reconnaissance, a wide-ranging investigation (which can, of course, have local applications). This reconnaissance, this investigation (all that I call intellectual nomadism) means a move through many cultures, not in view of international jamborees, but always in search of the fundamental.

It implies also a moving through many sciences, many philosophies, and across the territories. A sense of 'open system' would get rid of the infantile narcissism that marks so much art; a sense of communication as between man and universe rather than only between man and man would get rid of a lot of low-level discourse; the practice of leaps in logic would make so much thinking sound paralytic, just as the search for 'original areas' in philosophy would show up as heavy, opaque and useless what only a naive adolescent or a professor with blinkers would still value as thought.

We are badly in need of a new *discourse*, the creation of such a discourse being infinitely more creative than most 'creative art'. Art needs discourse. I mean a discourse behind art, I *don't* mean that semi-intellectual discourse that for the last twenty years or so now has surrounded even the most inept of art objects. I mean a *logos*. When Klee and Miro say that what matters in art is the poetry, that's what they have in mind. Discourse, of the deepest, most wide-ranging and vivifying type, is absolutely essential.

10

Out of so much movement, is it possible to list some principles?

At the beginning of this essay, I quoted the eleventh-century Chinese painter Kuo Hsi: 'In landscape painting there are principles and thoughts that cannot be expressed roughly and hurriedly... To paint in an unprincipled, careless manner, without realizing the great idea, is like flinging dung into the wind.'

In his *Principles of Chinese Painting*, George Rowley lays out thirteen such principles. I've whittled them down to five, inducing and extrapolating a little, as follows:

Poetic energy. Also sometimes called 'life-movement'. A poet-painter said of it that it 'grows out of the wanderings of the mind and the inspirations of heaven'.

Implicate coherence. Also called 'chaos-union', or the 'opening and joining of interacting forces'. This means the composition of the multifold field of energy, the ability to make a complex open unity out of heterogeneous multiplicity.

Illuminate penetration. This is like a lightning stroke in the complex field of energy. It's this penetrant thing that is most obviously lacking in most art, most literature. 'The thrust must go through to the white at least somewhere', says a modern poet, William Carlos Williams.

Design in depth. This means keeping the interaction live, never letting the lines go slack and inert. The lines of the design have to come up from the depths. These depths are biophysical and cultural. The connections made should have all the intense coherence of an ideogram.

The Void. Emptiness-plenitude. This is the most difficult space of all. With regard to painting, a Chinese artist of the seventeenth century said this: 'Modern painters apply their minds to brush and ink, whereas the ancients applied their minds to the absence of brush and ink.' This technique of 'absence' is called 'flying white' style.

There's enough there to be going on with.

The Music of the Landscape

Sounding earth
(André Breton)

1

As I begin to write this text, rain is beating on the window of my 'Atlantic studio' on Brittany's north coast. This light percussion – a rain *raga* – is punctuated now and then by gull cries. At such moments of, shall we say, biocosmopoetic pleni- tude, I often think I don't need any other music, any fabricated music, at all. I imagine certain hermits on the Western Isles, in Cappadocia, in the Himalaya or the Tian Shan, must have felt the same.

Here's Henry Thoreau, the hermit of Walden Pond, writing in his *Journal* under the date 13 June 1851:

> Walked to Walden last night (moon not quite full) by railroad and upland wood-path [...]. We do not commonly live our life out and full; we do not fill all our pores with our blood; we do not inspire and expire fully and entirely enough, so that the wave, the comber, of each inspiration shall break upon our extremest shores, rolling till it meets the sand which bounds us, and the sound of the surf come back to us. [...] He that hath ears to hear, let him hear. Employ your senses [...]. As I climbed the hill again toward my old bean-field, I listened to the ancient, familiar, immortal, dear cricket sound under all others, hearing at first some distinct chirps; but when these ceased I was aware of the general earth-song, which my hearing had not heard [...] and I wondered if behind or beneath this there was not some other chant yet more universal.

So, there's a music to be heard if we listen in to the earth.

And the paradox, the contradiction, is that it's often music, fabricated music, that prevents the listening in to that other music. In our society, music, at least a kind of music, is all over the place. You can't even pick up the telephone in the silence of your room without having music poured into your ears. We live in a perpetual cacotopian cacophony. Maybe society's always been more or less like that, it's just that ours has multi- plied the means of diffusion. Marius the Epicurean must have had trouble getting away from the blare and clamour of Rome. As for the Middle Ages, think of all the bells. There's an old Celtic poem I love which has this about those bells: 'Finn loved to hear the troating of the stag and the sound of the otter slipping into the water, he loved to hear the tide rolling over white pebbles, he did not love the noise of the christian bell.'

Once I plunged into the ocean of writing, I listened very little to music. I know painters who work to music, maybe there are writers who do so too. That for me is inconceivable. For long, the very notion of 'symphony' or 'concert' was repugnant to me (I didn't want to be 'carried away' into some orchestral empyrean).

Musically, I was looking for something else. Something that came to me from the universe, and which I tried to carry over into writing.

2

It was Erik Satie who reconciled me to music 'proper': a note every thirty seconds, and a good deal of humour. I'm thinking of the *Gymnopédies*, the *Gnossiennes*, the *Prélude Postume*, the *Danse maigre*, the *Avant-dernières pensées*... A decongestioning of culture, a laughing asceticism, a liberation of the mind. I liked to imagine Satie at the *Chat Noir*, or at the *Auberge du Clou*, or listening to the rain at 22, rue de Cauchy, at Arcueil.

Then there was jazz, those little erotic touches, those breaks, letting the instruments talk (*jaser*), instead of imposing an order on them. Sensitive improvisation.

But mostly it was Eastern music I'd listen to, from Hindu *raga* to Japanese bamboo flute. In Sanskrit poetics, from which it's all derived, at the basis of everything, there is Brahma, who is silence. Out of the silence comes Vak, which is thought and voice, intelligence and language, word and music. Vak is often personified in the form of Sarasvati ('she who flows'), who is the goddess of poetry, music and knowledge. She wears a white sari (primordial silence), travels on the back of a peacock (the bird of many eyes – to see all, know all), and carries in her hand a *vina* (representing music) and a scroll (representing poetry). The *raga* is a river of sonorous silence, accompanied by the physiological earth-beat of the drum. As for Zen music, I have a predilection for certain *shakuhachi* pieces such as *Empty Sky, Sea Mist, The Flight of the Cranes.*

On those bases, I gradually, tentatively, extended my network. I even became reconciled to Beethoven when I learned that the first theme in the *Fifth Symphony* was inspired by the song of an oriole.

Here's a letter of the pianist–composer Ferrucio Busoni, written to his wife from Columbus, USA, on 22 March 1910:

> I spoke to a Red Indian woman [...]. She said that her tribe ought to have an instrument something like this: a hole should be dug in the earth and strings stretched all round the edges of it. I said (in the spirit of the Red Indians): 'An instrument like that ought to be called The Voice of the Earth'. She was quite enthusiastic about this.

For Busoni, most Western music was infantile: 'How young our European music is', he says in a letter of 30 March 1904, 'still only a few hundred years, and our culture numbers many thousand. There must be a reason why music develops so late. Perhaps, because it does not find its models ready-made in nature as the other arts do, and the first impulse – to imitate – cannot arise.'

It was just that connection with nature that Busoni was after six years later, working with earthy, spatial Amerindian music, and imagining further developments. In 1912 (letter of 12 August), he speaks of 'joining time together with noise, movement and sensuality'. And in 1918 (letter of 18 August), he has this: 'You see what a lot has to be changed. That is why a composer must be *a poet too.*'

3

In 1913, the poet Luigi Russoli brought out a 'futurist manifesto' entitled *The Art of Noise.* It begins with a fierce attack on music as it is conceived, as it is practised. Musical creation is dead, he says, the whole organization of Western music tends to the commonplace: those concert halls with their 'hieratic atmosphere' and their 'stupid religious ecstasy'. Result, varying degrees of boredom and banality, never any real advance, never an 'extraordinary sensation'. As a basis for remedy, Russoli proposes noises 'with confused and irregular vibrations': the noises of wind, thunder, streams, waterfalls; the cries of animals; noises coming from the human mouth; the noises of towns – streets and stations. Some of all this is only provocative and one doesn't have to adhere to the futurist ideology, but the general tendency is in the direction of what I've already indicated: renew music from the ground up by getting out of 'facile traditional rhythms' and over-mathematical arrangements of sound, noise for Russoli being the very opposite of 'sound', an artificial notion.

From Luigi Russoli to John Cage, the road is not long. With Cage, there is similar provocation – it's just that, where the Futurist resorted provocatively to stridency, Cage resorts provocatively to silence. I'm thinking of that piece of 1952 entitled 4'33" which takes place in total silence, the pianist simply extending and contracting his arms. Beyond mere dadaistic-futuristic provocation, there's a similar desire also to give music a new *vocation*, by going back to first principles and changing postulates. 'Is it not a fact', said Cage in a lecture of 1958 (he considered his lectures as an integral part of his musical creation), 'that being a musician makes one automatically stupid and incapable of hearing? Would it not therefore be a good idea to stop the study of music altogether?'

Here's a list of some of Cage's musical compositions that constitutes in itself a little musicographical poem:

> *In a Landscape*
> *Totem Ancestor*
> *Prelude for Meditations*
> *Music of Changes*
> *Seven Haiku*
> *Atlas Eclipticalis*
> *Austral Studies*
> *Boreal Studies*
> *Ryoanji*
> *Mureau*

All of these speak for themselves (I'd simply draw attention to their geopoetic tonality) – except maybe Mureau, which is an amalgam of 'music' and 'Thoreau'.

What Cage appreciates in Thoreau (and in Satie), is their 'anarchistic', that is, non-monumental mentality. If music is an aggregation of sound, they go in for disaggregation and 'amusicality'. They set aside, for something more interesting, and rarer, all the 'resources' of musical art. The idea for Cage is to liberate sound–noise and discover new 'anarchistic' harmonies, or, as he says elsewhere, 'an indefinite poetry', 'a poetry of infinite possibility'.

Where most attempts to renew music in the twentieth century have taken place technically *inside* the sphere of music (Schönberg's atonality, Stravinsky's cubist formalism, etc.), Cage works in *from the outside*. This comes across best for me in his meteorological piece 'Lecture on the Weather', for twelve voices, a sound tape and a film. What Cage loathes in traditional music is an excessive humanism. He wants to let nature, the weather, the outside, have their say. That's why he calls his interviews *For the Birds*. He moves *out*. Chinese Taoism and Zen Buddhism helped him there. Which is why, in his postscript to *Mureau* he says that, in search of an activity other than 'art', he's leaving for China, which I interpret here as some kind of amusical atopia.

4

If Cage left 'for China', Glenn Gould went 'North'. A renowned interpreter of Bach, but disgusted with 'musical consumerdom', 'theatrical talent', and 'values depressingly orientated towards the city, that is, spiritually limited', Gould decided to quit the concert hall in 1964. Henceforth he wanted to play in a non-musical way, and attain to 'a kind of rigour and simplicity, absence of sophistication', for which it would be necessary to stay away from the piano as much as possible. That's when the 'idea of North' came into his head – the North as a place of isolation, silence, solitude: 'I've always considered that for each hour spent in human company, you need to spend X hours alone.' For a while, in Canada, he wrote critical articles on music under the name of Herbert von Hochmeister, supposedly a resident in the Northwest Territories. He also undertook, for the Canadian Broadcasting Company, a series of sound documentaries, 'The Idea of North', 'The Latecomers', and 'The Quiet in the Land' under the general title *The Trilogy of Solitude*. Using speech, and noises electronic and natural, these pieces aimed at a 'total art', the premises of which Gould saw in... Busoni, which would seem to indicate that there's some kind of coherence in these rambling musical explorations of mine.

5

It's possible to find elements of the 'total art' Busoni envisaged in musicians apparently less 'extravagant' than Cage or Gould – usually, as Busoni says, in their preparatory work, their preludes and transitions, where they could set aside questions of proportion and symmetry, and breathe freely. One thinks of Bartok, Varèse, Webern, Mahler, Messiaen and Debussy. In 1909, Debussy made this statement: 'One looks for ideas inside oneself, whereas one ought to look for them all around. We make combinations and constructions, but never listen to the thousand voices of nature. A new way lies open there. But I've only had a glimpse of it. There's so much to be done in that direction!'

It seems evident, then, that, since the beginning of the twentieth century, something is happening, or trying to happen, in the musical world, that is neither traditional sclerosis nor frenzied stridency, something that goes beyond a simple technical reformation (still more permutations and combinations) and looks more like an ontological revolution – a new, grounded poetics.

Arriving at this point in my geopoetico-musical meditation, I hear a gull crying out there in the mist and it sounds like approval.

An Outline of Geopoetics

Principles and elements.
                    (Aristotle)

1

Over the centuries, civilization has been carried by various powers: myth, religion, metaphysics. Although remnants of all these remain, usually in degraded forms, today civilization is carried by nothing – it just grows and spreads, like a cancer.

The last driving force was history itself, as put forward by Hegel, who claimed to see a *Weltgeist* ('spirit of the world') at work in it.

From Hegel on, the conviction would be that history was reasonable, that it had a purpose, and that it was leading somewhere. The ideology of Progress (with Growth and Prosperity as its motto) was born. The 'somewhere' supposedly on the horizon differed according to the various ideological contexts. In Bismarck's Germany, it was an all-powerful State, which would lead into the Nazi *Drittes Reich* (the 'Third Empire' – after that of the Romans and that of Charlemagne). In Marxist Russia, it would be the creation of a great State whose mission would be to put an end to all States and usher in World Communism. In the liberal West, it would be some kind of immense Supermarket, offering a package deal of happiness to all (provided you kept in line and didn't criticize the management). The Bismarck–Nazi project ended up among the smoking ruins of Berlin. The Marxist light faded into greater and greater gloom in the latter years of the twentieth century, and then suddenly sputtered out. Only the Supermarket still stands on the horizon.

And we have the Contemporary Situation. A hollowness, filled with more and more images, more and more noise. Mediocracy triumphant – the mediocre raised to a social and political power. Down the centre, a mindless helterskeltering. Along the rim, a literature, an art, that is little more than a reflection of this situation, this condition.

What is now evident – whatever people may have hoped,

229

even in a passing or tangential way, from nationalism, social-ism, national-socialism, communism, fascism, liberalism, or whatever – is that there is no strictly political solution to the condition described above. All politics on its own can do, and that is all we can expect from it, is try to cope with symptoms, in a more or less competent way.

The fundamental question is cultural rather than political, but only, as I have stressed, if the concept of culture is under-stood in a sense deeper than the one prevalent.

The sense of that word prevalent in our societies is strictly sociological. It covers everything that is done in the domains of theatre, cinema, literature, ballet and the visual arts. At times, some little distinctions are made, as between, say, 'élite culture' and 'popular culture', where the former means the products and activities of effete, disconnected minds, and the latter, not anything like the culture of a people, but the sort of pabulum certain social 'deciders' with mediocratic minds consider fit for the populace, and an easy sell. But mostly it's an indiscriminate hold-all term comprising the production of all kinds of objects, the exercise of all kinds of activities, outside the utilitarian sphere, and vaguely connected with the concept of 'leisure'. Underlying this conception lies the convic-tion that the more books, films, plays, paintings, sculptures, installations, concerts and so on a society produces (the best and most necessary gets lost in the rush), the more evolved it is. This is hardly the case. Real evolution can do with less, a lot less. In fact, this object-ridden, activity-frantic consumer-culture gets nobody anywhere and its marketing administration becomes a business in itself, blind to any deep purpose.

The question now is whether any 'deep purpose' is still possible, whether anything like a real turning of the times is possible, anything like a new epoch of being.

This is where geopoetics comes in, saying: perhaps.

At the very least, it presents itself as a beautiful gesture (a final gesture of sentient-intelligent humanity?) and as the most interesting thing around.

2

In order to see exactly where we now stand, and to see into the habitual contents of our mind, it's necessary to make an analysis of the progress of our (Western) civilization.

I propose to see this civilization as a motorway, with various stages. All of the stages have left traces on our conscience. As I go through the various stages, I'll be raising questions. It's to these questions that geopoetics brings answering elements.

The first stage, the Classical Age, is represented by Plato and Aristotle, who are written into the very language we use, the way we think.

Plato invented metaphysics, that is, idealism. When we say that someone is 'an idealist', it's vaguely complimentary. This is a person interested in something beyond 'mundane' concerns: the Good, the True, the Beautiful. At the same time, there is an implied criticism: this person needs to get his or her feet on the ground, and get back to 'the real world' (where, again implied, nobody gives a damn about the Good, the True, the Beautiful).

Might it be possible to get outside the opposition of idealism and realism? As well as outside the attempt to dialectize them (ideorealism, etc.)? And also beyond the punky nihilism that comes to the fore when idealism falls flat on its face? Might it be possible to get beyond the division of the intellectual and the sensitive on which metaphysics is based, a division leading, degeneratively, to empty intellectualism on the one hand and sentimentality on the other?

As to Aristotle, his contribution to the Motorway (the march of Western civilization) was classification, taxonomy. Classification is a useful tool. With ten books in your library, you have no problem. If you have three hundred or three thousand, without some kind of classification, you're going to waste a lot of time. Beyond that utilitarian aspect, there is an epistemological one: most of our knowledge is based on classification. We divide the real into parts, and we study the parts. A body, for example. We lay it, dead, on a table, and we cut it up. We learn a great deal that way about the respiratory system, the circulation of blood, the constitution of the various organs. And in cases of dysfunction, our medicine treats the various parts. The suspicion may arise, however, not only that the whole is more than the sum of its parts, and that the live whole may have a way of functioning that dissection cannot discover, but that health depends, not on the treatment of classified parts, but on a whole organism in an environment. Finally, if classifications are useful, they can become too narrow, the real living life of the world and the mind flows over them. There are, for example, books written which simply do not fit into the genre-systems of most histories of literature or the classifications of most bookshops. On a still more general plane, geopoetics is situated beyond the presently established and classified division of science, philosophy and poetry.

After the Classical Age come the so-called Middle Ages, stage 2 on the Motorway, marked largely by Christianity. Although life went on in the fields and gardens, as can be seen in so many of those beautiful miniatures in the Books of Hours, although St Francis talked almost paganly about Brother Sun and Sister Moon, although there were deviant movements and intellectual heretics, Christian culture tended to see the common-or-garden world as a vale of tears, to be passed through on the way to a life beyond. The accent was on a vertical relationship to a transcendence, as exemplified in those church towers and spires striving gothically up towards the heavens. In place of the Idea to be intellectually seized, there is God, to be adored and feared and loved via the Virgin Mary and the Christ. In place of Plato's intellectual and Aristotle's scientific field, you have a psychological theatre marked by the obsession of Original Sin: the world is agonizedly bemoralized. Another obsession is that of time. If Christ the Saviour rose to heaven after his sacrifice, one day he will return to Earth. One hopes and waits for the Second Coming. When hope runs out, one continues to wait – for Godot.

Stage 3 on the cultural Motorway: the Renaissance. The renaissance, that is the re-birth – of what? Of the Classical Age, of classical space. First of all, in the form of the works of Plato and Aristotle, lost in the Middle Ages, and preserved thanks to Arab scholars. Then, in the form of mythology: gods and goddesses, naiads and dryads. These mythical creatures were going to invade the mind massively. For long, no poem worthy of the name would be without its Venus, its Endymion, and so on, till, late in the nineteenth century, they were abandoned as an excrescence, an encumbrance, a nuisance. But these ancient mythical creatures served initially a significant cultural purpose. Before they became conventional, they were operative: the nymph of the forest aroused an interest in the forest, the muse of the mountain aroused an interest in the mountain. The natural world became again a focus of attention. Hence the rise of science: the attempt to probe into the secrets of nature. Hence an interest in this earthly world, and the desire to see beyond the boundaries of the small 'known world' of medieval maps. New worlds are discovered – notably to the West, across the Atlantic. But look what happens. It's much easier to impose a known system on the unknown than to expose oneself to that unknown. So that, in coming across an island, instead of taking a close look at it and naming it accordingly (a poetic, geopoetic act), as, say, 'Sharp Rock Island' or 'Palm Island', one dubs it 'St John' or 'St Martin', or tabs it with the name of some king, some governor, sticks a flag on it, and exterminates all former inhabitants, human or non-human. The result is that the so-called New World is never really a new world, only a blown-up caricature of some parts of the Old. At surface level, renaissances tend to be full of confused noise. Even at a deeper level, if some minds manage to reach into new-lighted, new-sounding space, most of what goes on is rehash: classical philosophy as taught in the humanist schools was only a pale reflection of the more radical areas of original Greek thought.

Modernity (stage 4 on the Motorway), as invented by René Descartes, was radical – both radical and ruthless. It reduced the whole world-complex to subject and object, and with that subject/object division went a project: mastery over Nature. With modernity, Nature becomes more and more objectified, considered exclusively as raw matter to be exploited. The disastrous ecological results of this are notorious. As to the subject, either it becomes completely robotized, wrapped up in some clinical, scientistic, astronautic, military uniform, or it ends up on the psychoanalyst's couch, rank with frustration, fantasy, mind-cinema of every conceivable variety. Meanwhile modernity raves on down the Motorway.

3

The first reaction came from what has been called Romanticism. This was private individuals realizing they had been deprived of everything, and trying to do something about it. 'What you're looking for is a world', says Hölderlin's hero, Hyperion (the man with hyper-demands), to himself. This meant, in the first place, a 'return to Nature', sometimes only in sentimental terms. But it also meant an attempt to get at some kind of wholeness of thinking and being, which took the form of transversal research, reaching out beyond the established divisions of knowledge and the compartmentalization of thought. Where psychology, biology and physics were separate departments in the 'correct' epistemological establishment, the Romantic tries to think in terms of a complex synthesis: psycho-biophysics. Carlyle has his caricature of a Romantic, Dr Teufelsdröckh ('Devil's dragon'), lodged at a university called Weissnichtwo ('God knows where'), talking about transcendental research, symbolism (windows into infinity) and natural supernaturalism.

The figures whom I've called 'intellectual nomads' are not Romantics, but they share a point of departure in the same context, and they raise some of the same questions, while trying to find new answers, while trying also to go beyond reaction into a new action (activity).

These figures are difficult to define and impossible to classify. They are not professional, without being vaguely amateurish. They are not persons, they are subjects. The social person is a congeries of heredity, coded emotion and fantasy. The nomadic subject is an intention and a trajectory. The person is an identity. The subject is a field of energy.

At the beginning of this book, I went in some detail into the movements of two of such figures, Nietzsche and Rimbaud, the two that meant most to me in my own trajectory. In the context of the present essay, I'll present only a rapid reminder, with maybe some additional flashes.

Nietzsche abandons his professional status as a classical philologist at the University of Basle, and thereafter nomadizes over Europe. We can trace his itinerary from Germany to Switzerland, and from Switzerland to France and Italy· 'I decided to go away out into foreign parts, meet what was strange to me. [...] Followed a long vagabondage, full of research and transformation, with no easy definition. [...] You feel space growing all around you, the horizon opens.' In the course of those travels and on those heights, Nietzsche writes a series of electrically charged books that analyse the context he has left behind and outline the new space in which he finds himself: *Human All-too Human, Dawn, Thus Spake Zarathustra, The Twilight of the Idols, Ecce Homo.* His final word, in the face of all transcendental belief and of technological earth-destruction, was 'Brothers, remain true to the earth.'

Close to Nietzsche, just as powerful a figure, being to poetry what Nietzsche was to philosophy, breaking out of bounds, desperate for new space, there is Rimbaud.

While he leaves two books on the literary scene, *A Season in Hell* and *The Illuminations*, Rimbaud's life is mainly move-ment across various territories. His first move takes him across the region of the Ardennes, between northern France and Belgium. Later, we find him crossing the Gothard Pass in Winter ('only whiteness to think of') between Switzerland and Italy. We can follow his journeys then through Germany and England. Thereafter, he leaves Europe for Indonesia. And at the end, we find him on the high plateau of Ogaden in Abyssinia. In one of his poems, he declares: 'If I have taste left for anything at all, it's for earth and stones.' I put this statement in connection with Nietzsche's 'Brothers, remain true to the earth', and see in both, as in the trajectories of these two figures, an approach to geopoetics.

It may be wondered why I was never interested to the same extent in any English writer. The simple fact is, in no English author (except maybe D.H. Lawrence in some rare passages) did I see the existential energy, the intellectual acumen and the poetic force I found in the German and the Frenchman.

It's in this context that my own itinerary has to be read.

Out from Glasgow (then rife with symptoms of Western civilization's latter phases), with early experience on the Atlan-tic coast of Scotland always in my mind, I moved across Europe in *Travels in the Drifting Dawn*, crossed over into Asia with *The Face of the East Wind*, and followed a path in the north of North America, with *The Blue Road*. Out of these areas (globally, 'the most difficult area') arose the poems of successive volumes, such as *Walking the Coast, Handbook for the Diamond Country, Atlantica, Limits and Margins*, gathered into the collected work *Open World*. After the itineraries and the poems came the essays, written for a long time mostly in French, of *The Outward Movement, A Quiet Apocalypse, The Nomad Mind, The Plateau of the Albatross*, which are attempts at a new poetic-theoretical cartography.

What I propose to do now is, not summarize these essays, but present synthetically the various affluents to geopoetics – scientific, philosophical, poetic – which they go into in more detail, and which the poems and waybooks incorporate and carry.

4

However infantile, nitwitted and irresponsible some techno-science will appear to the geopoetician, there is no doubt what-soever that much of what has gone and is going on in science flows naturally into the field of geopoetics.

Among the first ancestors of geopoetics, I rank Alexander von Humboldt. In one of the notes to his *Cosmos*, Humboldt says that science, poetry and philosophy are not fundamentally separate, that they come together in the mind of one who has achieved a state of unity. It is this unity which characterizes a 'complete work', in the sense I give that term. A similar unity can occur, in a more general kind of way, at certain periods in history. It is one of the theses of geopoetics that we may be able to open up such a period.

In many books on scientific thought published over the last ten years or so, the word 'poetics' turns up in the final chapter. This is because science has entered an area in which 'normal' language no longer seems adequate, and in which the structure of reality seems more poetic than mechanistic.

It all began with Einstein's *Cosmological Considerations* (1917). Suddenly the word 'cosmos' was back in human con-sciousness. Here was a scientist not content to simply measure and weigh, or hunt about for yet another particle, a scientist going against the established axiom that there is no science of the whole, only of parts, and who was not only talking about 'the whole', but who was using that ancient Greek word meaning 'the beautiful whole'.

This text undoubtedly marks a turning-point in science. But, for the purposes of this quick introduction to geopoetics, it's useful to look rather into Einstein's correspondence (notably with Max Born), where we get an insight into the working of this scientific mind, and see a scientist asking existential, cultural questions.

In the first place, there's the sense Einstein has of his own life: 'I find myself so much connected with all of life that it's impossible for me to say where the individual begins and where he ends.' Then he goes into his dilemma as a scientist: the division he feels between logical schematics and 'the loveliness of life'. If one aims at clarity, absolute clarity, the only efficient language is that of mathematics. But mathematics misses out on so much, the world becomes insubstantial, one loses 'the living context'. The question then arises: might it be possible, beyond this dilemma and division, which for Einstein amounts to a tragedy, to reconcile logical clarity and the 'loveliness of life'? For that, a new kind of thought is necessary. Einstein speaks of the 'wildly speculative' nature of his own mind, and stresses the need to set aside 'mechanical and specialized logic' and accomplish 'a great intellectual leap'.

It's this kind of 'leaping' we see in the liveliest scientific thought since Einstein. Not the leap back into metaphysics, or religion, that we see in some scientists, but the leap, forward, into an uncertain, undefined field.

For a start, it's the field of quantum physics where chance, chaos and the indeterminate are no longer considered as breaks in the order of things, but as an integral part of the moving universe-multiverse. The grammar henceforth is not that of classical order, but one based on fluctuation, irregularity, complexity.

In biology, Varela and Maturana use the term 'autopoetics' to indicate the work of a complex system able to use order and disorder in the structuring of a 'self'.

Lastly (in this outline), there is the contribution of linguistics. Here the key-figure, the seminal mind, is the French linguist Gustave Guillaume. Setting aside most of the 'scientific' work done on language as 'maximal knowledge based on limited understanding', the linguistic scientist Guillaume makes the radical point that 'the human being is present not only in the human context but in the context of the universe'.

5

In face of the mass of introverted complication that philosophy had largely become, many philosophically inclined minds have tended, in the late modern period, to move over into ethno-logy, sociology and other human sciences, when they didn't confine themselves, as so many did in the English language context, to logical positivism. But there has been a lot of interesting development and evolution within philosophy itself: a radical displacement, a topological transformation.

It begins with Nietzsche.

While knowing them thoroughly, Nietzsche abandons the precincts of academic and classical philosophy. Most philosophy, he says, is built on a blockage. Which is why, instead of posing heavy problems within a closed structure, instead of adding to the constructions ('Why is my intelligence so quick and sharp? Because I don't waste time asking questions that aren't real questions'), he undertakes a radical culture-analysis, and, instead of writing treatises, writes books of essays, fragments, ongoing autobiography.

Beyond the figure of the philosopher, Nietzsche invents that of the philosopher–artist (the 'poet–thinker', in my vocabulary), working both at a large concept stemming from 'universal symphony' (the poet–thinker is characterized by 'amplitude and diversity') and in a field of immediate experience, immediate perception.

The philosopher–artist is first and foremost a solitary traveller, who can settle into no comfortable, homely context, while always looking for a place, a space, a ground, where he can experience 'a humanly superhuman well-being'. Nietzsche moves across the no man's land of nihilism, trying to work his way back up beyond metaphysics and enter into a landscape–mindscape dominated by no transcendental idol, no religious ideology. He's moving out of the history of metaphysics and religion into a new intellectual–existential geography.

In one of his poems (while criticizing so much poetry, based

238

just as much on blockage and sickness as most philosophy, this philosopher–artist writes poems, calling himself 'a poet at the limit of the word'), Nietzsche evokes a band of crows flying raggedly out of town and calling over a wintered landscape. That's an image of the initial ground and movement of the radical poet–thinker.

Nietzsche's work has to be seen as a kind of wing-beat in larger and larger space. But the higher you go, as he says elsewhere, the less people will see you, just as they won't understand the nature of your work, simply because it doesn't fit into the usual categories. Nietzsche, then, was more or less resigned to being misunderstood in his lifetime and a long time after – until, I would say, the map of a new space could be drawn up, beyond an age, beyond a world (the Contemporary Situation) characterized by the ruins of idealism, remnants of Christianity, numb nihilism, short-sighted realism and various types of more or less wacky spirituality.

While looking to the opening of that new field, Nietzsche's final message to other solitary travellers was that 'remain true to the earth', along with an aesthetics of living and creativity based on 'a sense of what is lasting and few means'.

Another philosophical affluent to geopoetics is Martin Heidegger, again a much misunderstood thinker, considered even by some, who have read little or none of his work, as anathema, because of a passing acquaintance with national socialism. I make no attempt to cover up Heidegger's political mistake, on the contrary I try to see in his work exactly from what point that mistake stemmed. But I don't take that mistake as an excuse for neglecting some of the most interesting thought going on in the twentieth century.

Heidegger's starting point is the observation that the world, the world as phenomenon, the world as life-space, has been reduced to a universe of utensils, a stock of furnishings (a forest seen as so much timber, a mountain as a potential stone-quarry), and to a social context in which human beings have been left with no sense of world at all, no sense of deep being, no sense of presence-on-earth. So much has been lost sight of, lost sense of, that in some linguistic contexts there is no vocabulary available even to talk about such a condition (hence a multiplicity of confused debates), and in some ideological contexts not enough mental distance and perspective to see it for what it is, far less conceive of any worthwhile change.

For Heidegger, this condition is the end-point of a whole development of thought that can be traced back to the beginnings of metaphysics. Philosophy as metaphysics or ontology has never spoken about *being* deeply enough. Which is why Heidegger steps out of philosophy into what he calls a 'beginning thinking'. This kind of thinking tries to begin again from the ground up, following paths with no obvious destination (leading 'nowhere'), but which may potentially open out into a clearing. These paths are mental paths, but they are also real, physical paths. Heidegger spent his life between his seminar at the University of Freiburg and a hut in the Black Forest from which such paths radiated.

In his attempt to move out of the philosophical domain into 'more original districts' that philosophy 'has never heard of', in his attempt to find adequate language, Heidegger looks to the earliest of thinkers, mainly Greek (but he is also aware of Far-Eastern thought), and also to poets, in particular Hölderlin and Rilke. His own writing often approaches poetry, as in this note concerning the relationship between earth and world:

> *Earth*
> *protect the beginnings*
>
> *world*
> *be awake to the soundings*
>
> *world*
> *be grateful to the earth*
>
> *earth*
> *salute the world.*

6

A text can be written with versecraft and pass for a poem, but have no real 'sounding' in the sense just evoked in the quotation from Heidegger. Nietzsche was interested only in poetry that went 'to the limit'. For Rimbaud, very little poetry was of any radical or general interest, whereas real poetry was always 'out ahead': he looked to 'new theories penetrating into unknown places'. It's in the context of this kind of theory-practice that I use the word 'poetics'. While including poetry, it also has a larger application. It applies not only to poetry as literary form, but also to art and music, and can be extended beyond these domains into science and even social practice.

If, for Rimbaud, most poetry was fundamentally insignificant, it was because it had no ground: when it wasn't mere verbal tiddleywinks, its context was no more than personal, socio-personal. It rarely broke into a larger space. It was, one might say, a poetry without poetics. One could also say (thinking back to an old Far-Eastern distinction between poetry that 'has a world' and poetry that 'does not have a world') a poetry *without world.*

In its specifically poetic aspect, geopoetics breaks out of the platonist-aristotelian theory of *poiesis* as *mimesis*, which still lies at the basis of literary practice in general (reproduction, representation, reflection: mirror-writing) and moves over into presence-in-the-world, experience of field and territory, openness of style, in a relationship of configurational complicity with the cosmological 'poetics' of the universe.

Although the field was not yet recognized as such, it is possible to see strong elements of geopoetics in many of the most powerful and radiant poets of the past two centuries.

It's Novalis speaking of a 'writing of the earth' that can be found on birds' wings, on shells, in clouds, in snow, on mountain sides, in plants, in animals, in the lights of the sky, and which can be integrated into the language of human being.

It's Walt Whitman declaring that he's ready to abandon almost everything most people associate with the word 'poetry' – personal sentiment, imagination, neat prosody, a clutch of metaphors – if only he can manage to express the undulation of a wave, the breathing of the ocean. In Whitman's 'ebb and flow of endless motion' emerges, by abstraction, via a field of waves, a hydrodynamic power.

Another significant American proto-geopoetician of that time is Henry Thoreau, breaking out of identity ideology and common-sense philosophy in his journey to Ktaadn, exercising a perpetual, day-to-day extravagance (in the original sense of the word: Latin *extra vagare*, to wander out) and, in his random trip to Cape Cod, moving along the Atlantic edge ('A man may stand there and put all America behind him') into a poetic atopia.

It's Rilke speaking of 'pure space breaking in from afar' and declaring that his poetic project is 'to present the vastness, the variety, the completeness of the world in the form of pure proofs'. The language here is almost scientific-mathematical, in an Einsteinian way. The relationship with Einstein's universal identity appears even closer when we hear Rilke saying: 'I live my life in larger and larger circles.'

It's there in Ezra Pound who, after his antiquarian nostalgias and his fascist futurism, comes to realize, after Whitman, that the aim of any poetry worth its salt is to 'make cosmos'.

It's there in Charles Olson, also moving along the Atlantic edge ('Headland over the sea-shore'), having started out from the white-whaling of Herman Melville, having studied city civilizations around the world, finally coming to the post-historical, the post-humanist, the beautiful open-world thing, walking in 'the openness the exploiters have not beat out'.

Slightly further inland lies the work-field of William Carlos Williams, reaching out, along the Passaic River, beyond the 'staleness of most literature', to a new movement of poetic intelligence.

In Scotland, there has been Hugh MacDiarmid, descrying, out on his stony limits, from the heights of a raised beach, a field few in the English-language context had any notion of and into which he often, cogently and beautifully, enters.

It's there in Saint-John Perse speaking of 'the new writing enclosed in the schist' and asking the sea to teach him 'the major verse of the greatest order', the 'tone of the greatest art', the model of the 'greatest text'.

7

Lastly, some question of vocabulary and language.

In the first place, why call this great cultural work-field 'geopoetics'?

If we look at the cultures humanity has evolved around the globe, it's possible to discern that they all have at their centre a principal motif (inducive of motivation, conducive to action), a central concern. In paleolithic culture, it's a relationship with animals (a whole range of concerns going from subsistence to myth). In Chinese culture, it's a cosmic concentring of power.

In Greek culture, it's the platform of City-State politics. In medieval Western culture, it's the Virgin Mary and the Christ. The question is: what could be the central motif, the central concern for a world-culture today, able to be shared by all, North, South, East and West? A reasonable answer, an obvious answer one might say, would be: the very Earth on which we try to live. Hence the *geo* in geopoetics.

As to 'poetics', that word is hardly prevalent (except in debased forms) at the end-stage of the Motorway we have described, and is, to say the least, not an integral part of the vocabulary of Technocracy or Mediocracy. But if we look again at cultures round the world, cultures that have been live and enlivening, fertile and lasting, we find that they have a poetics at their centre. In paleolithic culture, we have the figure of the shaman, whose poetics are concerned with maintaining a contact between the human community and the larger, non-human environment. In Chinese culture, there is the *Book of Odes*, with 'the wind of the territories' blowing through its pages. In Greek culture, there is the oceanic poetics of Homer, without which the culture would be lopsided, without which the platform of politics itself would become dry and brittle.

It was part of my individual programme from the beginning, and integral to the geopoetics programme from its inception, to work out the equivalent of such poetics as have just been evoked for the world (the worlding) now. To give the word its full sense and force, I suggest we go back, here in the West, to Aristotle's *nous poietikos* ('the poetic intelligence'). Which is to say that geopoetics is more than 'poetry concerned with the environment', more than literature with some kind of geographical content (just as what I call 'waybooks' are a lot more than travel literature). Geopoetics is concerned, fundamentally, with a relationship to the earth and with the opening of a world.

Unless it is very clearly articulated, the word 'geopoetics' will often be confused with the word 'geopolitics', at present much more widely known and extensively practised. This phonetic juxtaposition provides another occasion for definition. Geopolitics is concerned with the power-relationships between State and State on a global scale, conceiving of space exclusively in terms of exploitable resources. Geopoetics is a deeper, more radical enterprise. Its concern is not territorial power-mongering among States, but the state of the human being in the universe, the relationship between human being and the planet Earth, presence in the world. Geopoetics is the antidote to world-poisoning.

'World' – there is another difficult concept, open to multi-layered and often indiscriminate usage. If we look to (Germanic) etymology, this Anglo-Saxon word may be seen as going back to something like *wer-alt*, meaning no more than 'an age of man'. It's this sense of 'world' as some particular stage of civilization, some particular social set-up, that Wordsworth had in mind when he said: 'The world is too much with us', expressing a desire for some larger sense of being, some more expansive contact with the universe. It's from this kind of world, because it so often weighs heavy on them and hems them in, that people take refuge in personal worlds of fantasy, seek relief in other worlds of a religious nature, or just look around for the nearest amusement.

Is it possible (as soon as you start digging into meaning, the questions start) to conceive of a world that is not overcoded, an 'open' world that is not merely personal, that is not other-worldly, and that offers more than distraction?

Before attempting anything like an answer at this stage, let's look at some more etymology.

In the Romance languages, latent in the word for 'world' (*monde* in French, *mundo* in Spanish, *mondo* in Italian), there's an aesthetic sense, going back to the Latin *mundus*, indicating a focus of fertile interconnections, a nexus of communicative forces. It's significant for the progress of civilization that this aesthetic sense has been preserved only in the negative, as in the French *immonde*, meaning 'disgusting and repulsive', just as English has retained the *mundus* root only in *mundane*, meaning 'platitudinous and uninteresting'.

The word 'cosmos' also, originally, had an aesthetic connotation, meaning 'a beautiful, harmonious totality' (Greek *kosmos*). We've retained that aesthetic sense only in the word 'cosmetics'. But it may be time to get back to that larger context, those more extensive connotations.

With those definitions in mind, the question now is: how to get, in the first instance conceptually, into a live field?

Moving from etymology to active terminology and working

thought, I propose this: a world emerges from the contact between the human being and the cosmos, represented by the Earth. When that contact is intelligent, sensitive, subtle, you have a world in the full and positive sense: a satisfying context, an interesting and life-enhancing place. When the contact is unintelligent, insensitive, heavy-handed and clumsy, what you have instead of a world is a diminished context, if not a precinct of horror.

Of course one can get used to a diminished context (the human being, marked by versatile adaptiveness, can get used to almost anything), one can identify with it, out of inured familiarity, local patriotism, and so on. One can even, out of perversity, and a deep despair of ever changing things and opening up a larger context, choose to exalt and multiply the horror.

With geopoetics, we are concerned with keeping the larger context open. Without a sense of that larger context, even the will to change society (reform, revolution) can proceed, as we have seen repeatedly, on overnarrow rails, this process leading often to situations actually worse than the original context.

A world is a place, a space that one cultivates. And in order to be up to that world-cultivation, one has to cultivate oneself.

This brings us back again to that vexed and much abused word: culture.

The working definition of culture, in the context of the individual (we begin with the individual, who can always move faster than a society), proposed by geopoetics, is this: the way human beings conceive of, work at, and direct themselves. Culture implies some conception of the human being. The human being has been seen, for example, as 'made in the image of God' (as in Christianity), or as 'master and possessor of nature' (as in Modernity). In place of these definitions, I propose 'inhabitant of the Earth', and, more precisely (thinking here of Hölderlin's 'man lives poetically on the Earth'), 'poetic inhabitant of the Earth'. After this general conception, comes work. There is no real culture without work. If agriculture means working at a field to help it produce the best crop, then human culture means working at the most harmonious growth of the individual. And then, lastly, there is a direction: some sense of a horizon of the possible.

A culture, in the collective sense, begins when, within a group of individuals – whether tribe, nation or community – there is consensus as to the essential.

To come back to the notion of 'world'. In the ongoing debate between commercially high-powered, multinational globalism on the one hand, and, on the other, localism, geared to identity ideology, narrow nationalism, sectarianism, provincial complacency, geopoetics sides with neither party. 'World' for geopoetics is open world. Open world begins with place, not with simple piety of place (from homey couthiness to spooky animism via racial rootedness), but with *knowledge* (informed, sentient, intelligent) of place. Thoroughly known, every place is open. From the smallest rivulet, via a network of rivers, one arrives at the ocean. A little geology allows one to know that not all the stones on the local beach are necessarily of local origin, that glaciers may have brought them in from elsewhere. Likewise, from a layer of local rock one can move across nations and continents. An informed look at the sky will see not only wind-driven cloud, but the tracks of migratory birds. To all of which must be added the movements of population and language.

There we come to another aspect of the world-culture potentially emergent from the great work-field: its grounded universalism. In the context of confusion, anxiety and emptiness that mark the end-stage of the Motorway, people, in the search for some more coherent space, will convert to practically anything, and we have all sorts and varieties. In this situation, there are those who think they are working for world-culture when they organize oecumenical jamborees. This may perhaps encourage a spirit of mutual tolerance, which, in a trigger-happy context, is not to be neglected – but it is somewhat short of active, radical work. The intellectual nomad who quits the monolinear, monocultural, monomaniac Motorway will pass through as many cultures as possible, but will go beyond the relativistic ('You in your own small corner and I in mine'), pluralistic ('The more, the merrier') vision of things. The fact is that all cultures are partial. A culture will insist principally on one aspect of the human being, to the neglect of others. For example, Western culture will insist more on sociality ('No man is an island'), whereas Eastern culture will insist more on the potential development of the self (the Buddhist: 'Be an island unto yourself').

The passage through many cultures in order to arrive at a potential world-culture is the work of the intellectual nomad. The work of the geopoetician is to integrate aspects of many cultures into a new coherence. This new coherence is not colourless. There can be all kinds of local colouration and tonality. The sense of unity prevalent and operative in geopoetics is that of an archipelago.

Finally, it has to be said that, for geopoetics, world is connected to Earth. To some, this may seem so self-evident as to be hardly worthy of consideration, let alone thought. To others, it will seem myopic and retrograde. These are the people for whom the Earth is a small thing, a thing of the past, a thing of little or no account. They think in terms of cosmic space. They want to build cities in space. They want to colonize Mars and other more distant planets. Man may not be biologically adapted to them, but that is no great hindrance. On some planets, it may be convenient to be nine foot tall and skinny, on others three foot tall and rotund – no problem, genetic manipulation will do the trick. The geopoetician knows that, according to biology and other fields of knowledge, the optimal conditions for the harmonious development of the human being are here on Earth. This perspective neither ignores nor neglects the cosmos – an early word I used before coming to 'geopoetics' was 'biocosmopoetics'. But the fact is that, by living on Earth, one is in the cosmos; whereas one can be in the cosmos (in a capsule and a special suit) and totally disconnected. As to the connection between world and Earth, between the human being and the Earth–cosmic context, this has, as aforesaid, very rarely been fully experienced, fully thought out, fully expressed. It is the aim of geopoetics to do so.

Geopoetics implies new wording, new working, new worlding.

Bibliographical Note

The essay 'The Re-mapping of Scotland' was originally a lecture, the Consignia lecture, delivered at the Edinburgh International Book Festival on 23 August 2001. It was later published by the Edinburgh International Book Festival as a pamphlet (Edbookfest Editions, 2002).

An earlier form of the essay 'An Outline of Geopoetics' was published as a booklet by the Scottish Centre for Geopoetics, at its new imprint, Alba Editions (2003), under the title *Geopoetics – Place, Culture, World.*